THE ANTHROPOCENE

Perhaps no concept has become dominant in so many fields as rapidly as the Anthropocene. Meaning "The Age of Humans," the Anthropocene is the proposed name for our current geological epoch, beginning when human activities started to have a noticeable impact on Earth's geology and ecosystems. Long embraced by the natural sciences, the Anthropocene has now become commonplace in the humanities and social sciences, where it has taken firm enough hold to engender a thoroughgoing assessment and critique. Why and how has the geological concept of the Anthropocene become important to the humanities? What new approaches and insights do the humanities offer? What narratives and critiques of the Anthropocene do the humanities produce? What does it mean to study literature of the Anthropocene? These are the central questions that this collection explores. Each chapter takes a decidedly different humanist approach to the Anthropocene, from environmental humanities to queer theory to race, illuminating the important contributions of the humanities to the myriad discourses on the Anthropocene. This volume is designed to provide concise overviews of particular approaches and texts, as well as compelling and original interventions in the study of the Anthropocene. Written in an accessible style free from disciplinary-specific jargon, many chapters focus on well-known authors and texts, making this collection especially useful to teachers developing a course on the Anthropocene and students undertaking introductory research. This collection provides truly innovative arguments regarding how and why the Anthropocene concept is important to literature and the humanities.

Seth T. Reno is Distinguished Research Associate Professor of English at Auburn University Montgomery. He is author of *Early Anthropocene Literature in Britain, 1750–1884* (2020) and *Amorous Aesthetics: Intellectual Love in Romantic Poetry and Poetics, 1788–1853* (2019); editor of *Romanticism and Affect Studies* (2018); and coeditor of *Wordsworth and the Green Romantics: Affect and Ecology in the Nineteenth Century* (2016). He has also published dozens of journal articles, book chapters, book reviews, and encyclopedia entries on eighteenth- and nineteenth-century literature, art, and science.

THE ANTHROPOCENE

Approaches and Contexts for Literature and the Humanities

Edited by Seth T. Reno

NEW YORK AND LONDON

First published 2022
by Routledge
605 Third Avenue, New York, NY 10158

and by Routledge
2 Park Square, Milton Park, Abingdon, Oxon OX14 4RN

Routledge is an imprint of the Taylor & Francis Group, an informa business

© 2022 selection and editorial matter, Seth T. Reno; individual chapters, the contributors

The right of Seth T. Reno to be identified as the author of the editorial material, and of the authors for their individual chapters, has been asserted in accordance with sections 77 and 78 of the Copyright, Designs and Patents Act 1988.

All rights reserved. No part of this book may be reprinted or reproduced or utilised in any form or by any electronic, mechanical, or other means, now known or hereafter invented, including photocopying and recording, or in any information storage or retrieval system, without permission in writing from the publishers.

Trademark notice: Product or corporate names may be trademarks or registered trademarks, and are used only for identification and explanation without intent to infringe.

Library of Congress Cataloging-in-Publication Data
A catalog record for this title has been requested

ISBN: 978-0-367-55839-0 (hbk)
ISBN: 978-0-367-55837-6 (pbk)
ISBN: 978-1-003-09534-7 (ebk)

DOI: 10.4324/9781003095347

Typeset in Bembo
by Newgen Publishing UK

CONTENTS

List of Figures vii
List of Contributors viii

Introduction: The Anthropocene and the Humanities 1
Seth T. Reno

PART 1
Approaches 11

1 The Deep Time Life Kit: Thinking Tools for the Anthropocene 13
  Lisa Ottum

2 The Two Households: Economics and Ecology 26
  Scott R. MacKenzie

3 Energy and the Anthropocene 38
  Kent Linthicum

4 Environmental Racism, Environmental Justice: Centering
  Indigenous Responses to the Colonial Logics of the Anthropocene 50
  Rebecca Macklin

5 The World Is Burning: Racialized Regimes of Eco-Terror and
  the Anthropocene as Eurocene 64
  Nicolás Juárez

6	Trans★Plantationocene *Nicholas Tyler Reich*	76
7	The Anthropocene and Critical Method *Stephen Tedeschi*	87

PART 2
Contexts   97

8	"One Life" and One Death: Mary Shelley's *The Last Man* *Matthew Rowney*	99
9	Henry David Thoreau: A New Anthropocenic Persona *Robert Klevay*	111
10	It's the End of the World: Can We Know It? *Tobias Wilson-Bates*	118
11	*Orlando* in the Anthropocene: Climate Change and Changing Times *Naomi Perez*	125
12	Corporeal Matters: J.P. Clark's *The Wives' Revolt* and the Embodied Politics of the Anthropocene *Kimberly Skye Richards*	134
13	What Global South Critics Do *Antonette Talaue-Arogo*	147
14	Queering the Modest Witness in the Chthulucene: Jeff VanderMeer's *Borne* (a New Weird Case Study) *Kristin Girten*	159
15	Contemporary Cli-fi as Anthropocene Literature: Kim Stanley Robinson's *New York 2140* *Seth T. Reno*	171

Index   *183*

FIGURES

0.1 Simon Lewis and Mark Maslin, "Orbis Spike," in "Defining the Anthropocene," *Nature* 519 (2015)   4
0.2 Adriane Lam and Jen Bauer, "Temperature and CO_2 for the Last 1,000 Years," in "CO_2: Past, Present, and Future," Time Scavengers, https://i0.wp.com/timescavengers.blog/wp-content/uploads/2017/06/1000-2000_co2temp-01.jpg?ssl=1   4
0.3 Simon Lewis and Mark Maslin, "Bomb Spike," in "Defining the Anthropocene," *Nature* 519 (2015)   5
1.1 Lisa Ottum, "Anthropocene Thinkfeel Axis"   18

CONTRIBUTORS

Kristin Girten is Associate Professor of English and Assistant Vice Chancellor for Arts and Humanities at the University of Nebraska Omaha. Her research and teaching focus on intersections between literature, philosophy, and science in the British Enlightenment and the twenty-first century, giving special emphasis to how women and other marginalized groups contribute to and feel the effects of such intersections. Her essay collection *British Literature and Technology, 1600–1830*, which she is coediting with Aaron Hanlon (Colby College), is forthcoming with Bucknell University Press. She is also completing a monograph focused on Epicureanism, the sublime, and the sensitive witness in British women's literature, philosophy, and science of the long Enlightenment.

Nicolás Juárez is a native, diasporic descendent of the Tsotsil Maya and a first-generation Chiapaneco living in the ancestral homelands, taken through genocide, of the Alabama-Coushatta, Caddo, Carrizo/Comecrudo, Coahuiltecan, Comanche, Kickapoo, Lipan Apache, Tonkawa, and Ysleta Del Sur Pueblo, among others. As a graduate student at the University of Texas Austin in Social Work, his research examines the libidinal economy of anti-blackness and settler colonialism and its implications for clinical mental health practice.

Robert Klevay is Associate Professor of English at Auburn University Montgomery, where his teaching and research focus on American and Classical literature. He specializes in American Transcendentalism and the work of Henry David Thoreau.

Kent Linthicum is Marion L. Brittain Postdoctoral Fellow at the Georgia Institute of Technology. His work has appeared in the *European Romantic Review*, *Nineteenth-Century Contexts*, and *Studies in English Literature*. His current book project

List of Contributors ix

analyzes the ways eighteenth- and nineteenth-century literature facilitated the expansion of British coal and American slavery through the development of fossil fuel aesthetics.

Rebecca Macklin holds a PhD from the University of Leeds and is currently Mellon Postdoctoral Fellow at the University of Pennsylvania. Her writing has been published in journals including *Interventions, ARIEL,* and *Transmotion,* and she is currently working on a monograph, titled *Unsettling Fictions: Relationality and Resistance in Native American and South African Literature.* Her postdoctoral research is focused on Indigenous literatures, gender, and narratives of resource extraction.

Scott R. MacKenzie is Associate Professor of English at the University of Mississippi. He is author of *Be It Ever So Humble: Poverty, Fiction, and the Invention of the Middle-Class Home* (2013), which won the Walker Cowen Prize for a study on an eighteenth-century topic. He has also published articles in *PMLA, Eighteenth-Century Studies, ELH, Studies in Romanticism, European Romantic Review, Novel,* and other journals. His current project is concerned with the history of generalized scarcity.

Lisa Ottum is Associate Professor of English at Xavier University, where she teaches British literature, literature and the environment, literary criticism, and other courses. She is coeditor of *Wordsworth and the Green Romantics: Affect and Ecology in the Nineteenth Century* (2016), and she has published on a variety of Romantic-era texts, as well as twentieth- and twenty-first-century artifacts.

Naomi Perez holds a Bachelor of Arts in English from Troy University, a Master of Teaching Writing from Auburn University Montgomery, and a Master of Secondary Education in English Language Arts from Auburn University Montgomery. Her master's thesis focuses on workplace inequalities for adjunct instructors of first-year composition. She currently works as a middle school English Language Arts teacher in central Alabama.

Nicholas Tyler Reich is a doctoral student and Russell G. Hamilton Scholar in Vanderbilt University's Department of English, where he studies queer and trans★ ecologies, literatures of the US Deep South and Appalachia, energy ontologies, film, and digital media. Their work has been published or is forthcoming in *ISLE: Interdisciplinary Studies in Literature and Environment, TSQ: Transgender Studies Quarterly, The Encyclopedia of LGBTQIA+ Portrayals in American Film,* and elsewhere.

Seth T. Reno is Distinguished Research Associate Professor of English at Auburn University Montgomery. He is author of *Early Anthropocene Literature in Britain, 1750–1884* (2020) and *Amorous Aesthetics: Intellectual Love in Romantic Poetry and*

Poetics, 1788–1853 (2019); editor of *Romanticism and Affect Studies* (2018); and coeditor of *Wordsworth and the Green Romantics: Affect and Ecology in the Nineteenth Century* (2016). He has also published dozens of journal articles, book chapters, book reviews, and encyclopedia entries on eighteenth- and nineteenth-century literature, art, and science.

Kimberly Skye Richards holds a PhD in Performance Studies from the University of California Berkeley. Her research examines how Indigenous and anti-colonial artists and activists use embodied practices to disrupt the development of new extractive infrastructure, foster a "petro-political consciousness," and inspire a just energy transition. She recently coedited an issue of *Canadian Theatre Review* on "Extractivism and Performance" (2020). She has also published in *TDR: The Drama Review, Theatre Journal, Theatre Research in Canada, Sustainable Tools for Precarious Times*, and *An Ecotopian Lexicon: Loanwords to Live With*.

Matthew Rowney is Assistant Professor of English at the University of North Carolina Charlotte. He is author of *In Common Things: Commerce, Culture, and Ecology in British Romantic Literature* (forthcoming), and he has published ecocritical articles in *European Romantic Review* and the *Journal of Literature and Science*.

Antonette Talaue-Arogo is Associate Professor of Literature at De La Salle University Manila, where she obtained her PhD in 2016. She was also a participant in the School of Criticism and Theory at Cornell University (2009). Her research interests include critical theory, especially postcolonialism and cosmopolitanism, continental philosophy, and translation studies.

Stephen Tedeschi is Associate Professor of English at the University of Alabama. He is author of *Urbanization and English Romantic Poetry* (2017), and he has published articles in *European Romantic Review, Keats-Shelley Journal, Keats-Shelley Review*, and *Essays in Romanticism*. His current book project centers on Percy Bysshe Shelley's poetics.

Tobias Wilson-Bates is Assistant Professor of English at Georgia Gwinnet College. His research examines novels as participating both conceptually and materially in the techno-cultural discourses that shaped the nineteenth century. At the center of his work is the concept of the "time machine," an idea he reads as emerging from the combination of narrative modes with assumptions of scientific and technological objectivity.

INTRODUCTION

The Anthropocene and the Humanities

Seth T. Reno

In the 1990s, no one had heard about the "Anthropocene" other than a handful of geologists and climate scientists. At that time, it wasn't even a widely used term. Most scholars credit Paul Crutzen with popularizing the term—he's an atmospheric chemist who won a Nobel Prize in 1995 for his work on the ozone layer. At an academic conference in 2000, Crutzen became agitated at presenters repeatedly referring to the Holocene—that's the geological epoch that began about 11,700 years ago at the end of the last Ice Age. Crutzen famously blurted out, "Stop saying the Holocene! We're not in the Holocene anymore." Instead, he proposed, we're in the "Anthropocene."[1] A few months later, he co-wrote an article with Eugene Stoermer on "The Anthropocene" in the *International Geosphere-Biosphere Programme Newsletter*, and then a follow-up essay in *Nature*, "The Geology of Mankind" (2002). These articles have been cited over 10,000 times in various publications, and they effectually started the field of Anthropocene studies.[2]

Two decades later, the Anthropocene pops up everywhere. There are new academic journals devoted solely to the Anthropocene, as well as numerous special issues of journals in fields like literature, history, and political science. Popular American novelist and YouTube personality John Greene has a successful podcast called *The Anthropocene Reviewed*. NPR and other major news outlets regularly run stories on the Anthropocene. Books on the Anthropocene have proliferated with academic and commercial presses, so much so that some scholars consider the concept to be "worn-out and déclassé."[3] The Anthropocene concept is widespread. It's everywhere. Everyone knows about the Anthropocene.

But not really. In my experience, and that of my colleagues at universities around the world, the vast majority of college students haven't heard of it. When I attend academic conferences and talk to others in academia, it seems that most college teachers may have heard the term used somewhere but have no clear

DOI: 10.4324/9781003095347-1

idea what Anthropocene studies is or what researchers in this area do. Despite widespread usage, the Anthropocene concept is still most familiar to scientists and academics doing specialized research in geology, the environmental sciences, and the environmental humanities—hardly the majority of people on this planet, or even in academia. Maybe this will change in the coming decades, especially if the Anthropocene becomes a formal geologic epoch (it's not yet), but maybe not. How many people do you know who could carry on a conversation about the Holocene epoch?

As I often ask my students: So what? Why should you or anyone else care about the Anthropocene? My response, unsurprisingly, is that there are many good reasons, especially for college students and instructors, not least to have some cultural currency with this interdisciplinary concept. Entering the mid-twenty-first century, we'll all be hard-pressed to find a career trajectory that's *not* interdisciplinary in some way; most students graduating college over the next few decades will change fields multiple times over the course of their lifetimes, in response to rapidly developing technologies and a rapidly changing global climate. Understanding how to adapt, and how to live, in this changing world will be essential. And the Anthropocene concept is necessarily interdisciplinary; to study it, we need to know a bit about geology, climate science, environmental justice, and literature, especially in the form of *stories*—the story of the Anthropocene itself. The Anthropocene is the proposed name for a new geologic epoch, but it's also the story of humans' relationship to the natural world, how we became geophysical agents capable of modifying Earth's ecosystems, raising global temperatures and sea levels, melting massive glaciers, changing the very physical makeup of the planet, and causing the Sixth Mass Extinction.[4] How'd we get here? Where might we go? How do we feel about and make sense of this new epoch that we've created? These are some of the questions that this book addresses.

This book is written for nonspecialists interested in but unfamiliar with the Anthropocene concept. But not exclusively. All of the chapters contain original research and arguments that engage with and develop key issues in Anthropocene studies. But they do so in accessible, jargon-free language suitable as an entry point for college teachers and students. Interested in new approaches to Henry David Thoreau? Check out Robert Klevay's chapter. Developing a course on the Environmental Humanities and want to design a unit on the Anthropocene? Check out chapters by Lisa Ottum, Kent Linthicum, and Stephen Tedeschi. Want to expand your reading lists with literature from the Global South? Read chapters by Rebecca Macklin, Kimberly Skye Richards, and Antonette Talaue-Arogo. Want to learn about contemporary cli-fi novels? Read chapters by Kristin Girten and Seth Reno. If you're a student, you can turn to any chapter as an introduction to a particular approach, author, or text as part of your studies.

All of the chapters in this book are short and focused (~4,000 words), designed to provide a concise overview or model of a particular approach or text, as well as a compelling and original intervention in the study of the Anthropocene. Part 1,

"Approaches," focuses on specific humanist approaches to the Anthropocene—the environmental humanities, economics, the energy humanities, environmental racism, queer theory, and literary criticism—though many of the chapters also engage literary texts. Part 2, "Contexts," focuses mainly on specific authors and literary works, though you'll also see overlap with the theoretical and historical approaches from Part 1. Authors include Mary Shelley, Henry David Thoreau, H.G. Wells, Virginia Woolf, J.P. Clark, Gina Apostol, Jeff VanderMeer, and Kim Stanley Robinson. There is no overarching argument to the collection, but, as a whole, this book shows how **the Anthropocene is simultaneously a geologic epoch, a scientific term, and a cultural concept with no single, definitive narrative**.

There are some central questions that drive this collection: Why is the Anthropocene important to the humanities and to literature in particular? How can humanists approach the Anthropocene? How can we teach the Anthropocene? Is there a literature of the Anthropocene? If so, how do we read it? Each chapter addresses one or more of these questions and offers an avenue into thinking about how literature and the humanities are central to understanding and living in this new epoch.

The Anthropocene: Definitions, Dating, and Debates

Meaning "The Age of Humans," the Anthropocene is the proposed name for the current geological epoch, beginning when human activities started to have a noticeable impact on Earth's geology and ecosystems. Paul Crutzen popularized the term in 2000, spurring two decades of debate, with most scholarship centered on defining the characteristics of the Anthropocene and in establishing its dates. Crutzen initially proposed that the Anthropocene began with the Industrial Revolution, citing James Watt's patent of the steam engine in 1784 as a possible cultural marker, while other scientists have since argued for the Orbis spike of 1610, the start of the nuclear age in 1945, and the "bomb spike" of 1964. These "spike" labels refer to what geologists call a "golden spike," or a Global Boundary Stratotype Section and Point (GSSP). This is an official geological marker with a set of specific international requirements that include identifying global change in rock layers of Earth.

Each of these proposed starting points offers a distinct narrative of the Anthropocene. The "Orbis spike" refers to a dramatic decrease in CO_2 levels in the Americas after the Columbian Exchange and a century of genocide resulted in unprecedented forest growth (see Figure 0.1). This narrative locates the origins of the Anthropocene in slavery, imperial colonialism, and global trade, all of which reshaped the trajectory of Earth's biosphere.[5] In contrast, the start date of 1784 coincides with the Industrial Revolution in Britain—an apt marker for the start of the global fossil fuel era—as well as the British Agricultural Revolution and the rise of capitalism and globalization. While these cultural phenomena do not

4 Seth T. Reno

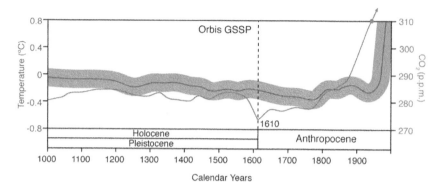

FIGURE 0.1 Simon Lewis and Mark Maslin, "Orbis Spike," in "Defining the Anthropocene," *Nature* 519 (2015).

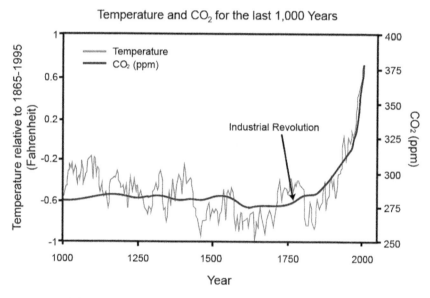

FIGURE 0.2 Adriane Lam and Jen Bauer, "Temperature and CO$_2$ for the Last 1,000 Years," in "CO$_2$: Past, Present, and Future," Time Scavengers, https://i0.wp.com/timescavengers.blog/wp-content/uploads/2017/06/1000-2000_co2temp-01.jpg?ssl=1.

have a specific start date or unambiguous geological marker, there is a clear rise in CO$_2$ beginning in the eighteenth century, which is a direct result of fossil fuels, and the Industrial Revolution in particular marks virtually every aspect of life on Earth (see Figure 0.2).[6] The more recent dates are the Trinity Nuclear Test in 1945 (the first detonation of an atomic bomb) and the "bomb spike" of 1964, the latter

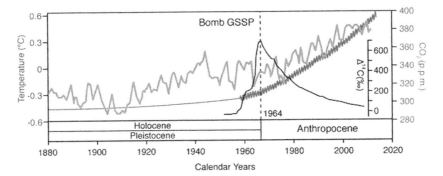

FIGURE 0.3 Simon Lewis and Mark Maslin, "Bomb Spike," in "Defining the Anthropocene," *Nature* 519 (2015).

of which shows a dramatic increase in radionuclides as a result of nuclear testing (see Figure 0.3). These twentieth-century markers center on what scholars call the Great Acceleration—that is, the concurrent accelerations of CO_2 emissions, global industrialization, species extinctions, and other related effects of intensified global warming since around 1950—as well as nuclear fallout, which will be detectable in Earth's crust for millions of years.[7] A mid-twentieth-century date is the leading candidate for the official start of the Anthropocene.[8]

However, scholars in the humanities and social sciences are less interested in golden spikes than the social, political, economic, and philosophical events and perspectives that have produced this new Age of Humans. While geologists are primarily concerned with determining a definitive stratigraphic boundary between the Holocene and Anthropocene, many humanists and social scientists challenge the unified notion of "Anthropos" by examining the unequal distribution of power, resources, and capital across the world. For many of these scholars, the very term "Anthropocene" is troubling, as only a handful of industrialized nations have produced the global ecological damage that characterizes this new epoch. Many scholars have therefore suggested alternative names, such as Capitalocene (to foreground capitalism), Plantationocene (to foreground colonialism and race), and Eurocene (to foreground the central role of European imperial colonialism). Meanwhile, humanities scholars are also rethinking the divisions of human and natural histories, as well as the human/nonhuman binary dominant in Western attitudes, through critical analyses of literary, scientific, artistic, and political texts. What stories do we tell about the Anthropocene, and who is telling those stories?[9]

For each of the "big three" dates (1610, 1784, and 1950), the major characteristics of the Anthropocene are fairly clear: dominance of the human species on Earth, in terms of population growth, land use, and resource consumption; widespread biodiversity loss and the sixth mass extinction; and increase of carbon dioxide in Earth's atmosphere, resulting in the accelerated effects of global warming (glacial ice melting, sea level rise, acidification of oceans, water shortages and food scarcity, widening social and economic inequality, and a planet increasingly hostile to human life). Chapters in this collection explore the Anthropocene in different ways, sometimes by focusing on a particular narrative about environmental change, but more often by showing how these changes coincide with the cultural phenomena of imperial colonialism, industrialization, and capitalism as driving forces of the modern world and of the Anthropocene itself.

How to Use This Book

While there is much overlap and connection between the fifteen chapters in this book, each chapter is a standalone piece that can be read and used independently. Each chapter ends with a reference list intended as "further reading" for scholars, teachers, and students in developing research projects, lesson plans, and courses (or course units). In order to write in an accessible manner, many citations and contextual/scholarly information are included in endnotes and references rather than in the body of the chapter itself. Chapter titles are also straightforward, giving readers a clear sense of the central approach and/or literary text. Regardless, I think it may be helpful to say a few words in summary of each part of this collection to orient readers.

In Part 1, "Approaches," you will find seven chapters that offer seven different theoretical approaches to the Anthropocene. The first three chapters illustrate broad contributions of the humanities to Anthropocene studies. In the opening chapter, "The Deep Time Life Kit," Lisa Ottum explains how a humanist approach to the Anthropocene can help us make sense of living in a time of environmental crisis, when we are asked on a daily basis to respond to a barrage of often conflicting information and stimuli. How does it feel to live in the Anthropocene? How might we channel those feelings into useful narratives to effect change, both personally and globally? She offers a set of "Anthropocene mantras" to help us understand, and cope with, the unique stress of living through the birth of a new geological epoch. The second chapter by Scott MacKenzie, "The Two Households: Economics and Ecology," reveals the intertwined developments of modern economic and ecological theory in the eighteenth century, which shed new light on the concept of the Capitalocene. While we often think of economics and ecology as oppositional, MacKenzie shows that eighteenth-century writers and theorists such as David Hume, Gilbert White, Thomas Malthus, and Edmund Burke thought of these fields as mutually constitutive, which continues to inform economic theory in the twenty-first century. Kent Linthicum's chapter on "Energy and the Anthropocene" provides a critical overview of the field of Energy Humanities, with case studies of three literary texts corresponding to the big three dates of the Anthropocene and their dominant energy source: wood in William Shakespeare's *The Tempest* (1611), coal in Jane Austen's *Mansfield Park* (1814), and petroleum in Wole Soyinka's "Telephone Conversation" (1962).

The next two chapters by Rebecca Macklin and Nicolás Juárez investigate environmental racism in the Anthropocene, but from different angles. Macklin draws from Indigenous studies and world literary studies to explore issues and instances of environmental racism and environmental justice in twentieth-century Native American literature, particularly the works of Simon Ortiz and Linda Hogan. She reveals how the lasting legacies of European colonialism and settler colonialism shape both the land of North America and Indigenous experiences of the Anthropocene. Juárez, on the other hand, takes a broader approach to environmental racism by showing how Black chattel slavery and Native American genocide mark each of the "big three" dates for the Anthropocene. He advocates for the alternative term Eurocene, which emphasizes the central role of European colonialism and conquest in producing the Anthropocene and our modern world. At its heart, Juárez suggests, is the question of who counts as human, and who gets to decide. Similarly, in his chapter "Trans*Plantationocene," Nicholas Reich discusses the Plantationocene, an alternative term that emphasizes how people of color, especially Black people in the US, are disproportionately marginalized and displaced by the Anthropocene. But Reich adds transgender people to the conversation, fusing approaches of critical race studies, queer theory, and gender studies, and thereby modeling a new kind of Anthropocene reading that uncovers the lives and voices of those most affected by the global climate emergency. He grounds this approach in an analysis of the 2015 film *Tangerine*.

In the final chapter of Part 1, Stephen Tedeschi offers an extensive critical review of major approaches to and studies of the Anthropocene in literature and the humanities, providing readers with a variety of methods and models. And he argues that what this renaissance of literary criticism suggests is a future where literature and the humanities provide us with "survival skills" for living in the Anthropocene, pointing to the pleasures of thinking and feeling above the economic- and capital-based pleasures that have produced the environmental catastrophe in which we now live. He sees something of a return to the aesthetic experience on the horizon, an appreciation of the beauty of life—something that requires careful attention, critical thinking, and the imagination.

In Part 2, "Contexts," each chapter treats one particular author and/or literary text, using the Anthropocene concept as a lens to analyze the text, or using the text to analyze the Anthropocene concept (and sometimes both). The author/text is named in the titles to most chapters, excepting two: Tobias Wilson-Bate's chapter, "It's the End of the World: Can We Know It?" focuses on H.G. Wells' novel *The Time Machine* (1895), and Antonette Talaue-Arogo's chapter, "What Global South Critics Do," focuses on Gina Apostol's novel *Insurrecto* (2018). The chapters in Part 2 are organized chronologically, spanning the early nineteenth century through the late-2010s. The first three chapters (Rowney, Klevay, and Wilson-Bates) analyze nineteenth-century texts, the next two (Perez and Richards) analyze twentieth-century texts, and the final three (Talaue-Arogo, Girten, and Reno) analyze twenty-first-century texts.

Ideally, readers of this book who are nonspecialists—teachers, scholars, and students—will find an accessible introduction to how and why the Anthropocene concept is important to literature and the humanities. The chapters offer a wide variety of ideas, texts, and models for course development, reading lists, and research projects. Readers who are specialists in literature and the environmental humanities will find truly innovative arguments that offer new and important contributions to the field of Anthropocene studies. The Anthropocene isn't going anywhere—we're in it—and what the field, and world, needs more of right now is the humanities.

Notes

1 Nicola Davidson, "The Anthropocene Epoch: Have We Entered a New Phase of Planetary History?" *The Guardian*, 30 May 2019.
2 See Paul J. Crutzen and Eugene F. Stoermer, "The 'Anthropocene,'" *IGBP Newsletter* 41 (2000): 17; and Paul J. Crutzen, "Geology of Mankind," *Nature* 415 (2002): 23.
3 Jeremy Davies, *The Birth of the Anthropocene* (Oakland: University of California Press, 2016), 6.
4 See Elizabeth Kolbert, *The Sixth Extinction: An Unnatural History* (New York: Henry Holt and Company, 2014).
5 See Simon Lewis and Mark Maslin, "Defining the Anthropocene," *Nature* 519 (2015): 171–180; Richard H. Grove, *Green Imperialism: Colonial Expansion, Tropical Island Edens, and the Origins of Environmentalism, 1600–1860* (Cambridge: Cambridge University Press, 1995); Steve Mentz, "Enter Anthropocene, circa 1610," in *Anthropocene Reading: Literary History in Geologic Times*, ed. Tobias Menely and Jesse Oak Taylor (University Park: Pennsylvania State University Press, 2017), 43–58; and Kathryn Yusoff, *A Billion Black Anthropocenes or None* (Minneapolis: University of Minnesota Press, 2018).
6 See Crutzen and Stoermer; Crutzen; Will Steffen, Paul J. Crutzen, and John R. McNeill, "The Anthropocene: Are Humans Now Overwhelming the Great Forces of Nature?" *AMBIO: A Journal of the Human Environment* 36, no. 8 (2007): 614–621; Jesse Oak Taylor, *The Sky of Our Manufacture: The London Fog in British Fiction from Dickens to Woolf* (Charlottesville: University of Virginia Press, 2016); Andreas Malm, *Fossil Capital: The Rise of Steam Power and the Roots of Global Warming* (London: Verso, 2016); and Seth T. Reno, *Early Anthropocene Literature in Britain, 1750–1884* (London: Palgrave Macmillan, 2020).
7 See J.R. McNeill and Peter Engelke, *The Great Acceleration: An Environmental History of the Anthropocene Since 1945* (Cambridge: Belknap Press, 2014); Clive Hamilton and Jacques Grinevald, "Was the Anthropocene Anticipated?" *The Anthropocene Review* 2, no. 1 (2015): 59–72; and Will Steffen, Wendy Broadgate, Lisa Deutsch, Owen Gaffney, and Cornelia Ludwig, "The Trajectory of the Anthropocene: The Great Acceleration," *The Anthropocene Review* 2, no. 1 (2015): 81–98.
8 In 2019, the Anthropocene Working Group, part of the International Commission of Stratigraphy, completed a binding vote to move forward with identifying a mid-twentieth-century golden spike to determine the start of the Anthropocene as a formally defined geological unit within the Geological Time Scale. See "Working Group on the 'Anthropocene'" (http://quaternary.stratigraphy.org/working-groups/anthropocene/). At the time of completing this book in mid-2021, a 2022 vote is planned to determine the Anthropocene golden spike, and the frontrunner is 1952. For useful overviews

of these dating debates, see Christophe Bonneuil, "The Geological Turn: Narratives of the Anthropocene," in *The Anthropocene and the Global Environmental Crisis: Rethinking Modernity in a New Epoch*, ed. Clive Hamilton, Christophe Bonneuil, and Francois Gemenne (New York: Routledge, 2014), 15–31; Christophe Bonneuil and Jean-Baptiste Fressoz, *The Shock of the Anthropocene: The Earth, History, and Us*, trans. David Fernbach (London: Verso, 2015); Davies; Simon L. Lewis and Mark A. Maslin, *The Human Planet: How We Created the Anthropocene* (New Haven: Yale University Press, 2018); and Jan Zalasiewicz, Colin N. Waters, Mark Williams, and Colin P. Summerhayes, eds., *The Anthropocene as a Geological Time Unit: A Guide to the Scientific Evidence and Current Debate* (Cambridge: Cambridge University Press, 2019).
9 For geology, see Lewis and Maslin; and Jan Zalasiewicz, et al., "Making the Case for a Formal Anthropocene Epoch: An Analysis of Ongoing Critiques," *Newsletters on Stratigraphy* 50, no. 2 (2017): 205–226. For the social sciences, see Andreas Malm and Alf Hornborg, "The Geology of Mankind? A Critique of the Anthropocene Narrative," *The Anthropocene Review* 24, no. 1 (2014): 62–69; and Cameron Harrington and Clifford Shearing, *Security in the Anthropocene: Reflections on Safety and Care* (New York: Columbia University Press, 2017). For the humanities, see Dipesh Chakrabarty, "The Climate of History: Four Theses," *Critical Inquiry* 35 (2009): 197–222; and Donna J. Haraway, *Staying with the Trouble: Making Kin in the Chthulucene* (Durham: Duke University Press, 2016).

References

Bonneuil, Christophe. "The Geological Turn: Narratives of the Anthropocene." In *The Anthropocene and the Global Environmental Crisis: Rethinking Modernity in a New Epoch*. Edited by Clive Hamilton, Christophe Bonneuil, and Francois Gemenne. New York: Routledge, 2014. 15–31.
Bonneuil, Christophe, and Jean-Baptiste Fressoz. *The Shock of the Anthropocene: The Earth, History, and Us*. Translated by David Fernbach. London: Verso, 2015.
Chakrabarty, Dipesh. "The Climate of History: Four Theses." *Critical Inquiry* 35 (2009): 197–222.
Crutzen, Paul J. "Geology of Mankind." *Nature* 415 (2002): 23.
Crutzen, Paul J., and Eugene F. Stoermer. "The 'Anthropocene.'" *IGBP Newsletter* 41 (2000): 17.
Davidson, Nicola. "The Anthropocene Epoch: Have We Entered a New Phase of Planetary History?" *The Guardian*. 30 May 2019.
Davies, Jeremy. *The Birth of the Anthropocene*. Oakland: University of California Press, 2016.
Grove, Richard H. *Green Imperialism: Colonial Expansion, Tropical Island Edens, and the Origins of Environmentalism, 1600–1860*. Cambridge: Cambridge University Press, 1995.
Hamilton, Clive, and Jacques Grinevald. "Was the Anthropocene Anticipated?" *The Anthropocene Review* 2, no. 1 (2015): 59–72.
Haraway, Donna J. *Staying with the Trouble: Making Kin in the Chthulucene*. Durham: Duke University Press, 2016.
Harrington, Cameron, and Clifford Shearing. *Security in the Anthropocene: Reflections on Safety and Care*. New York: Columbia University Press, 2017.
Kolbert, Elizabeth. *The Sixth Extinction: An Unnatural History*. New York: Henry Holt and Company, 2014.
Lewis, Simon L., and Mark A. Maslin. *The Human Planet: How We Created the Anthropocene*. New Haven: Yale University Press, 2018.

Malm, Andreas. *Fossil Capital: The Rise of Steam Power and the Roots of Global Warming.* London: Verso, 2016.

Malm, Andreas, and Alf Hornborg. "The Geology of Mankind? A Critique of the Anthropocene Narrative." *The Anthropocene Review* 24, no. 1 (2014): 62–69.

McNeill, J.R., and Peter Engelke. *The Great Acceleration: An Environmental History of the Anthropocene Since 1945.* Cambridge: Belknap Press, 2014.

Mentz, Steve. "Enter Anthropocene, circa 1610." In *Anthropocene Reading: Literary History in Geologic Times.* Edited by Tobias Menely and Jesse Oak Taylor. University Park: Pennsylvania State University Press, 2017. 43–58.

Reno, Seth T. *Early Anthropocene Literature in Britain, 1750–1884.* London: Palgrave Macmillan, 2020.

Steffen, Will, Paul J. Crutzen, and John R. McNeill. "The Anthropocene: Are Humans Now Overwhelming the Great Forces of Nature?" *AMBIO: A Journal of the Human Environment* 36, no. 8 (2007): 614–621.

Steffen, Will, Wendy Broadgate, Lisa Deutsch, Owen Gaffney, and Cornelia Ludwig. "The Trajectory of the Anthropocene: The Great Acceleration." *The Anthropocene Review* 2, no. 1 (2015): 81–98.

Taylor, Jesse Oak. *The Sky of Our Manufacture: The London Fog in British Fiction from Dickens to Woolf.* Charlottesville: University of Virginia Press, 2016.

"Working Group on the 'Athropocene.'" http://quaternary.stratigraphy.org/working-groups/anthropocene/.

Yusoff, Kathryn. *A Billion Black Anthropocenes or None.* Minneapolis: University of Minnesota Press, 2018.

Zalasiewicz, Jan, Colin N. Waters, Mark Williams, and Colin P. Summerhayes, eds. *The Anthropocene as a Geological Time Unit: A Guide to the Scientific Evidence and Current Debate.* Cambridge: Cambridge University Press, 2019.

Zalasiewicz, Jan, et al. "Making the Case for a Formal Anthropocene Epoch: An Analysis of Ongoing Critiques." *Newsletters on Stratigraphy* 50, no. 2 (2017): 205–226.

PART 1
Approaches

1
THE DEEP TIME LIFE KIT
Thinking Tools for the Anthropocene

Lisa Ottum

Imagine you're at home on the couch, scrolling through pictures of kittens, or Kardashians, or something. It's late (or maybe it's early—the time doesn't really matter). You hear "breaking news" chimes on the TV and look up. *It's one of those depressing environment stories.* You've seen these before: in fact, you could practically script the entire thing. There's the familiar red "Alert!" banner next to a worried-looking expert. In the background, there's footage of something on fire, or something melting, or some awful-looking pile of trash. Even though the sound is down, you can pick out the phrases "scientists warn" and "without further action." *Ugh.* You sigh loudly. You look away. You feel bad about this latest catastrophe ... but also irritated. Isn't this someone else's fault—all those stupid people more wasteful and shortsighted than you? Screw *those* people, whoever they are. *You*—you didn't cause this, at least not directly. Besides, maybe they're just exaggerating—hopefully. The media exaggerates, right? You flip off the TV. Still, you can't shake a lingering sense of unease. None of this is really your *fault*, and yet you also feel a little stab of guilt—or maybe it's sadness? It's something unnamable, a sensation in search of a word.

This is life in the Anthropocene—or one part of it, anyway: the unsettling feeling that Earth is off-kilter, and that everyone, but no one in particular, is responsible. It's not your imagination. Climatologically speaking, we *are* living in momentous times. According to the United Nations, the last six years (2015–2020) were the hottest on record; temperatures in the Arctic have risen three degrees Celsius since 1990.[1] Globally, July 2019 was the hottest July ever recorded by the National Oceanic and Atmospheric Administration.[2] According to NASA, arctic sea ice is melting at a record pace.[3] I could list other alarming developments, although most people—even climate skeptics—can tell without consulting statistics that

DOI: 10.4324/9781003095347-3

that weather outside their window is changing, and that things seem similarly out-of-whack elsewhere.

For scientists, the term "Anthropocene" refers to changes in Earth's systems—to the myriad ways humans have altered the oceans, the land, and the air. Humanists, meanwhile, invoke the Anthropocene as a historical or cultural label. This chapter examines the Anthropocene from both of these perspectives, as well as a third perspective: that of the nonspecialist struggling to make sense of their role in creating, and responding to, climate change and other large-scale environmental disasters. For many people, the sheer magnitude of today's environmental problems forms an emotional barrier to engagement. (Think back to that couch example from a moment ago.) What if ordinary people—and not just specialists—were to embrace the Anthropocene in both our private and public deliberations about the environment? By introducing geologic time into the conversation, the Anthropocene reframes partisan debates about climate change. It also invites us to imagine new ways of relating to environmentalism. While the idea of the Anthropocene is not a panacea for anger or anxiety, it might help us to cultivate affective stances that are more sustainable, and thus more compatible with action, than amorphous feelings of guilt and helplessness. In the pages that follow, I offer a brief history of the Anthropocene concept, before turning to an in-depth analysis of "Anthropocenic" thinking and its affordances.

The term "Anthropocene" surfaced in scientific literature as early as the 1980s, though its formal emergence is usually traced to a 2000 article in a rather obscure geology publication. In this article, Earth scientist Paul Crutzen and ecologist Eugene Stoermer proposed the term "Anthropocene" to describe a global environment dominated by human activity. Mankind, they asserted, has become a geological force whose influence seems likely to endure "for many millennia, maybe millions of years to come." Therefore, they conclude, "it seems to us more than appropriate to emphasize the central role of mankind in geology and ecology by proposing to use the term 'anthropocene' for the current geological epoch."[4] Crutzen reiterated this view in a 2002 article for the journal *Nature*; it was then that the term "Anthropocene" came into widespread usage, catapulting from obscurity to common usage in less than a decade.[5]

As with any paradigm shift, the notion of an "Anthropocene" has been controversial, not only among geologists but among other scientists. At issue is the way we measure and describe planetary history: when exactly does one era of Earth's history become a new one? For geologists, the question of whether we are indeed in a new era is a matter of stratigraphic evidence.[6] Until the debate over the Anthropocene arrived, geologists placed our present day in the Holocene, an epoch that began about 11,500 years ago after the last glacial period. Compared to previous epochs in Earth's history, this one has been pretty stable, ecologically speaking: Earth's temperatures have stayed within a 1-degree Celsius range, and, as a result, human civilization emerged and has flourished. Yet things are changing fast—especially the temperature, which, even in most optimistic projections, is set to rise 1.5 degrees Celsius. Moreover, life on Earth is changing in ways that suggest a catastrophic rupture in the Holocene. On the geologic timescale, several key turning points correspond to mass extinction events (the so-called "Big Five" extinctions). Many experts believe that such an event—a Sixth Mass Extinction—is currently underway. Now, if you're picturing "mass extinction" as the kind of event that wiped out the dinosaurs, this might seem far-fetched: there are no flaming meteorites raining from the sky outdoors. Not all mass extinctions are this cinematic, though. For example, the so-called Great Dying that took place at the end of the Paleozoic Era 250 million years ago may have included an enormous volcanic event; if this is true, then what actually killed everything was the global warming and ocean acidification that followed. In our own moment, species are going extinct at a rate that far exceeds the "background rate"—that is, the estimated natural rate at which species go extinct, absent catastrophe. (For reference, according to a 2015 study, for mammals, this rate is 2 species per 10,000 per 100 years. A recent study estimates that the current rate of vertebrate loss is 100 times that pace.)[7]

If previous geologic eras are marked by mass extinctions, and if we are currently in a mass extinction, then it stands to reason that we have entered a new moment in geologic time. It takes time for extinction events to show up in the rock record, though. Will geologists thousands of years in the future be able to pinpoint this event in Earth's underlayers? Even if the answer is no, we've made other changes to the planet that may register stratigraphically. For example, humans have massively reshaped Earth's surface through mining, agriculture, and the building of dams, all of which adds up to some pretty wicked erosion. We've also introduced millions of tons of manufactured stuff into the environment. A 2017 article in *The Anthropocene Review* estimates that the material output of humans—what the authors call the "physical technosphere"—weighs about 30 trillion tons. This technosphere "includes a large, rapidly growing diversity of complex objects that are potential trace fossil or 'technofossils'."[8] In other words, our junk is creating a new Earth layer—one that "already exceeds known estimates of biological diversity as measured by richness, far exceeds recognized fossil diversity, and may exceed total biological diversity through Earth's history."[9]

Given all of these signs that humans are a planet-altering force, it might seem that the Anthropocene discussion is settled. Geologists are not in agreement, though, about whether to amend the geologic timescale. As geologist Jill Schneiderman explains, "formal stratigraphic practice requires a systematic approach to define, delineate, and correlate sequences of rocks and to identify stratigraphically constrained units of time based on contained rocks, minerals, and fossils as well as chemical and physical parameters."[10] The conditions do not yet exist to perform this sort of analysis because, in terms of geologic time, humans basically just got here. Another difficulty is that "certain indicators of the Anthropocene," such as the rise of greenhouse gases in the atmosphere, "do not leave abrupt boundary layers in strata that would delineate the Anthropocene clearly."[11] Some other markers are not globally synchronous. For instance, if farming marks a significant turning point in Earth's history, its traces will appear to start at different times, since some parts of the world were cultivated on a mass scale before others.

Here, we arrive at some questions that are interesting to people *other* than geologists, whose debates might seem arcane to those of us outside the field. Broken down its roots, the term "Anthropocene" names the "age of humans"; it is commonplace to use collective pronouns in discussing "our" imprint on the planet. However, as numerous critics of the term "Anthropocene" point out, our current environmental dilemmas are hardly the fault of "humankind." Consider for a moment your personal carbon footprint compared to that of someone—an anonymous member of "humankind"—in a developing country. The resources brought to bear on housing, transporting, and feeding those of us in the Global North are enormous. To say that "humans" have mucked up the air, or the soil, or the oceans is to ignore profound differentials in responsibility. It also means ignoring the uneven distribution of environment-related burdens. To cite an obvious example, sea level rise is an acute problem for only some places, even though we have all contributed to the carbon emissions that drive sea level rise. For now, at least, people not living along coastlines have the luxury of simply ignoring the ocean, while some communities, and even entire island nations in the Pacific, scramble to cope with regular inundation, land loss, freshwater contamination, and other problems.

The disparities that underwrite the Anthropocene manifest in individual bodies, too. Children living near open waste dumps, or near polluting factories, bear the costs of "progress" at the level of their very cells. Thanks to a practice known as "regulatory arbitrage," in which companies exploit weak environmental regulations in certain areas in order to comply with stiffer regulations elsewhere, toxins associated with a European or American product often end up in African bodies. For example, as historian Gabrielle Hecht explains, commodity traders purchase fossil fuels from refineries and then blend these fuels differently for different destinations, sending high-sulfur gasoline to African countries and cleaner blends to the U.S. and Europe.[12] This profit-maximizing strategy is one reason why air pollution in African cities is so much worse than air pollution elsewhere: European oil companies profit from offloading pollutants into African airspace. If we examine the "age of humans" through the lens of individual human bodies, the blind spots of a universalizing, purely geological perspective become starkly obvious. Rock layer or no, the Anthropocene is viscerally real for some people in ways that is not for others. For these reasons, many humanist scholars see the Anthropocene as a useful framework for analyzing structures of power. What does it say about "the Anthropos" that natural resources have been disproportionately exploited by certain groups of people—often in conjunction with the violent subjugation of other groups of people?

Humans have always affected ecosystems: ever since there was settled agriculture, people were using fire to clear land. In fact, throughout history, indigenous communities have actively managed natural resources; one hazard to the term "Anthropocene" is that it risks naturalizing a pernicious view of "human nature." It is actually *not* "human nature" to pillage natural resources beyond recovery, pollute our surroundings, enslave one another, or hunt animals to extinction: plenty of communities across time and in different regions have managed *not* to do any of these things. Hence, many humanists argue that *culture* drives unsustainable and unjust decisions. Colonialism and the ecological depredations that followed unfolded in a particular cultural and historical context; so, too, did the Industrial Revolution, and the so-called Great Acceleration of the twentieth century. Thus, whether we say that the Anthropocene began with the Columbian exchange, or with the massive scaling up of fossil fuel extraction, or with some other marker, it does not necessarily follow that current trends were always already in motion. For this reason, some scholars have proposed alternatives to the term "Anthropocene," including the "Capitalocene," a term popularized by historian Jason W. Moore and favored by Marxist thinkers. Moore argues that the warming, increasingly unstable planet we inhabit was created not by humankind but by the power relations dictated by capitalism.

By now, it is hopefully clear that the Anthropocene is both a scientific concept and a narrative, a story about how we got where we are today. Like any story, the Anthropocene relies on plot and characters—and this is one reason the Anthropocene interests literature scholars. In some versions, late 1700s Britain with its harnessing of coal is the bad guy, whereas in others, the villain is someone or something else. The hero also changes with the teller. Will technology swoop in and save us? A visionary and charismatic political leader? The market? Grass-fed beef? (Actually, that last one definitely won't work—sorry.) One important feature of narratives is that they involve us emotionally, sometimes even without our realization. Cognitive science shows that we require only the barest details about a fictional person to begin making inferences about their motivations and empathizing (or not) with their actions.

The way we think about environmental crises and our role in addressing them has as much to do with narrative as it does science. Here is a visual representation of what I mean (Figure 1.1). I call this the Anthropocene Thinkfeel Axis (and I borrow the term "thinkfeel," meaning "the sensation of having an idea," from Timothy Morton).[13] The horizontal axis represents both time and our feelings about time. It is easier to feel connected to events that we imagine as recent, whereas events from the distant past tend to feel less proximate, or relevant, to our experience. The vertical axis represents a spectrum of perceived urgency: in our minds, some social issues seem, well, *urgent*, and worthy of action, whereas others seem less pressing. Most of us fall into one of these four quadrants in our thinking about the environment. In the upper left quadrant is the "we didn't start the fire" crowd. For these folks, things between humans and the Earth went south a long time ago—so long ago that it's difficult to feel intense *personal* guilt or shame about CO_2 levels, mass extinction, and other problems. Put differently, this group doesn't

18 Lisa Ottum

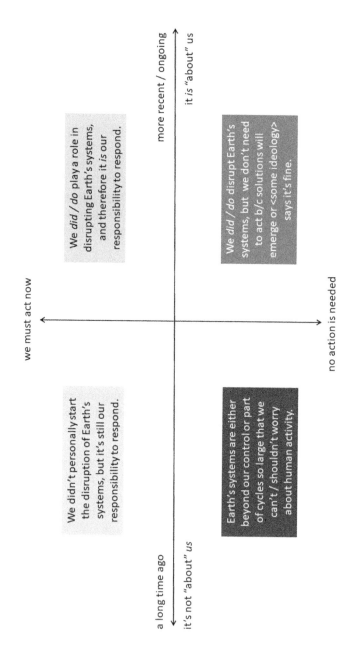

FIGURE 1.1 Lisa Ottum, "Anthropocene Thinkfeel Axis."

feel that climate change is "about" them—but unlike the people in the lower left quadrant, they *do* feel that action is needed. We'll return to this intriguing cohort in a moment.

In contrast, the group in the lower left takes a longer "long view," one *so* long that they don't see humans as having meaningful agency. Adherents to this view include the "sun-is-going-to-expand-someday-and-kill-us-all" crowd. This quadrant also incorporates two views that might at first seem incompatible: (1) a belief in the awesome power of Mother Nature to do whatever she wants, including violently "reset" herself, and (2) the circular logic that if humans are part of nature, and we do something, then that thing must be "natural" and thus accounted for, in some way or another, by nature. The important commonality between these groups is they take geologic time seriously: seen through the lens of Earth's entire history, what's going now is not that bad. Across evolutionary time, there is little evidence that the universe cares about one particular mammal. Shift your context, and suddenly environmentalism seems quixotic or just unnecessary.

The people in the lower *right* quadrant are skeptical of environmentalism for different reasons. This group acknowledges that yes, humans are the cause of enormous disruption to Earth's systems—however, optimism and a faith in human enterprise insulates them from panic. This is where we find proponents of geoengineering and other techno-optimists. They may feel anxious or even guilty about their personal environmental impact; they may even be proponents of "sustainability," the notion that with the right tweaks to existing economic and social systems, we can transition from a "dirty," resource-intensive culture to a "cleaner," more efficient one. Interestingly, this quadrant also contains a few fringier constituencies. These include religious thinkers for whom present-day reality is distressing, but ultimately a prelude to something much better—heaven, or maybe the apocalypse. If you believe yourself to be favored by God or some other force, then it's possible to justify your role in creating the Anthropocene. Why did God put oil in the ground if he didn't mean for to use it?

Finally, in the top right corner are honest-to-goodness *environmentalists*, people who feel *both* personally implicated in the ongoing, up-to-the-minute disruption of Earth's systems *and* compelled to act on these feelings. For these people, environmental problems are palpable and therefore difficult to ignore. They feel impelled to act—and they do. Sometimes, their actions are ambitious and collective: they run for office or join EarthFirst! Sometimes, their actions are modest and individual—they give up meat, or drive a Prius. A challenge this group faces is that it has a pretty bad reputation in popular culture. The term "environmentalist" tends to evoke unpleasant caricatures of smug hippies. To be sure, environmentalists can be mightily annoying, especially to people in the lower right, who feel that all of this freaking out about things that might never come to pass is silly.

Let's return to the top left corner, the group that feels compelled to support environmental causes *even though* they do not, themselves, feel close to the events that have created environmental problems. How do these people reconcile the feeling that they are only minor characters in the story with the feeling of agency normally reserved for protagonists? How do they empathize with a narrative with which they do not strongly identify? Queer theorists have been asking related questions about affect and futurity for some time. As Lee Edelman and others point out, the discourse of futurity is closely tied to heterosexual reproduction. In our culture, the child is the figure of the future; thus, the green movement asks us to "save the whales" or "save the rain forest" for our children, whose bodies are our externalized, concretized vision of "the future." This so-called "reproductive futurism" excludes a great number of queer people, whose stake in the future may not include children at all or at least not children to whom they are biologically attached. Of course, this does not mean that queer people cannot or should not be environmentalists; rather, it suggests that a "queer environmentalism" might pose different, nonreproductive ways of investing in the world around us. Sarah Ensor has theorized the notion of "spinster ecology" to describe a way of caring for the future. In contrast to a mother figure, whose relationship to the future is a direct line from herself to her child, the spinster aunt's future "proceeds far less predictably, is far less invested in replication and repetition, [and] is far more open to unanticipated effects."[14] The spinster, Ensor argues, is well-equipped for a present that is already marked by "variation … nonlinearity … and illegibility"—in other words, a present that is Anthropocenic.[15] To return to the coordinate axis: different positions in this matrix imply different relationships to the idea of past-ness and how one fits into historical time, not all of which are neatly linear or logical. The person inhabiting the upper left might be someone a bit like Ensor's "spinster aunt" figure—not necessarily literally an unmarried, childless woman, but someone with a self-consciously ironic, playful, or otherwise "queer" relationship to environmentalism itself.

In some sense, the term "Anthropocene" is already queer, a shape-shifting, paradoxical concept that defies rigid binaries. The term "Anthropocene" unavoidably evokes The Story (capitalized) of itself *and* the many dueling (lowercase) stories it contains; it inhabits multiple genres at the same time. In this way, the Anthropocene licenses us to sit with cognitive dissonance. Think back to that moment I described at the beginning of this chapter, when you found yourself at first irritated, and then momentarily belligerent, and then apathetic about the news all in the space of a minute. I'm not a psychologist, but I bet that what happened there was a clash between two or more contradictory beliefs jostling around in your brain. There was the thought: "*this is horrible: we must do something!*" bumping up against the thought: "*this is horrible: we can't do anything!*" There might be other contradictions, too: "This is my fault" colliding with "It's not my fault," or "time is running out!" colliding with "we still have time to fix this!" The thing about cognitive dissonance is that humans will go to great lengths to resolve it, hardwired as we are to favor internal consistency. In the case of difficult Anthropocenic issues, that resolution may take the form of disengagement or denialism.

The key challenge of the Anthropocene is that we must channel dissonance into ethical action, knowing that the action may not—and in fact, almost certainly *will not*—fully dispel our unease. To thrive in the Anthropocene, we need to borrow a bit from each of the four quadrants of our diagram. We need the perspective afforded by deep time and its irreducible alterity (the lower left). We need calm and sense of resolution that comes from a degree of detachment (the upper left). We need the sense of urgency afforded by guilt and shame (the upper right). And we also need the hope that we may—just maybe—catch a break (the lower right). Perhaps it's not possible to stand in all four quadrants at once. Still, I think we can use some precepts to anchor our efforts.

In closing, I offer a few mantras for the Anthropocene—aids to reflection that might help us to sit with discomfort. Now: if you're not the meditating type, stick with me a moment: these kernels are crafted less in the spirit of a Hinduist mantra (that "om" from yoga class), and more on the model of a Zen Buddhist kōan. Kōans are short riddles, questions, or stories that might at first seem paradoxical or puzzling; one reflects on a kōan in order to arrive at greater truths about oneself and about the world. Importantly, the kōan is meant to engage the practitioner's intuition, since, according to Buddhist teaching, the rational mind can actually hinder enlightenment. We *definitely* need rationality to confront the Anthropocene, yet we also need habits of mind that are less clearly rational: equanimity, bravery, compassion, a sense of humor. There are no shortcuts here: we'll have to work hard to achieve an attitude commensurate to the Anthropocene's complexities. The following propositions are a first step in that direction. Try them on for size.

Mantra 1: Nature Is Resilient, Surprising, and Not Attached to "Nature"

Nature is one of the slipperiest words in English, mired in such a tangle of meaning, and in so many layers of culture, that it's hard to know which version we are talking about at any moment. Numerous critics have exposed "Nature" and similar concepts (such as wilderness) as thoroughly constructed; one could cite Raymond Williams, or William Cronon, or any number of other scholars on this point. Still, the stuff of nature—the grass and bugs and birds and so on—is very real and remarkably persistent. In fact, if there is one lesson in deep time, it is that nature has grit. Burn it, drown it, freeze it, blast it to bits with an asteroid, and nature will shake it off, stand up, and keep going if we give it a few hundred million years. Nature's resilience should comfort us. It should unsettle us, too, because this resilience is not necessarily directed toward our desires, or our ideas about what "Nature" is, or what is good. We will have nature in generations to come—it just might not resemble Nature. Put differently, in the Anthropocene, nature is getting less and less like itself. One of our challenges moving forward is to cherish an unnatural nature.

Mantra 2: Hippies Rejoice: It's All Connected (for Better—and for Worse)

This mantra is inspired by Timothy Morton's concept of "the ecological thought."[16] This is the simultaneously awesome and discomfiting recognition that everything is ecologically interconnected. Everything includes flowers, and wind, and the haunting sound of wolves howling in moonlight. It also includes toxic chemicals, nuclear waste, and microplastics. A good thing about being interconnected is that we automatically share common interests with every other being on the planet. The bad news is that there is no magical "away" where our trash goes when we throw it out, or where the earth magically transform plastic into something organic and harmless. Interconnectedness *can* be wonderful in situations where we hope to effect change. It complicates these efforts, though, for, as in a woven net (or to use Morton's term, the "mesh"), a tug in one place means tightening and/or loosening in another. In the Anthropocene, we are entangled with other species in fluid, dynamic networks that involve technology, plants, animals, microbes, elements, and natural forces that we don't control. This intimacy is empowering and dangerous at the same time. We would be wise to approach it with love and humility instead of defensiveness about whether climate change is "our fault."

Mantra 3: Climate Change Is Everything Else Change

Climate change is certainly an important part of the Anthropocene no matter how we define it. However, it's often the cascading effects of climate change that we mean when we refer to "climate change." Some time ago, the promoters of climate change skepticism figured out that swapping the term "climate change" for "global warming" was a smart branding move. Warming sounds scary. *Change* isn't necessarily bad. Regardless of how you personally feel, follow me for a moment on embracing the changeability of "change." The thing about climate change is that it alters the rules of the game, so to speak: climate tends to bump into or inflect other systems in ways that are complex and unpredictable. This is why we cannot be sure what exactly the climate of a post-Anthropocene will look like. The trouble with visualizing a thermometer going up and up is that this metaphor makes climate change seem incremental, unidirectional, and uniform; the effects of climate change have none of these features. By embracing the idea of "everything else change," we may be better positioned to face climate change down clearheadedly. We don't have to start public debates with "climate change," either. The most salient aspect of climate change for a farmer in Iowa might be changes to rain patterns; a conversation about "rain change" might succeed where one about climate change might not.

Mantra 4: It's Too Late to Save the Planet, but Also Too Early Not To

To everyone worried that we can't save the planet, relax: we actually cannot save the planet, at least not the version of the planet underpinned by the stable, capitalized Nature that used to seem so natural. What can we accomplish freed from the fear that we must save the planet? One, we can embrace initiates that are experimental, flawed, or even quixotic—and that's good, because so far, we do not actually have a surefire way to combat ocean acidification and other processes already in motion. Two, we can focus attention on how best to distribute the burdens and suffering that will certainly accompany future environmental change. At the moment, people in the first world do not inhabit a postapocalyptic nightmare where we can focus only on our immediate survival. There is time to ask questions such as how can we make the suffering that accompanies habitat loss less bad for people and for nonhuman animals? How can we ensure that our century sees something less than the maximum possible number of climate refugees? Saving the planet need not be an all or nothing proposition.

Mantra 5: The World Isn't Going to End (and Also: Your Kids Will Be There When It Doesn't)

This final mantra is closely related to the fourth one. If there is any insight to draw from deep time, it is this: Earth, like the Dude, abides. Life goes on even when more than 90% of it disappears. On one hand, this thought might seem like the ultimate abdication of responsibility: why worry about mass extinction or anything else when in the big picture, life on Earth is an imponderable cycle of destruction and renewal? On the other hand, the planet's persistence can attune us humankind's legacy, both in the near future and in the distant future. Earth will survive no matter what we do—so we had better decide what kind of post-Anthropocene is morally, ecologically, and aesthetically acceptable. This is not impossible leap of moral imagining. At some point, most of us probably plan for a world after our own death: we know that *we* won't be around, but we try to set things in a direction that is what we would like to see if we were around. Apocalyptic thinking is a cop-out, in that we use it to avoid imagining a future we personally will not inhabit.

These mantras may not change your life—or perhaps they will. At the very least, I hope that they offer some insight into how we might utilize the idea of the Anthropocene to cope with some very overwhelming problems. I'm not an optimist—far from it—but I believe the future is worth betting on. After all, if there is such a thing as "the Anthropocene," there is also such a thing as the post-Anthropocene—the era after this "age of humans" when life on Earth will exist in some form, and more likely than not, in a way that still includes human beings. So, in addition to asking: *where is the Anthropocene going?* let's also ask: *what will the Anthropocene have been?* We're in new territory, which means that anything could happen, even a day when "the Anthropocene" recedes into the distant reaches of cultural memory.

Notes

1. António Guterres, "The Climate Emergency and the Next Generation," http://un.org/sg/en/content/sg/articles/2019-03-15/the-climate-emergency-and-the-next-generation.
2. "July 2019 Was Hottest Month on Record for the Planet," National Oceanic and Atmospheric Administration, http://noaa.gov/news/july-2019-was-hottest-month-on-record-for-planet.
3. Kate Ramsayer, "2020 Arctic Sea Ice Minimum at Second Lowest on Record," National Aeronautics and Space Association, https://climate.nasa.gov/news/3023/2020-arctic-sea-ice-minimum-at-second-lowest-on-record/.
4. Paul J. Crutzen and Eugene F. Stoermer, "The 'Anthropocene,'" *IGBP Newsletter*, no. 41 (2000): 17.
5. Paul J. Crutzen, "Geology of Mankind," *Nature* 415 (2002): 23.
6. Rock layers, or "strata," are studied by stratigraphy, a branch of geology. For some time, geologists have debated how, and whether, human activity might register in the rock record. For more on this point, see Jill S. Schneiderman, "The Anthropocene Controversy," in *Anthropocene Feminism*, ed. Richard Grusin (Minneapolis: University of Minnesota Press, 2017), 169–196.
7. Gerardo Ceballos, et al., "Accelerated Modern Human-Induced Species Losses: Entering the Sixth Mass Extinction," *Science Advances* 1, no. 5 (June 2015): 4.
8. Jan Zalasiewicz, et al., "Scale and Diversity of the Physical Technosphere: A Geological Perspective," *The Anthropocene Review* 4, no. 1 (2017): 9.
9. Ibid., 10.
10. Schneiderman, "Anthropocene Controversy," 185.
11. Ibid., 185.
12. Gabrielle Hecht, "The African Anthropocene," *Aeon*, 6 February 2018.
13. Timothy Morton, *Being Ecological* (Cambridge: MIT Press, 2019): 3.
14. Sarah Ensor, "Spinster Ecology: Rachel Carson, Sarah Orne Jewett, and Nonreproductive Futurity," *American Literature* 84, no. 2 (2012): 419.
15. Ibid., 419.
16. For more, see Timothy Morton, *The Ecological Thought* (Cambridge: Harvard University Press, 2010).

References

Ceballos, Gerardo, Paul R. Ehrlich, Anthony D. Barnosky, Andrés García, Robert M. Pringle, and Todd M. Palmer. "Accelerated Modern Human-Induced Species Losses: Entering the Sixth Mass Extinction." *Science Advances* 1, no. 5 (2015): 1–5.

Crutzen, Paul J. "Geology of Mankind." *Nature* 415 (2002): 23.

Crutzen, Paul J. and Eugene F. Stoermer. "The 'Anthropocene.'" *IGBP Newsletter*, no. 41 (2000): 16–18.

Ensor, Sarah. "Spinster Ecology: Rachel Carson, Sarah Orne Jewett, and Nonreproductive Futurity." *American Literature* 84, no. 2 (2012): 409–435.
Guterres. António. "The Climate Emergency and the Next Generation." 2019. http://un.org/sg/en/content/sg/articles/2019-03-15/the-climate-emergency-and-the-next-generation.
Hecht, Gabrielle. "The African Anthropocene." *Aeon*. 6 February 2018.
National Oceanic and Atmospheric Administration. "July 2019 Was Hottest Month on Record for the Planet." 2019. http://noaa.gov/news/july-2019-was-hottest-month-on-record-for-planet.
Morton, Timothy. *The Ecological Thought*. Cambridge: Harvard University Press, 2010.
———. *Being Ecological*. Cambridge: MIT Press, 2019.
Ramsayer, Kate. "2020 Arctic Sea Ice Minimum at Second Lowest on Record." *National Aeronautics and Space Association*. 2020. https://climate.nasa.gov/news/3023/2020-arctic-sea-ice-minimum-at-second-lowest-on-record/.
Schneiderman, Jill S. "The Anthropocene Controversy." In *Anthropocene Feminism*. Edited by Richard Grusin. Minneapolis: University of Minnesota Press, 2017. 169–196.
Zalasiewicz, Jan, Mark Williams, Colin N. Waters, Anthony D. Barnosky, John Pamesino, Ann-Sofi Rönsskog, Matt Edgeworth, et al. "Scale and Diversity of the Physical Technosphere: A Geological Perspective." *The Anthropocene Review* 4, no. 1 (2017): 9–22.

2
THE TWO HOUSEHOLDS
Economics and Ecology

Scott R. MacKenzie

The idea that we are in an Anthropocene epoch is based on an assumption that human activity is significantly different from other forces that shape the geologic record. There must be something in the way humans affect the planet that sets them apart. In what might that difference consist? Humans are not the only producers of carbon dioxide, nor the only modifiers of ecosystems, nor the only predators that consume other organisms—even to extinction. Part of the answer has to do with the vast scale at which anthropogenic change is leaving traces in earth, rock, air, and water. But humans have not always wrought such immense effects. Only in the last 200–400 years has humanity begun to alter the planet substantially, and since the 1950s, we have seen a "great acceleration" in all aspects of human production and consumption that is rapidly increasing carbon emissions and other harmful outputs.[1] The Anthropocene epoch does not coincide with the duration of humanity's existence as a species.

Whether it began in the sixteenth century or the twentieth century, the Anthropocene is linked to the history of what Karl Marx called the mode of production—capitalism. Over the past 500 years or so, capitalism has become the dominant system of organization for the manufacturing and consuming of what we need and what we desire. Marx's vision of a communist mode of production was also designed around industrialization, but there can be little dispute that the massive expansion of human capacities to make, distribute, and use since the seventeenth and eighteenth centuries has been primarily driven by capitalism.

In the twenty-first century, "no society can be seen to exist in complete isolation from capitalism."[2] Even though there are places and social groups that remain technically outside the systems of property and exchange that come with capitalism, those places and populations are affected by the environmental impacts of

DOI: 10.4324/9781003095347-4

large-scale industry and transportation. Some scholars have argued that *Capitalocene* would be a better term for this epoch than Anthropocene because only a small proportion of humanity is directing the world-altering processes, and many non-human participants are caught up in them (e.g., organisms produced by agriculture or minerals used to generate energy).[3] Even the class of humans who possess major wealth and capital are not primarily interested in creating climate change and environmental degradation, so how is it that capitalism so consistently wreaks disruptive effects on the earth, air, water, and organisms in its path?

Part of what has made the great acceleration possible has been the dominant methods of talking about, studying, and organizing capitalist activity—economics. Not all economic thought is only concerned with capitalism, nor do all economists accept that capitalism is the best possible economic system (Marx is a major figure in nineteenth-century economic thought). Mainstream economics does, nonetheless, generally promote and adhere to capitalist objectives. Pro-capitalist economics has separated itself from fields of knowledge that deal with the natural world (including many aspects of human living conditions) and neglected what industry and commerce are doing to those spheres. "For much of the twentieth century," Fraser Murison Smith argues, "most economists steadfastly maintained that … economics did not need to consider all the other messy, bothersome problems outside the study of markets."[4] Smith is himself an economist and proposes a plan to develop "a future, stable economy in alignment with natural systems," which may mitigate some kinds of exploitation but sustains the premise that nature and "the economy" are two distinct entities.[5]

Economists do not claim that their discipline has nothing whatsoever to do with nature; they see nature as important to economics because it is the repository of primary resources and its biological systems govern human capacities to produce and consume. But as far as mainstream economics is concerned, nature has not required much in the way of care or stewardship. It may be that resources sometimes run short, but, at least until recently, economists have generally insisted that "flexibility, not rigidity, characterizes the relationship of modern man to the physical universe … Nature imposes particular scarcities, not an inescapable general scarcity."[6] General scarcity is "impossible for economists," according to Michael Perelman, "because they maintain that everything always has a substitute."[7] "Advances in fundamental science," Burnett and Morse assert, "have made it possible to take advantage of the uniformity of energy/matter—a uniformity that makes it feasible, without preassignable limit, to escape the quantitative constraints imposed by the character of the earth's crust."[8] They seem to imagine that human technical progress works like the replicator device from *Star Trek, The Next Generation*, which can transform amorphous matter into whatever the user desires. They see little reason to bother preserving "particular resources for later use."[9] Because economists play such a significant role in planning and organizing capitalist activity and government policy, it is not hard to see how viewpoints like Burnett's and Morse's have helped to facilitate the exploitation and destruction of Earth's environments. Economics, Kate Raworth writes, "is the mother tongue of public policy, the language of public life and the mindset that shapes society."[10]

Smith, Raworth, and other economists have begun to acknowledge that environmental degradation and resource exhaustion is imposing limits on the expansion of human activity.[11] Smith argues that "today's economy is locked into a coevolution with nature," allowing economics to modify itself by drawing examples "not from the self-maximizing rational actor but from the self-regulating natural system."[12] But the idea that nature is a self-regulating system is still an economic conception. It imagines nature as analogous to a market where, instead of prices and supplies balancing one another, populations and means of survival do the same thing. Such a view of nature offers a glimpse into the history of the relationship between natural science and economics and the shared premises that persist in both fields of knowledge, despite their two-centuries-long separation. Their division into different spheres of knowledge has always been something of an illusion, and the environmental crises of the Anthropocene are increasingly forcing them back together again.

A brief exploration of the history of the natural sciences reveals that ideas of what is natural have in fact been deeply entangled with economic theory for as long as there has been economic theory. In *The Natural Origins of Economics* (2005), Margaret Schabas demonstrates that "until the mid-nineteenth century, economic theorists regarded the phenomena of their discourse as part of the same natural world studied by natural philosophers."[13] She terms the separation of disciplines "the denaturalization of the economic order."[14] The term *economy* itself long predates the concept of "the economy." It originated in ancient Greece, compounded from the words *oikos* (household) and *nomos* (law). *Oikonomikē* meant the art of household management. It had been adapted in European languages to define ideas such as the "oeconomy of nature" and "animal oeconomy" by the beginning of the eighteenth century.[15] More recently, the Greek *oikos* has been rendered as the prefix *eco-* in English.

These economic theories of nature were founded on the recognition that living beings and nonliving matter were enmeshed in dynamic and circulating systems where the various components affected and depended upon each other. For instance, David Hume wrote in 1779:

> Is there a system, an order, an oeconomy of things, by which matter can preserve that perpetual agitation, which seems essential to it, and yet maintain a constancy in the forms, which it produces? There certainly is such an oeconomy.[16]

So, rather than saying nature is understood as analogous to markets, we should say that markets are imagined as analogous to natural systems. This model is the basis for what would, in the nineteenth century, come to be called *ecology*, adapting that root concept *oikos* for an economized understanding of nature. An ecosystem is a kind of household, even a home, for its inhabitants.

In 1749, the Swedish naturalist Carl Linnaeus published an essay titled *Oeconomia Naturae*, which described "the Creator's wise arrangement and deposition of all things according to which they fulfil their purpose for the glory of God and the happiness of Man."[17] It focuses on "the fundamental processes or stages in the life cycle," showing "how these processes create a flow of matter through nature—what we would refer to as the great biogeochemical cycles—so that everything is connected and nothing is really lost."[18] Donald Worster calls Linnaeus' essay "a primitive first step" in ecological thought.[19] The theological basis on which Linnaeus constructs his argument clearly distinguishes him from later scientific understandings, which define natural systems as self-generating and self-sustaining. Another feature of the Linnaean natural economy that differs from modern ecology is its "thoroughly static portrait of the geo-biological interactions in nature," which is to say, Linnaeus believed that

> All movement takes place in a single confined sphere, planetary in scope. Like the classical Greek naturalists, Linnaeus allows only one kind of change in the natural economic system, a cyclical pattern that keeps returning to its point of departure.[20]

In his poem *The Seasons* (1730), James Thomson envisions the same kind of mechanism:

> Unresting, changless, matchless, in their course;
> To night and day, with the delightful round
> Of *Seasons,* faithful; not excentric once:
> So pois'd, and perfect is the vast machine.[21]

Nothing really changes in such a world system; it has no room for evolution, extinction, or significant environmental transformations.

For Worster, Gilbert White is the key figure who began the transition from Linnaeus' static natural economy to the evolving ecosystem model that we now use. White was a clergyman who lived in Hampshire in the eighteenth century. His highly popular and influential book *The Natural History and Antiquities of Selborne* (1789) takes as its premise that "Nature is a great economist," but, unlike Linnaeus, White envisions the economy of nature as a fully dynamic system, affected and altered by scarcity and abundance: "the most insignificant insects and reptiles are of much more consequence, and have much more influence in the economy of nature, than the incurious are ever aware of, and are mighty in their effect"; "nature is such an economist, that the most incongruous animals can avail themselves of each other!"[22] To say nature is an economist, then, means understanding all parts of the system as connected by their needs and interactions, in the same way that human economics sees all of its constituent parts and actors as interrelated through the credit/value system.

White's influential modification of the economy of nature remains central to biological science: "the structural explanations in which the [Economy of Nature] features continue to play a vital purpose ... in the life sciences over a range of theories as varied as Linnaean classification and population genetics."[23] Andrew Ross is more emphatic: "the vestigial influence exercised over biological thought by ... economics has been quite tenacious ... The law of competition and the condition of scarcity ... continue to play a role akin to that of default settings within the life sciences."[24] This passage, from *The Journal of Insect Behavior*, exemplifies the proximity between economic and biological sciences:

> Cannibalism ... is inversely proportional to the *abundance* of primary prey. Under conditions of prey *scarcity*, cannibals may *choose* to feed on either conspecifics or on the ... less nourishing plant substrate ... There are two primary advantages for an individual to engage in cannibalism: reduction of *competition* and a high *quality* food source ... These *advantages* are balanced against the *costs* of foraging for a less *abundant* and potentially well defended prey type ... In scorpions, the smaller, immature stages can access food that the larger, adults cannot, thereby serving as *consumers*.[25]

This excerpt is rich with terms and concepts that might appear in an economics journal: abundance and scarcity, choice, cost/benefit analysis, competition, consumption. The two households of economics and ecology are, in many respects, really just one.

An important consequence of this shared economism has been the naturalization of generalized scarcity. Scarcity, according to Lionel Robbins, takes the form of "that conflict of choice which is one of the permanent characteristics of human existence."[26] From this perspective, "human behaviour [is] a relationship between ends and scarce means which have alternative uses."[27] Paradoxically, the enormous productive power generated by capitalism has fostered, and depended on, perpetuation of deficiency, poverty, and depletion. "Where production and distribution are arranged through the behavior of prices," Marshall Sahlins explains, "and all livelihoods depend on getting and spending, insufficiency of material means becomes the explicit, calculable starting point of all economic activity."[28] According to this logic, nonhuman nature is just one part of the "means" by which the economy does its work ("means" also include wealth, labor power, and other factors assumed to be already separated from the natural world), and it is presumed to be scarce, which is to say always in danger of running out.

A second paradox follows from the presumption that we are always falling short of what we need (or desire), at both personal and societal levels. James O'Connor has called this paradox the second contradiction of capitalism.[29] Costas Panayotakis summarizes O'Connor's thesis: "capitalism's compulsive growth ...

tends to destroy the natural preconditions of production, such as land, natural resources, and so on," an effect that "can be seen as a socially produced natural scarcity."[30] The systems of capitalism never cease responding to declining demand for a commodity or depletion of a productive resource by moving on to another, more intensive, opportunity for value realization and growth.

At the end of the eighteenth century, Thomas Malthus blamed this recurrent growth cycle on what he saw as the tendency of population to increase at a much faster rate than the productive resources that can sustain it: "the increase of the human species can only be kept commensurate to the increase of the means of subsistence by the constant operation of the strong law of necessity acting as a check upon the greater power."[31] In other words, Malthus argues that continual expansion is structurally guaranteed to result in what he calls "oscillations," between prosperity and crisis, a "constantly subsisting cause of periodical misery."[32] It is important to note that Malthus saw this process as natural, rather than unique to capitalism, but his ideas gained traction in both ecological sciences and capitalist economics. Malthus demonstrates what we have already observed: although economists treat ideas like market circulation and resource competition as self-contained capitalist processes, they have historical and ongoing links to biological and ecological science. For example, historians have found compelling evidence that the idea of commerce as a circulatory system was first derived from William Harvey's 1628 discovery of the circulation of blood in the human body.[33]

Malthus' thesis—which has been strongly contested by scholars who study population dynamics—is often identified as a crucial influence in Charles Darwin's development of the concept of natural selection.[34] Darwin himself wrote in his autobiography:

> I happened to read for amusement Malthus on Population, and being prepared to appreciate the struggle for existence which everywhere goes on … it at once struck me that under these circumstances favorable variables would tend to be preserved and unfavorable ones destroyed.[35]

Natural selection remains an accepted component of evolutionary theory in what is usually called the modern synthesis.[36] It presumes that a permanent state of looming scarcity—analogous to that of human socioeconomics—governs nonhuman ecologies. Darwin's famous "wedge" metaphor, which he used repeatedly in his discussions of natural selection, captures this sense: "The face of Nature may be compared to a yielding surface, with ten thousand sharp wedges packed close together and driven inwards by incessant blows, sometimes one wedge being struck, and then another with greater force."[37] Each wedge is a species or organism competing to find space within its environment to survive and flourish. Those which are forced out die off.

One of the earliest analyses to identify the role of scarcity in the complex relationships between human markets and nonhuman ecosystems was written in

1795 (though not published until 1800) by Edmund Burke, a prominent politician and philosopher, best known for *Reflections on the Revolution in France* (1790). In *Thoughts and Details on Scarcity*, Burke discusses crop failures in Britain during the years 1794–1795 and the shortages that resulted. He demonstrates a clear conception of what we would call an ecosystem model: "All the productions of the earth link in with each other. All the sources of plenty, in all and every article, were dried or frozen up. The scarcity was not as gentlemen seem to suppose in wheat only." From crops, the shortfall passed on to other kinds of agricultural production, including pork, and from there to the food supply system as a whole: the "failure of so very large a supply of flesh in one species, naturally throws the whole demand of the consumer on the diminished supply of all kinds of flesh, and, indeed, on all the matters of human sustenance." The crisis, however, was by no means simply a disruption in nature's cycles: Burke argues that the "sole *cause* of scarcity in" pork "arose from the proceedings of men themselves." What he means is that pork supplies ran low because government responded to the shortage of grain by halting distillation of liquor, whose "waste wash" was, according to Burke, a far more efficient hog feed than unprocessed grain.[38]

For Burke, scarcity involves both human (economic) and nonhuman (natural) factors. He clearly distinguishes between the human and the nonhuman, but he also insists that human economics have a basis in nature: "the laws of commerce, are the laws of nature, and consequently the laws of God." For that reason, Burke insists that economic systems must be allowed to operate without external intervention: "Of all things, an indiscreet tampering with the trade of provisions is the most dangerous, and it is always worst in the time when men are most disposed to it:—that is, in the time of scarcity." He blames the shortages of 1794–1795 on "indiscreet tampering" and not on intractable natural scarcity. "Never since I have known England," he asserts, "have I known more than comparative scarcity."[39] Some years may see less abundance than others, he claims, but there is never genuinely too little to go around.

Burke's pamphlet demonstrates the paradox of *laissez faire* economics: commerce is supposed to be an entirely human field of endeavor, but human interference with its processes is to be discouraged. This way of imagining capitalism's apparatus has been facilitated by another historical development in which Burke participated: the reform of the royal household, which is to say the administrative offices of British government. In 1780, serving as a member of parliament, he introduced legislation aimed at modernizing the financial systems of government, which had been arranged around the royal household and a myriad of official positions that tended to be handed out as favors and sinecures, rather than with the goal of efficient administration. In a long speech aimed at persuading MPs to vote for the bills, Burke argued that the royal household "is formed upon manners and customs, that have long since expired … it is formed, in many respects, upon feudal principles." In such a system, the household or office is defined by its patron and may come to an end when the patron departs (or dies). The goal of Burke's legislation was to ensure that "when officers are removed ... the offices remain."[40]

Although Burke's bills did not pass, equivalent reforms were instituted a few years afterward, transforming the bases on which institutions were founded from personal (depending on the personal qualities of the office holder) to impersonal (defined by the functions of the institution and its relation to other entities). The concept of household entailed by the *eco-* in economics and ecology came to be defined by the same logic. Modern economics is concerned with interchangeable functions and substitutable relations between components whose particular qualities only matter insofar as they contribute to exchangeable value. Prior to this transformation of institutional norms, monetary value (including national wealth) had been indexed to gold, which was considered to be a stable embodiment of measurable value. Since roughly the mid-eighteenth century, gold has ceased to have special monetary status: it only has value in relation to the credit system as a whole and is always presumed to be substitutable. So, for instance, there is no major functional difference between paper currency, gold coins, checks, or liquid credit in terms of exchange. In fact, the valuation of gold itself can fluctuate according to market forces, just like any commodity. It is traded globally in the same kind of exchange markets as oil, grain, and other primary commodities. As recently as 2000, gold was valued at less than a quarter (in adjusted terms) of what it costs as I write this chapter.

What happened in the mid-eighteenth century to establish this change was the widespread acceptance in Britain of paper credit—written notes, and later bank notes, that stated their value verbally. Initially, paper credit was understood as an inferior substitute for gold, which is why the Bank of England held reserves of bullion to ensure that paper credit was backed up by a supply of "real" value. But strict bullionism was gradually displaced by a full acceptance that the symbolic value of bank notes was as good as "real" value. Although many currencies continued to be indexed to gold reserves (the "gold standard") into the twentieth century, Britain had recognized before the end of the eighteenth century that the amount of monetary value held as symbolic credit far outstripped the quantity of gold that was supposed to secure that value. For that reason, the 1797 Restriction Act suspended the Bank of England's obligation to exchange paper currency for gold on demand. Even though Britain's gold standard was restored in 1821, it was well understood that the monetary value contained in global economies vastly exceeded all gold reserves. Thus, economics does not treat any given exchangeable item as significantly different from all others. Wealth and value are expressed in complex interrelations and equivalences that can change without preset limits. This state of relativity and interchangeability also applies to social factors like wages and salaries, consumer goods and services, and rent and real estate prices. Hence, Marx criticized capitalist economic systems for their tendency to distort all aspects of human existence.

Like human societies in the age of commerce, ecosystems are also understood as transformable groupings of components and relations. Although scientists study every ecosystem as a particular set of participants and interrelations, they assume that any given component can be changed or removed, and the ecosystem will adapt itself to the new arrangement. There will still be an ecosystem, even if it changes dramatically. Prior to the development of this consensus, the "oeconomy of nature" was understood to be organized by divine providence. God was the head of the "household," dispensing or withholding abundance. Every creature and substance had an unchangeable place in the natural order, what was often called "the Great Chain of Being." In the last 200 years, scarcity has taken the place of providence, pitting all organisms against one another in a perpetual contest for subsistence. This economized world is the medium in which the Anthropocene has developed.

Paradoxically, economism places humanity at the center of planetary systems but also means nobody in particular is responsible for the effects of capitalism. Because economic relationships are always defined by function, rather than the personal attributes of the participants, every component of the economic system can be substituted or even eliminated without stopping the process. Indeed, disruption and adaptation are themselves intrinsic to capitalism's operation. That is why disruption is taught in business schools as a goal to be pursued. Marx recognized capitalism's "constant revolutionising of production, [and] uninterrupted disturbance of all social conditions" but did not see it as a desirable feature.[41] The biological sciences understand ecosystems in analogous ways; consider, for instance, the theory that major fires are a part of the normal cycles by which many forests maintain themselves. Upheaval and crisis are actually business as usual for economists and ecologists.

Because the relations and institutions of capitalism are so fungible, not even the wealthiest capitalists and most powerful politicians are the kind of villains whose elimination would bring capitalism and planetary crises to an end. Institutions, power structures, and economic relations sustain the processes of capitalism, even as they transform in seemingly radical ways. For example, corporations like IBM, Shell, and Disney have reconfigured themselves profoundly in the last 100 years, and the US federal government has seen a huge variety of representatives and appointees come and go but has never abandoned the fundamental goal of increasing the national gross domestic product. The economization of the world has not only made humanity sovereign over all of nature but also made it virtually impossible to abdicate and end our calamitous reign. We cannot simply stop what we have been doing. As far as global economies are concerned, even large numbers of people wishing to end ruinous patterns of consumption are simply expressing a kind of consumer desire. Such desire can easily be accommodated by global capitalism. When one consumer does not buy a product, other consumers will be sought and other products developed. The system that produces massive arrays of choice does not offer the choice to opt out of that system, much less switch it off, and as long as economics continues to treat the system as natural, it will have a very hard time finding ways to break its destructive patterns.

Notes

1 See J. R. McNeill, *The Great Acceleration: An Environmental History of the Anthropocene since 1945* (Cambridge: Harvard University Press, 2014).
2 Lyla Mehta, "The Scare: Naturalization and Politicization of Scarcity," in *The Limits to Scarcity: Contesting the Politics of Allocation*, ed. Lyla Mehta (New York: Earthscan, 2010), 18.
3 See, for example, Jason W. Moore, ed., *Anthropocene or Capitalocene? Nature, History, and the Crisis of Capitalism* (Oakland: PM Press, 2016); and Jeremy Davies, *The Birth of the Anthropocene* (Oakland: University of California Press, 2016), esp. 94–95.
4 Fraser Murison Smith, *Economics of a Crowded Planet* (London: Palgrave MacMillan, 2019), 3.
5 Ibid., vii.
6 Harold J. Burnett and Chandler Morse, *Scarcity and Growth: The Economics of Natural Resource Availability* (Baltimore: Johns Hopkins University Press, 1963), 11.
7 Michael Perelman, "Scarcity and Environmental Disaster: Why Hotelling's Price Theory Doesn't Apply," *Capitalism, Nature, Socialism* 18, no. 1 (2007): 83.
8 Burnett and Morse, 11.
9 Ibid.
10 Kate Raworth, *Doughnut Economics: Seven Ways to Think Like a 21st Century Economist* (White River Junction: Chelsea Green Publishing, 2017), 5.
11 See, for instance, Edward B. Barbier, *Nature and Wealth: Overcoming Environmental Scarcity and Inequality* (London: Palgrave MacMillan, 2015).
12 Fraser Murison Smith, *Economics of a Crowded Planet* (London: Palgrave MacMillan, 2019), vii–viii.
13 Margaret Schabas, *The Natural Origins of Economics* (Chicago: University of Chicago Press, 2005), 2. "Natural philosophy" is a term that predates but roughly equates to natural science.
14 Ibid., 2.
15 Ibid., 4.
16 Ibid., 4.
17 Geir Hestmark, "*Oeconomia Naturae* L.," *Nature* 405, no. 4 (2000): 19.
18 Ibid.
19 Donald Worster, *Nature's Economy: A History of Ecological Ideas*, 2nd ed. (Cambridge: Cambridge University Press, 1994), 33. See also Frank N. Egerton, "A History of the Ecological Sciences, Part 23: Linnaeus and the Economy of Nature," *Bulletin of the Ecological Society of America* 88, no.1 (2007): 72–88.
20 Ibid., 34.
21 James Thomson, *The Four Seasons, and Other Poems* (London: J. Millan and A. Millar, 1735), 5.
22 Worster, 7–9.
23 Charles H. Pence and Daniel G. Swaim, "The Economy of Nature: The Structure of Evolution in Linnaeus, Darwin, and the Modern Synthesis," *European Journal in the Philosophy of Science* 8 (2018): 450.

24 Andrew Ross, *The Chicago Gangster Theory of Life: Nature's Debt to Society* (London: Verso, 1994), 260.
25 Amie Laycock, Edith Camm, Sherah Van Laerhoven, and Dave Gillespie, "Cannibalism in a Zoophytophagous Omnivore Is Mediated by Prey Availability and Plant Substrate," *Journal of Insect Behavior* 19, no. 2 (2006): 219–227, emphasis added.
26 Lionel Robbins, *An Essay on the Nature and Significance of Economic Science* (London: MacMillan, 1932), 29. Robbins played a significant part in the rise of the London School of Economics.
27 Ibid., 15.
28 Marshall Sahlins, *Stone Age Economics* (Chicago: Aldine Atherton, 1972), 4, 3.
29 See James O'Connor, "Capitalism, Nature, Socialism: A Theoretical Introduction," *Capitalism, Nature, Socialism* 1, no. 1 (1988): 11–38.
30 Costas Panayotakis, "Capitalism's 'Dialectic of Scarcity' and the Emancipatory Project," *Capitalism, Nature, Socialism* 14, no. 1 (2003): 106.
31 Thomas Malthus, *An Essay on the Principle of Population*, ed. Geoffrey Gilbert (Oxford: Oxford University Press, 1993), 18.
32 Ibid., 66.
33 See Richard Kroll, *Restoration Drama and "The Circle of Commerce"* (Cambridge, Cambridge University Press, 2007), 37–39.
34 For a summation of anti-Malthusian scholarship, see Erik Millstone, "Chronic Hunger: A Problem of Scarcity or Inequality?" in *The Limits to Scarcity*, 179–194.
35 Qtd. in Heather Remoff, "Malthus, Darwin, and the Descent of Economics," *American Journal of Economics and Sociology* 74, no. 4 (2016): 864.
36 See, for instance, Pence and Swaim. The modern synthesis refers to the combining of Darwinian theory with more recently developed models of genetic heredity and variation.
37 Qtd. in Pence and Swaim, 9.
38 Edmund Burke, *Thoughts and Details on Scarcity, Originally Presented to the Right Hon. William Pitt, in the Month of November 1795* (London: F. and C. Rivington, 1800), 40, 39.
39 Ibid., 1, 32, 44.
40 Edmund Burke, *The Writings and Speeches of Edmund Burke*, vol. 3, ed. W.M. Elofson and John A. Woods (Oxford: Clarendon Press, 1996), 508, 485.
41 Karl Marx and Friedrich Engels, *The Communist Manifesto*, ed. Jeffrey C. Isaac (New Haven: Yale University Press, 2012), 77.

References

Barbier, Edward B. *Nature and Wealth: Overcoming Environmental Scarcity and Inequality*. London: Palgrave MacMillan, 2015.
Burke, Edmund. *Thoughts and Details on Scarcity, Originally Presented to the Right Hon. William Pitt, in the Month of November 1795*. London: F. and C. Rivington, 1800.
———. *The Writings and Speeches of Edmund Burke*. Vol. 3. Edited by W.M. Elofson and John A. Woods. Oxford: Clarendon Press, 1996.
Burnett, Harold J., and Chandler Morse. *Scarcity and Growth: The Economics of Natural Resource Availability*. Baltimore: Johns Hopkins University Press, 1963.
Davies, Jeremy. *The Birth of the Anthropocene*. Oakland: University of California Press, 2016.
Egerton, Frank N. "A History of the Ecological Sciences, Part 23: Linnaeus and the Economy of Nature." *Bulletin of the Ecological Society of America* 88, no. 1 (2007): 72–88.

Hestmark, Geir. "*Oeconomia Naturae* L." *Nature* 405, no. 4 (2000): 19.
Kroll, Richard. *Restoration Drama and "The Circle of Commerce."* Cambridge: Cambridge University Press, 2007.
Laycock, Amie, Edith Camm, Sherah Van Laerhoven, and Dave Gillespie. "Cannibalism in a Zoophytophagous Omnivore Is Mediated by Prey Availability and Plant Substrate." *Journal of Insect Behavior* 19, no. 2 (2006): 219–229.
Malthus, Thomas. *An Essay on the Principle of Population*. Edited by Geoffrey Gilbert. Oxford: Oxford University Press, 1993.
Marx, Karl, and Friedrich Engels. *The Communist Manifesto*. Edited by Jeffrey C. Isaac. New Haven: Yale University Press, 2012.
Mehta, Lyla, ed. *The Limits to Scarcity: Contesting the Politics of Allocation*. New York: Earthscan, 2010.
———. "The Scare: Naturalization and Politicization of Scarcity." In *The Limits to Scarcity: Contesting the Politics of Allocation*. Edited by Lyla Mehta. New York: Earthscan, 2010. 13–30.
Millstone, Erik. "Chronic Hunger: A Problem of Scarcity or Inequality?" In *The Limits to Scarcity: Contesting the Politics of Allocation*. Edited by Lyla Mehta. New York: Earthscan, 2010. 179–194.
McNeill, J. R. *The Great Acceleration: An Environmental History of the Anthropocene since 1945*. Cambridge: Harvard University Press, 2014.
Moore, Jason W., ed. *Anthropocene or Capitalocene? Nature, History, and the Crisis of Capitalism*. Oakland: PM Press, 2016.
O'Connor, James. "Capitalism, Nature, Socialism: A Theoretical Introduction." *Capitalism, Nature, Socialism* 1, no. 1 (1988): 11–38.
Panayotakis, Costas. "Capitalism's 'Dialectic of Scarcity' and the Emancipatory Project." *Capitalism, Nature, Socialism* 14, no. 1 (2003): 88–107.
Pence, Charles H. and Daniel G. Swaim. "The Economy of Nature: The Structure of Evolution in Linnaeus, Darwin, and the Modern Synthesis." *European Journal in the Philosophy of Science* 8 (2018): 435–454.
Perelman, Michael. "Scarcity and Environmental Disaster: Why Hotelling's Price Theory Doesn't Apply." *Capitalism, Nature, Socialism* 18, no. 1 (2007): 81–98.
Raworth, Kate. *Doughnut Economics: Seven Ways to Think Like a 21st Century Economist*. White River Junction: Chelsea Green Publishing, 2017.
Remoff, Heather. "Malthus, Darwin, and the Descent of Economics." *American Journal of Economics and Sociology* 74, no. 4 (2016): 862–903.
Robbins, Lionel. *An Essay on the Nature and Significance of Economic Science*. London: MacMillan, 1932.
Ross, Andrew. *The Chicago Gangster Theory of Life: Nature's Debt to Society*. London: Verso, 1994.
Sahlins, Marshall. *Stone Age Economics*. Chicago: Aldine Atherton, 1972.
Schabas, Margaret. *The Natural Origins of Economics*. Chicago: University of Chicago Press, 2005.
Smith, Fraser Murison. *Economics of a Crowded Planet*. London: Palgrave MacMillan, 2019.
Thomson, James. *The Four Seasons, and Other Poems*. London: J. Millan and A. Millar, 1735.
Worster, Donald. *Nature's Economy: A History of Ecological Ideas*. 2nd ed. Cambridge: Cambridge University Press, 1994.

3
ENERGY AND THE ANTHROPOCENE

Kent Linthicum

Energy and fuel define the Anthropocene. Energy and culture are co-constitutive: cultures use energy to accomplish ideological goals, and energy systems shape culture. Despite these connections, the link between the Anthropocene and the energy humanities is often implicit. Understanding the Anthropocene requires understanding the energy regimes of the past 400 years. This chapter examines the interplay between culture and energy as a defining feature of the Anthropocene. First, it reviews energy humanities' research. Then, it connects works of Anglophone literature in the early modern, romantic, and postmodern periods with their energy systems. This brief study will show how energy can be traced through Anthropocene cultures. Understanding Anthropocene cultures means understanding the ways they used and were shaped by energy. Only by understanding this can new energy cultures be developed for a sustainable future.

The Energy Humanities

Scholarly research on energy and culture stretches back almost a century. Lewis Mumford in *Technics and Civilization* (1934) divides history into three phases based on energy systems: biomass/labor (1000–1800), coal/steam (1700–1900), and electricity (1900–1930). After Mumford, other scholars such as Leslie White, Jean-Claude Debeir, Jean-Paul Deléage, Daniel Hémery, Vaclav Smil, and David E. Nye expanded upon the study of energy and society. The field of energy humanities has its roots in the 1990s when Amitav Ghosh published his essay on "Petrofiction," noting a dearth of literary works that grapple with petroleum.[1] His essay, along with the rise of ecocriticism and the growing climate crisis, would catalyze the energy humanities. In 2011, Patricia Yaegar made one of the first calls for the

DOI: 10.4324/9781003095347-5

energy humanities, asking "Instead of divvying up literary works into hundred-year intervals ... or categories harnessing the history of ideas ... what happens if we sort texts according to the energy sources that made them?"[2] Soon thereafter, the first energy humanities studies appeared: Stephanie LeMenegar's *Living Oil* (2014), Bob Johnson's *Carbon Nation* (2014), and Ross Barrett and Daniel Worden's *Oil Culture* (2014). LeMenager articulates the clearest energy humanities thesis, arguing "Energy systems are shot through with largely unexamined cultural values, with ethical and ecological consequences."[3] Only a few years later, Imre Szeman and Dominic Boyer's *Energy Humanities* (2017); Sheena Wilson, Adam Carlson, and Imre Szeman's *Petrocultures* (2017); and Imre Szeman, Jennifer Wenzel, and Patricia Yaeger's *Fueling Culture* (2017) arrived. To date, the energy humanities are a growing interdisciplinary field.

The energy humanities, though, have not kept pace with conversations about the Anthropocene. The Anthropocene is a useful concept for demarcating the dramatic changes caused by human beings. However, many scholars have argued it flattens humanity into a singular force. Some scholars argue capitalism is to blame for the crisis, others settler colonialism, others racism.[4] The energy humanities' focus on oil—what Jones describes as petromyopia[5]—leads it to be too focused on the twentieth century and a narrow definition of the Anthropocene. This focus causes the energy humanities to foreshorten its histories of racism, colonialism, and capitalism. Critiques of the Anthropocene, though, argue for earlier markers because of the ways settler colonialism in the Americas, for example, creates the conditions for fossil capitalism and global warming.[6] And, despite leaving the coal-smothered and steam-powered industrial revolution behind, Yaeger notes, "the age of coal is not close to being over."[7] Energy transitions are hardly transitions at all, merely additions with new stresses on old circuits.[8] More work needs to be done to embrace a broader range of fuels and ages so that the energy humanities can help us truly understand how we became "the citizens and subjects of fossil fuels."[9]

The energy humanities methodology is critical to various definitions of the Anthropocene. To show this, this chapter analyzes three proposed markers: (1) the 1610 Orbis spike, biomass, and slavery in the early modern period, focusing on Shakespeare's *The Tempest* (1610–1611); (2) the 1784 spike, focusing on Jane Austen's *Mansfield Park* (1814) and the relationship between coal, slavery, and culture; and the 1964 bomb spike, through Wole Soyinka's "Telephone Conversation" (1962), which sees advances in electrification as new tools for racism. These three stratigraphic-literary case studies show how energy is an important catalyst for the Anthropocene. It is important to remember that energy is not a neutral concept that is equal across all periods. Energy is both a reality and a culturally defined concept. Regardless of epoch, all life requires energy to exist. Yet, the way cultures have defined that necessity has changed over time, and our modern understanding of energy is arguably only about 120 years old.[10] Energy in text still represents a material reality, but one that is lensed through culture; other periods did not have the same assumptions about energy as today. Nevertheless, because of its essential nature, energy can still be traced and used to understand different cultures. Together, these three case studies show that the energy humanities are a necessary tool to understand the full scope of the Anthropocene.

Early Modern Period

The early modern period and its intensive use of biomass is a precursor to today's crises. In early modern England, biomass, especially wood, was important both as a fuel and as a building material for structures and ships. Wood was also cooked into charcoal, which was then used in industries such as iron making.[11] Like petroleum today, wood was a "substrate" of early modern culture, a condition for its existence.[12] Around the turn of the seventeenth century, England was facing a wood shortage, specifically for shipbuilding, to the anxiety of some of the era's thinkers.[13] One answer to this concern, rather than increased trade, was American colonialism. The author of *Nova Britannia* (1609) and the author of *A Trve Declaration of the Estate of the Colonie in Virginia* (1610) both promote colonization, arguing that the "new world" was the solution to England's shortages.[14] This shortage made American forests seem like "treasure chests of fuel and raw materials" to colonial explorers.[15]

The Orbis spike of 1610 is marked by the dramatic *reforestation* of North America, as European diseases swept through Native American populations, reducing the amount of biomass those people would have otherwise harvested. Lewis and Maslin argue that 1610 (alongside 1964) is one of the strongest markers for the start of the Anthropocene because it derives from a "globally synchronous" event.[16] This event, in 1610, is a drop in atmospheric carbon dioxide from a previously stable level. Lewis and Maslin argue this decrease is a result of the genocide of Native Americans started in 1492, which by 1650 had reduced a Native American population of roughly 54 million down to 6 million. These millions dead lead to the "near-cessation of farming and reduction in fire use [which] resulted in the regeneration of over 50 million hectares of forest, woody savanna and grassland with a carbon uptake by vegetation and soils."[17] Forests, woody savannas, and grasslands were now easily taken by European colonizers. The abundance and the demand for wood helps demarcate this Anthropocene spike, which is visible in the literature of the period.

William Shakespeare is arguably the most famous English writer, and his influence on English is felt all the way down to syntax and diction. Importantly, he also lived through this cooler period of Earth's history, known as the Little Ice Age.[18] *The Tempest* is likely one of the last plays Shakespeare wrote and has long been an important text for colonial and postcolonial studies, in addition to the energy humanities.[19] Vincent Nardizzi, in *Wooden Os* (2013) and elsewhere, examines wood in early modern culture and the ways the period can be described as an "age of wood."[20] *The Tempest* demonstrates this with its emphasis on wood harvesting: Caliban's first line is "There's wood enough within," indicating he'd rather not gather more fuel for Prospero's fire.[21] Nardizzi notes that throughout the play, "Caliban keys us into the indispensability of wood as the primary energy source under-pinning subsistence and manufacture in the preindustrial era."[22] *The Tempest* responds to the colonial fantasy of new world logging, but euphemizes the labor of that extraction through Prospero's magic.[23] While Nardizzi analyzes the various instances of wood in the play, this critique will focus on Ariel's enslavement and its relationship to wood to show how *The Tempest* engenders a colonial fantasy of slavery too.

Ariel, the other being besides Caliban who is enslaved by Prospero, appears to be a djinn who can control the elements. The tempest that initiates the play is created by Ariel.[24] And Ariel seems to have a wide range of powers, notably the ability to transport Prospero through air, water, and fire.[25] Ariel is a magical engine in a pre-engine age. This association with energy is reinforced by Ariel's prior imprisonment in a "cloven pine."[26] Ariel becomes part of the "physical and social—[energy economy that] circulates in this play," their body at one point synonymous with the fuel logs Caliban hates.[27] Ariel's tortured groans when imprisoned are compared to the sound of the "mill-wheel strike," reinforcing their engine-like nature.[28] While the combination of Ariel's power over the elements and their association with wood and mills would suggest a kind of early modern steam engine, that kind of engine was 200 years away.[29]

Ariel's enslavement, though, would have been much more relevant to *The Tempest*'s contemporary audience. A subplot of the play is Ariel's plea for "liberty."[30] Prospero responds to this plea by accusing Ariel of lying and threatening to "rend an oak/And peg thee in his knotty entrails" before agreeing to free Ariel in two days.[31] At the end of the play, Ariel, after performing their tasks "bravely," is freed by Prospero.[32] Ariel's enslavement and labor are significant for Anthropocene energy studies. Unlike the rebellious Caliban, Ariel, according to Cohen, has submitted to enslavement in the hopes of freedom.[33] They represent the "magic" of slavery, the ability to extract energy for "nothing" from the world—nothing except dehumanization, torture, and murder. Slavery is a managerial and energy technology predicated on using violence to maximize labor, and Prospero's treatment of Ariel and Caliban shows the bleeding edge of a culture that would find its nadir in the middle of the nineteenth century.[34] While slavery was not widespread in English colonies in 1610, the expansion of the British Caribbean and the growth of tobacco, cotton, and sugar industries meant that by the 1690s the English were the dominant slave traders in West Africa.[35] Ariel's portrayal suggests slavery can be benign, even good, because Prospero "rescued" Ariel from even worse torment.[36] Ultimately, Prospero does grant Ariel's freedom, defusing the question about whether Prospero was right to enslave Ariel in the first place. So, while wood is a significant part of the play and the play responds to concerns about the scarcity of wood, this lens of fuel reveals slavery as an energy regime that would catapult the English toward the "magic" of the industrial revolution through human violence and suffering.

Industrialization

The Industrial Revolution is tied directly to the systematized application of fossil fuels. Unlike 1610 or 1964, this spike involves energy directly, as coal would fuel a dramatic shift in British culture. Yet, imagining this date as exclusively the result of fossilized carbon, steam, and entrepreneurial spirit forgets the other energy circuits that facilitated industrialization. Britain's industrial revolution did not happen alone; it was part of a system of energy and commodities including, "South American silver, Caribbean sugar, North American cotton, African slaves, and the consumer goods that flowed into and out of the advanced population centers of northwest Europe, China, and India."[37] While industrialized coal and steam are dramatic markers of a changing world, they did not act alone.

Paul Crutzen chose 1784 as the first definition of the Anthropocene because of a conjunction between James Watt's "design of the steam engine" and the "growing global concentrations of carbon dioxide."[38] Watt was one of many working on the machines that would define the Industrial Revolution. Thomas Newcomen built the first industrial steam engine in 1712, himself iterating off the designs of Thomas Savery and others.[39] Watt then iterated on Newcomen's designs, adding a separate condenser in 1765 and parallel motion in 1784. Watt and business partner, Matthew Boulton, were able to profit by selling steam engines to mills, first to recirculate water and then to power the mill itself.[40] They were responding to the dramatic growth of cotton manufacturing, produced by protectionist measures against Indian cotton and the expansion of slave-grown cotton in the West Indies.[41] After 1802, the United States would become the "single most important supplier of cotton to the British market."[42] Coal and Watt's engine did not immediately supplant other kinds of energy; they helped co-opt and intensify previous systems, like the labor necessary to harvest cotton, work the mills, and mine the coal. Watt, like a number of other industrialists, was financed by capital derived from slave labor.[43] While the 1784 spike is often used to point to the industrial ascension of fossil fuels, it is critical to see this spike as an intensification of all energy regimes—labor, wind, water, biomass, and fossil fuels.

Jane Austen's *Mansfield Park* seems to be far away from the soot of coal and the sweat of slavery. However, the trials of Fanny Price as she navigates the domestic politics of Mansfield Park have been famously linked to slavery. Edward Said, in *Culture and Imperialism* (1993), argues that *Mansfield Park* silently endorses slavery because the characters benefit from Sir Thomas Bertram's plantation without questioning it, and Austen gives the reader rich descriptions of country house life without attendant reflection on the violence that purchased the house.[44] Although the novel mostly takes place in the East Midlands, the plantation is a critical plot point. Sir Thomas leaves for Antigua early in the novel.[45] This absence allows for indecent enterprises, like the attempted staging of the salacious *Lover's Vows*. Upon Sir Thomas' return, there is little discussion of the plantation. To her credit, Fanny does ask her uncle about the slave trade, but the conversation ends in "dead silence" as no one else wants to talk about slavery.[46] Subsequent scholars, though, have questioned Said's claims regarding this silence and whether Austen or *Mansfield Park* endorse slavery.[47] For an Anthropocene energy reading, it is crucial to connect *Mansfield Park* with slavery, as slavery (despite the abolition of the slave trade in 1807) supported an industrializing Britain.

Slave labor extended beyond the field: it was fed into products consumed by the wealthy. The novel does not say what Sir Thomas' plantation grows, but it is likely either cotton or sugar. Antigua was an "important producer of cotton" in the eighteenth century and, like many Caribbean colonies, transitioned to sugar in the early nineteenth.[48] In these ways, the energy of slaves is polymerized and congealed into the goods of the era.[49] Cotton was polymerized in the form of muslin, a delicate, thin fabric that "transformed life during Austen's generation."[50] Despite increasing domestic production, muslin gowns evoked the tropics in their delicacy and sheerness.[51] Muslin is not specifically mentioned in the novel, but given its popularity, it is likely the wealthy characters were wearing it.[52] For instance, at one point, Fanny warns Maria against jumping a fence to explore more of James Rushworth's estate for fear she will "tear her gown," an allusion to the delicacy of muslin and to the indecency of Maria traipsing alone with young men.[53] Slave labor created the flirty, revealing dresses that facilitated courtship in the era. This polymerized slave energy helped construct the British social sphere. Slave-produced sugar helped build that same sphere. Sugar was increasingly popular in Britain for both tea and sweets in the late eighteenth and early nineteenth centuries.[54] Again, Austen does not use the word "sugar," but it is still in her characters' social world. For example, as Henry Crawford doggedly flirts with an uninterested Fanny, it is the entry of the servants with the "tea-board, urn, and cake-bearers" that saves Fanny.[55] The rituals of sugar give Fanny an escape. The labor of slaves helps build Fanny's social world: British culture was slave-powered.

Like the condensed energies of slave-grown cotton or sugar, coal largely exists in a hidden fashion in *Mansfield Park*. Steam was being adopted in cotton manufactures; thus, some of the dresses in the novel might have been fossil produced. And coal was used to refine sugar, and steam engines were being imported into the Caribbean to power cane mills.[56] In these ways, coal parallels slave labor, while also showing how life at Mansfield Park required a vast energy network. Unlike slaves, though, coal does make a few brief appearances in *Mansfield Park*. When Fanny returns to her parents, she is welcomed by Mrs. Price, who wants to make her daughter comfortable after a long journey,

> "Dear me!" continued the anxious mother, "what a sad fire we have got, and I dare say you are both starved with cold. Draw your chair nearer, my dear. I cannot think what Rebecca has been about. I am sure I told her to bring some coals half an hour ago. Susan, you should have taken care of the fire."[57]

This request seems innocuous, but in Austenian style, it is revealing. The issue is not the coal: coal was burnt by the wealthy and the poor—the wealthy just burned less noxious coal along with other fuels like wood.[58] Rather, the fact that the Price daughters have to attend to the fire (instead of servants) and that they have failed to do so reveals social standing.[59] The ambient energy of burning fossil fuels becomes a metonym for class, as previously Fanny enjoyed the warm fires of Mansfield Park but in Portsmouth sits without one.[60] Energy, then, is a building block of social space and difference. So, while Austen might have been in favor of abolition, her culture was accommodating itself to the increasingly widespread violence of slavery and fossil fuels.

Postmodern Period

The bomb spike of 1964 is the most stratigraphically defensible definition of the Anthropocene because of the dramatic increase in atmospheric carbon, the fallout from nuclear weapons tests, and the proliferation of new anthropogenic materials like concrete. For the energy humanities, this era is the most familiar: widespread electrification, gasoline-fueled cars, and nuclear power plants. This expansion of energy use has come to define "the experience of modernity."[61] The period, accordingly, has been a fruitful space for energy humanist scholarship, especially on petroleum. However, petroleum is not the only energy of the latter half of the twentieth century. Even as new energy technologies have developed, old circuits have not fallen out of use, but rather have intensified in unexpected ways.[62] The intensification of some of these circuits in the latter half of the twentieth century has accelerated the crisis of climate change.

The United Kingdom of the 1960s has many recognizable features. While coal was still the dominant source of electricity, the first nuclear power plant had been connected to the electrical grid. What would become Heathrow airport had been open for commercial use since 1946. Power and mobility were more accessible than ever. Critically, the British Nationality Act of 1948 gave citizenship and the rights of entry and settlement to all peoples living in British colonies. This coincided with the arrival of the *HMT Empire Windrush* from Jamaica (the first members of what is known as the Windrush Generation) and inaugurated the expansion of the Black British population. While not a member of the Windrush Generation, Akinwande Oluwole Babatunde Soyinka, or Wole Soyinka, was studying in England in the 1950s. Soyinka is a Nigerian writer and, in 1986, the first African to be awarded the Nobel Prize in Literature. He is most famous for the play *Death and the King's Horseman* (1975), although his corpus covers a range of genres and mediums. His often-anthologized poem "Telephone Conversation" dramatizes a racist incident that would surely be familiar to any British person of color from the period. At the same time, the poem also reveals the shifting energy culture of Britain.

"Telephone Conversation" is a short poem about a man trying to rent an apartment over the phone. The man is Black and the landlord a bigot. Their conversation quickly degrades as the landlord asks a series of racist questions. The poem crystalizes the prejudices faced by British people of color into a banal interaction. "Telephone Conversation" also outlines the modern energy infrastructure that allows for the conversation. The speaker, during the conversation, reflects on the "Red booth. Red pillar box. Red double-tiered / Omnibus squelching tar."[63] This urban scene is recognizably modern. The bus and the tarmac both use petroleum, in different ways, to promote transport and communication. Likewise, the phone and the mailbox improve communication, using electricity and petroleum, respectively. The speaker's emphasis on red is notable: these red British symbols contrast with the conversation about shades of brown. These symbols were also covered in petroleum—the red paint—as petroleum polymers were used to manufacture paint by this time.[64] Petroleum is used to present a vision of British society where color does not matter—the red of Britain represents all its people. Instead, the petroleum polymers merely help cover up white supremacy. The new fossil fuel technologies of the Bomb Spike reinforce barriers rather than breaking them down.

The telephone of the eponymous conversation was not new in 1962. Telephones were invented in the nineteenth century, and the iconic red telephone kiosks—the "Red booth" of the poem—were designed in 1924. The poem highlights the acceptance of the phone as both the speaker and the landlord are comfortable with renting an apartment over the phone. The phone allows for an extension of business and efficiency, as the speaker notes, "I hated a wasted journey."[65] The speaker is able to avoid wasting time because of this technology. The phone's efficiency, though, cuts both ways. While the technology removed the landlord's ability to be subtly racist, it extends her racism through space. Although the reader surely laughs at the landlord's indignation at the end, the poetic speaker still is wounded by the questions.[66] A technology that seems to have the capacity to reduce racism, by removing sight, instead forces the practice to occur in other ways. This is how technologies are reshaped by culture: even though phones offer a utopian promise of bringing people closer together, they also facilitate the extension of dystopian cruelty. The system of coal-powered electrification, batteries, and copper wires—not to mention petroleum-fueled transport—amalgamates into a prosthesis of white supremacy. Therefore, while culture at times shapes itself to energy, at other times culture reshapes energy and technology to suit its ends. Both the speaker and the landlord have saved time in "Telephone Conversation," but the landlord wins by inflicting a verbal wound and still being able to extract rent from her apartment.

Conclusion

Energy will always shape human culture. Human cultures, though, are not passive consumers of energy; cultures direct the energies they use toward outcomes they perceive as acceptable or good. The Anthropocene, regardless of when it starts, is an epoch shaped by changes in energy use, from globalized slavery, to fossil fuels, to nuclear power. These are not the only features of the Anthropocene, but tracing the threads of energy through culture can show in part how the Anthropocene came to be. Energy will always be slippery due to its ubiquity. Today, energy arrives through both literal and figurative transmission lines, causing it to recede or vanish altogether from art and literature. And throughout human history, the mundanity of energy use has again kept it from preservation. Yet, as shown above energy is traceable in culture. By tracing energy and the ways that it influences culture, we can start to rethink our current energy systems and direct them toward a more sustainable world.

Notes

1. Amitav Ghosh, "Petrofiction: The Oil Encounter and the Novel," *The New Republic* 206, no. 9 (1992): 29–30.
2. Patricia Yaeger, "Literature in the Ages of Wood, Tallow, Coal, Whale Oil, Gasoline, Atomic Power, and Other Energy Sources," *PMLA* 126, no. 2 (2011): 305.
3. Stephanie LeMenager, *Living Oil* (Oxford: Oxford University Press, 2014), 4.
4. See Jeremy Davies, *The Birth of the Anthropocene* (Oakland: University of California Press, 2016), esp. 8–9, 41–68.
5. Christopher F. Jones, "Petromyopia: Oil and the Energy Humanities," *Humanities* 5, no. 2 (2016): 36.
6. Heather Davis and Zoe Todd, "On the Importance of a Date, or Decolonizing the Anthropocene," *ACME: An International E-Journal for Critical Geographies* 16, no. 4 (2017): 774–776.
7. Yaeger, 307–308.
8. On Barak, *Powering Empire* (Oakland: University of California Press, 2020), 33–40.
9. Imre Szeman and Dominic Boyer, *Energy Humanities* (Baltimore: Johns Hopkins University Press, 2017), 1.
10. Cara New Daggett, *The Birth of Energy* (Durham: Duke University Press, 2019).
11. Heidi C. M. Scott, *Fuel* (New York: Bloomsbury Academic, 2018), 95–97.
12. Vincent Joseph Nardizzi, *Wooden Os* (Toronto: University of Toronto Press, 2013), 10.
13. Michael Williams, *Deforesting the Earth* (Chicago: University of Chicago Press, 2003), 168–173.
14. Nardizzi, 120.
15. Scott, 78.
16. Simon L. Lewis and Mark A. Maslin, "Defining the Anthropocene," *Nature* 519 (2015): 80.
17. Ibid., 175.
18. See Brian M. Fagan, *The Little Ice Age* (New York: Basic Books, 2002).
19. See Meredith Anne Skura, "Discourse and the Individual: The Case of Colonialism in 'The Tempest,'" *Shakespeare Quarterly* 40, no. 1 (1989): 42–69.
20. Vincent Joseph Nardizzi, "Wooden Slavery," *PMLA* 126, no. 2 (2011): 313–315.
21. William Shakespeare, *The Tempest*, in *The Riverside Shakespeare*, 2nd ed., ed. G. Blakemore Evans and J.J.M. Tobin (Boston: Houghton Mifflin, 1997), 1.2.314.
22. Nardizzi, "Wooden Slavery," 313.
23. Nardizzi, *Wooden Os*, 118–122.

24 Shakespeare, 1.2.193–1.2.206.
25 Ibid., 1.2.190–1.2.192.
26 Ibid., 1.2.274–1.2.293.
27 Nardizzi, *Wooden Os*, 123.
28 Shakespeare, 1.2.280–1.2.281.
29 See Andreas Malm, *Fossil Capital* (New York: Verso, 2016), 199–218.
30 Shakespeare, 1.2.245.
31 Ibid., 1.2.294–1.2.295.
32 Ibid., 5.1.240–5.1.241, 5.1.317–5.1.319.
33 Derek Cohen, "The Culture of Slavery: Caliban and Ariel," *The Dalhousie Review* 76, no. 2 (1996): 160.
34 Edward E. Baptist, *The Half Has Never Been Told* (New York: Basic Books, 2016), 141–143; and Caitlin Rosenthal, "Slavery's Scientific Management: Accounting for Mastery," in *Slavery's Capitalism*, ed. Sven Beckert and Seth Rockman (Philadelphia: University of Pennsylvania Press, 2016), 63.
35 Hilary McD. Beckles, "The 'Hub of Empire': The Caribbean and Britain in the Seventeenth Century," in *Origins of Empire: British Overseas Enterprise to the Close of the Seventeenth Century*, ed. Nicholas Canny (Oxford: Oxford University Press, 2001), 219–227; Paul E.H. Hair and Robin Law, "The English in Western Africa to 1700," in *Origins of Empire*, 257.
36 Shakespeare, 1.2.242–1.2.293.
37 Davies, 95–99.
38 Paul J. Crutzen, "Geology of Mankind," *Nature* 415, no. 23 (2002), 23.
39 Richard Leslie Hills, *Power from Steam* (Cambridge: Cambridge University Press, 1989), 20–30.
40 Malm, *Fossil Capital*, 53–57.
41 Sven Beckert, *Empire of Cotton* (New York: Alfred A. Knopf, 2014), 42, 47–48.
42 Beckert, 104.
43 Eric Williams, *Capitalism and Slavery* (New York: Capricorn Books, 1966), 102–103; and Kathryn Yusoff, *A Billion Black Anthropocenes or None* (Minneapolis: University of Minnesota Press, 2019), 41–43.
44 Edward Said, *Culture and Imperialism* (New York: Alfred A. Knopf, 1993), 80–97.
45 Jane Austen, *Mansfield Park* (New York: W.W. Norton, 1998), 25.
46 Ibid., 136.
47 Corinne Fowler, "Revisiting Mansfield Park: The Critical and Literary Legacies of Edward W. Said's Essay 'Jane Austen and Empire' in Culture and Imperialism (1993)," *The Cambridge Journal of Postcolonial Literary Inquiry* 4, no. 3 (2017): 362–367.
48 Barry W. Higman, *Slave Populations of the British Caribbean, 1807–1834* (Kingston: University of the West Indies Press, 1995), 52–53.
49 Bob Johnson, *Mineral Rites* (Baltimore: Johns Hopkins University Press, 2019), 150–158.
50 Hilary Davidson, *Dress in the Age of Jane Austen* (New Haven: Yale University Press, 2019), 269–270.
51 Laura George, "Austen's Muslins," in *Crossings in Text and Textile*, ed. Katherine Joslin and Daneen Wardrop (Lebanon: University of New Hampshire Press, 2015), 73–102.
52 Davidson, 269.
53 Austen, 71; and George, 82–83.
54 Sidney W. Mintz, *Sweetness and Power* (New York: Penguin Publishing Group, 1986), 112–121.

55 Austen, 234.
56 Barrie Stuart Trinder, *Britain's Industrial Revolution* (Lancaster: Carnegie Publishing, 2013); Jennifer Tann, "Steam and Sugar: The Diffusion of the Stationary Steam Engine to the Caribbean Sugar Industry 1770–1840," in *History of Technology*, vol. 19, ed. Graham Hollister-Short (New York: Bloomsbury, 1997), 63–84.
57 Austen, 257.
58 William M. Cavert, *The Smoke of London* (Cambridge: Cambridge University Press, 2016), 26–27.
59 Scott, 90–91.
60 Austen, 101, 270.
61 Szeman and Boyer, 2.
62 Barak, 33.
63 Wole Soyinka, "Telephone Conversation," in *The Norton Anthology of English Literature*, 9th ed., vol. F, ed. by Stephen Greenblatt, Jahan Ramazani, and Jon Stallworthy (New York: W.W. Norton, 2012), 13–14.
64 Harriet A.L. Standeven, *House Paints, 1900–1960* (Los Angeles: Getty Publications, 2011), 15.
65 Soyinka, line 5.
66 Soyinka, lines 14–16.

References

Austen, Jane. *Mansfield Park*. New York: W.W. Norton, 1998.
Baptist, Edward E. *The Half Has Never Been Told*. New York: Basic Books, 2016.
Barak, On. *Powering Empire*. Oakland: University of California Press, 2020.
Beckert, Sven. *Empire of Cotton*. New York: Alfred A. Knopf, 2014.
Beckles, Hilary McD. "The 'Hub of Empire': The Caribbean and Britain in the Seventeenth Century." In *Origins of Empire: British Overseas Enterprise to the Close of the Seventeenth Century*. Edited by Nicholas Canny. Oxford: Oxford University Press, 2001. 218–240.
Cavert, William M. *The Smoke of London*. Cambridge: Cambridge University Press, 2016.
Cohen, Derek. "The Culture of Slavery: Caliban and Ariel." *The Dalhousie Review* 76, no. 2 (1996): 153–175.
Crutzen, Paul J. "Geology of Mankind." *Nature* 415 (2002): 23.
Daggett, Cara New. *The Birth of Energy*. Durham: Duke University Press, 2019.
Davidson, Hilary. *Dress in the Age of Jane Austen*. New Haven: Yale University Press, 2019.
Davies, Jeremy. *The Birth of the Anthropocene*. Oakland: University of California Press, 2016.
Davis, Heather, and Zoe Todd. "On the Importance of a Date, or Decolonizing the Anthropocene." *ACME: An International E-Journal for Critical Geographies* 16, no. 4 (2017): 761–780.
Fagan, Brian M. *The Little Ice Age*. New York: Basic Books, 2002.
Fowler, Corinne. "Revisiting Mansfield Park: The Critical and Literary Legacies of Edward W. Said's Essay 'Jane Austen and Empire' in Culture and Imperialism (1993)." *The Cambridge Journal of Postcolonial Literary Inquiry* 4, no. 3 (2017): 362–381.
George, Laura. "Austen's Muslins." In *Crossings in Text and Textile*. Edited by Katherine Joslin and Daneen Wardrop. Lebanon: University of New Hampshire Press, 2015. 73–102.
Ghosh, Amitav. "Petrofiction: The Oil Encounter and the Novel." *The New Republic* 206, no. 9 (1992): 29–34.

Hair, Paul E.H., and Robin Law. "The English in Western Africa to 1700." In *Origins of Empire: British Overseas Enterprise to the Close of the Seventeenth Century*. Edited by Nicholas Canny. Oxford: Oxford University Press, 2001. 241–263.

Higman, Barry W. *Slave Populations of the British Caribbean, 1807–1834*. Kingston: University of the West Indies Press, 1995.

Hills, Richard Leslie. *Power from Steam*. Cambridge: Cambridge University Press, 1989.

Jones, Christopher F. "Petromyopia: Oil and the Energy Humanities." *Humanities* 5, no. 2 (2016): 36–46.

LeMenager, Stephanie. *Living Oil*. Oxford: Oxford University Press, 2014.

Lewis, Simon L., and Mark A. Maslin. "Defining the Anthropocene." *Nature* 519 (2015): 171–180.

Malm, Andreas. *Fossil Capital*. New York: Verso, 2016.

Mintz, Sidney W. *Sweetness and Power*. New York: Penguin Publishing Group, 1986.

Nardizzi, Vincent Joseph. "Wooden Slavery." *PMLA* 126, no. 2 (2011): 313–315.

———. *Wooden Os*. Toronto: University of Toronto Press, 2013.

Rosenthal, Caitlin, "Slavery's Scientific Management: Accounting for Mastery." In *Slavery's Capitalism*. Edited by Sven Beckert and Seth Rockman. Philadelphia: University of Pennsylvania Press, 2016. 62–86.

Said, Edward. *Culture and Imperialism*. New York: Alfred A. Knopf, 1993.

Scott, Heidi C.M. *Fuel*. New York: Bloomsbury Academic, 2018.

Shakespeare, William. *The Tempest*. In *The Riverside Shakespeare*. 2nd ed. Edited by G. Blakemore Evans and J.J.M. Tobin. Boston: Houghton Mifflin, 1997.

Skura, Meredith Anne. "Discourse and the Individual: The Case of Colonialism in 'The Tempest.'" *Shakespeare Quarterly* 40, no. 1 (1989): 42–69.

Soyinka, Wole. "Telephone Conversation." In *The Norton Anthology of English Literature*. 9th ed. Vol. F. Edited by Stephen Greenblatt, Jahan Ramazani, and Jon Stallworthy. New York: W.W. Norton, 2012.

Standeven, Harriet A.L. *House Paints, 1900–1960*. Los Angeles: Getty Publications, 2011.

Szeman, Imre and Dominic Boyer. *Energy Humanities*. Baltimore: Johns Hopkins University Press, 2017.

Tann, Jennifer. "Steam and Sugar: The Diffusion of the Stationary Steam Engine to the Caribbean Sugar Industry 1770–1840." In *History of Technology*. Vol. 19. Edited by Graham Hollister-Short. New York: Bloomsbury, 1997. 63–84.

Trinder, Barrie Stuart. *Britain's Industrial Revolution*. Lancaster: Carnegie Publishing, 2013.

Williams, Eric. *Capitalism and Slavery*. New York: Capricorn Books, 1966.

Williams, Michael. *Deforesting the Earth*. Chicago: University of Chicago Press, 2003.

Yaeger, Patricia. "Literature in the Ages of Wood, Tallow, Coal, Whale Oil, Gasoline, Atomic Power, and Other Energy Sources." *PMLA* 126, no. 2 (2011): 305–310.

Yusoff, Kathryn. *A Billion Black Anthropocenes or None*. Minneapolis: University of Minnesota Press, 2019.

4
ENVIRONMENTAL RACISM, ENVIRONMENTAL JUSTICE

Centering Indigenous Responses to the Colonial Logics of the Anthropocene

Rebecca Macklin

While the mainstream adoption of the term "Anthropocene" is a relatively recent development, the impacts of the epoch it names are not new. As Indigenous and allied scholars have long argued, anthropogenic (human-caused) climate change marks an intensification of environmental changes that have been imposed upon racialized peoples for centuries through colonialism.[1] What is new, perhaps, is how these changes have begun to infiltrate the lives of those who previously were exempt. As Kathryn Yusoff argues, "The Anthropocene might seem to offer a dystopic future that laments the end of the world, but imperialism and ongoing (settler) colonialisms have been ending worlds for as long as they have been in existence."[2] Charges to "decolonize" the Anthropocene assert the need to locate the contested start date of the epoch with the arrival of Europeans in the Americas, directly locating the origins of anthropogenic climate change in relation to the colonial project. Doing so, according to Zoe Todd and Heather Davis, would be a recognition "that the ecocidal logics that now govern our world are not inevitable or 'human nature,' but are the result of a series of decisions that have their origins and reverberations in colonization."[3]

To understand how such reverberations manifest in our presents and, inevitably, our futures, it is necessary to examine how the effects of the Anthropocene are shaped by the enduring legacies of European colonialism and subsequent settler colonial projects. As has been well documented, the effects of the Anthropocene are not the same for everyone. Instead, the human forms of vulnerability that are a product of climate change are uneven—and the lines on which they fall are inseparable from historic and ongoing forms of inequality. Globally, those who have historically been oppressed in terms of race, gender, and class disproportionately suffer the consequences of our changing environment. Environmental

DOI: 10.4324/9781003095347-6

racism is a term that can be used to understand the multiple and intersecting ways that structural racism and environmental degradation together impact the health and well-being of people of color. As Ingrid Waldron has argued, this emphasis on race does not detract from discussions of class or other intersecting characteristics of inequality. Rather, these concerns are always interlinked. For non-white or racialized peoples, Waldron asserts, "the added burden of racism deepens existing inequalities and disadvantages they are already experiencing related to class, such as unemployment, low income, poverty, food insecurity, and residence in under-resourced neighbourhoods."[4] Crucially, the impacts are not limited to the conditions of Earth's changing climate, such as hotter temperatures and rising waters, though these too pose very real threats to Indigenous and other historically marginalized populations. Instead, Black and Indigenous communities, as well as other people of color, disproportionately experience the negative impacts of environmental degradation, whatever form this might take.

While environmental racism recurs around the globe, often as a long-temporal consequence of European imperialism, in this chapter, I will specifically discuss the experiences of Indigenous populations in the United States and Canada. In doing so, I seek to center Indigenous perspectives that are all too frequently sidelined in discussions of the Anthropocene. I understand environmental racism as a strategy of settler colonialism: a process distinct from other forms of colonialism "in that settlers come with the intention of making a new home on the land, a homemaking that insists on settler sovereignty over all things in their new domain."[5] The overarching aim of settler colonialism, as Patrick Wolfe has argued, is to obtain land. Settler access to territory is only made possible through "elimination of the native," whether through genocide, forced removal, assimilation, or other means.[6] One way in which this is achieved is through "wastelanding," a term that names the process whereby settler colonizers determine which lands are classed as undesirable and therefore made available for degradation. In explaining this concept, Traci Brynn Voyles argues that

> remaking Native land as settler home involves the exploitation of environmental resources, to be sure, but it also involves a deeply complex construction of that land as either always already belonging to the settler—his manifest destiny—or as undesirable, unproductive, or unappealing: in short, as wasteland.[7]

This process has historically occurred through legislation that has sought to undermine Indigenous sovereignty or remove Indigenous groups from their ancestral lands altogether. In the United States, the system of federal Indian law has shaped the relationship between the government and tribal nations since the early nineteenth century, while in Canada, the 1876 Indian Act is the primary legislation through which the federal government manages reserve land and relations with Indigenous groups.

Frequently, Indigenous environments are transformed by industries that make their territories into wastelands and mark their bodies as disposable. In the United States and Canada, the settler colonial state produces conditions of environmental precarity, a term I use to refer to the disproportionate vulnerability that many Black and Indigenous people of color experience as a result of the combined effects of colonial legacies and the increased influence of neoliberal capitalism on the nation-state. In the Southwest US, for example, uranium mining in the late twentieth century led to over two million tons of uranium tailings being dumped on Native American reservations. As a consequence, Navajo, Pueblo, and other tribal communities in the region experience rates of cancer far greater than the national average. Navajo children are affected by reproductive organ cancer at fifteen times the rate of other populations.[8] Across Canada, the proximity of First Nations reserves to sites of resource extraction means that Indigenous communities are exposed to increased environmental risks including unclean drinking water. As of February 2020, there were sixty-one long-term drinking water advisories in place in First Nations communities. For women and two-spirit people,[9] the presence of extractive industries also means the increased risk of sexual assault. As the 2019 Canadian National Inquiry found, the geographic proximity of male-dominated oil drilling sites to reservations directly contributes to a rise in incidences of sexual violence and sex trafficking, crimes that are predominantly perpetrated by non-Native men.[10]

Such examples of environmental racism exemplify the imbricated forms of sudden and "slow violence" that render certain bodies precarious under the settler colonial state.[11] In the United States and Canada, the settler state reaps harm on Indigenous bodies, violence that is not always spectacular or newsworthy. While state violence is often thought of as something overt, it also "commonly manifests as a short-circuited life."[12] Further, environmental racism should be understood as relating not only to physiological health but also to spiritual and cultural health. Writing of the geothermal drilling of the active Mauna Loa volcano in Hawai'i, Greta Gaard and Lori Gruen argue that "such drilling is an act of environmental racism in that it violates the religious and cultural beliefs of the native Hawaiians, for whom the Mauna Loa volcano is a manifestation of the Goddess Pele."[13] This broader conceptualization of environmental racism is necessary in order to understand the reasons for Indigenous opposition to many extractive projects and other forms of industrialized development.

Within the environmental and social sciences, scholars have demonstrated the need for analyses of the Anthropocene that focus on the enduring legacies of colonialism. Yusoff's vital work *A Billion Black Anthropocenes or None* (2018) urgently counters what she describes as the willful "racial blindness" of geology, contesting that any discussion of the "Anthropos" should begin with an analysis that attends to how the category of Man has always been an inherently racialized formation.[14] Arguing for the necessity of an analysis of race in how extraction is conceptualized, Yusoff writes:

> As the Anthropocene proclaims the language of species-life—anthropos—through a universalist geologic commons, it neatly erases histories of racism that were incubated through the regulatory structure of geologic relations. The racial categorization of Blackness shares its natality with mining the New World ... That is, racialization belongs to a material categorization of the division of matter (corporeal and mineralogical) into active and inert.[15]

Yusoff's work urgently brings scholarship from critical race studies and biopolitics into dialogue with geology. Projects including those by Yusoff, Todd, and Davis demonstrate the necessity of interdisciplinary research that works across boundaries to contend with how colonial legacies, including histories of racialization, inform the study of the Anthropocene. Bearing these projects in mind, we must ask what work is required of the humanities to contribute to this project of decolonizing the Anthropocene. And what role specifically does literature play in this challenge?

With its potential to reach audiences across cultural, geographic, and temporal borders, literature offers the possibility of rendering visible the forms of environmental harm that are all too frequently hidden in the public sphere. As Rob Nixon has argued, literature is able to make visible "sights unseen," overcoming the "representational" challenge posed by the long-temporal frame of slow violence. Nixon writes, "In the long arc between the emergence of slow violence and its delayed effects, both the causes and the memory of catastrophe readily fade from view as the casualties incurred typically pass untallied and unremembered." The imaginative capacity of literature means that it can "bring home—and bring emotionally to life—threats that take time to wreak their havoc, threats that never materialize in one spectacular, explosive, cinematic scene."[16] While Nixon focuses on the representational challenge of slow violence, others have discussed literature's potential to surpass the sociopolitical limitations that inform the question of visibility. Sharae Deckard has advocated for the subversive potential of world-literature, a term that she understands to be literature of the capitalist world-system. Imagining world-literary texts as "beacons that shine light onto obscured terrains and subjects," Deckard writes that "world-literature has the potential to reveal the objects of erasure and contradict the discourses which obfuscate the historical conditions and victims of capitalism."[17] Yet, as Deckard stresses, as a commodity that exists within the capitalist world-system, literature—and therefore its more radical mechanism for highlighting inequality—is complicated by the opportunities for circulation offered by the global literary industry.

In the second half of this chapter, I place these approaches into dialogue in order to understand the ways that selected Indigenous authors have used literature in order to highlight instances of environmental racism and, crucially, imagine the possibility of environmental justice. Following Deckard and Nixon, I understand the examples of environmental harm that are highlighted to be products of capitalism. Yet, by focusing on Indigenous North American literatures, I highlight the centrality of settler colonialism—and settler colonial technologies such as wastelanding—in these histories. In doing so, I echo Indigenous paradigms that assert the inseparability of decolonization from environmental justice and remediation. When reckoning with conditions of environmental racism, texts by Indigenous authors frequently emphasize the question of environmental justice. Understanding environmental justice as the necessary other side of the (colonial-capitalist) coin to environmental racism, this chapter asks how different forms of literary expression are being used to advocate for and imagine more just futures for human and nonhuman creatures. By reading together two classic examples of Indigenous literary environmentalism, Simon Ortiz's *Fight Back* (1980) and Linda Hogan's *Solar Storms* (1994), this chapter frames the struggle of environmental justice as a continuation of historic anticolonial resistance.

Indigenous authors have employed literature as an anticolonial tool since the colonial era and up to the contemporary moment. In *Why Indigenous Literatures Matter* (2018), Cherokee author and scholar Daniel Heath Justice considers literature to be "just one more vital way that we have countered ... forces of erasure and given shape to our own ways of being in the world."[18] An early example of this is the *Cherokee Phoenix*, the first Native American newspaper, which was published from 1828 to 1834. The publication arose directly in response to federal and state pressures placed on the Cherokee Nation to surrender their territory to Georgia. Cherokee dispossession was cemented through the 1830 Indian Removal Act, but the publication helped to delay removal for a number of years, enabling communication between tribal members and spreading awareness of the nation's plight to a wider audience. In the contemporary period, Acoma Pueblo poet Simon Ortiz is one writer who has worked to develop this tradition by highlighting forms of environmental racism that have been directed at Indigenous peoples in the United States. Through poetry and prose, the collection *Fight Back: For the Sake of the People, for the Sake of the Land* (1980) documents the impacts of uranium mining on Laguna lands and communities in New Mexico, presenting a necessary counternarrative to hegemonic colonial narratives. It testifies to Ortiz's experiences as a former mine worker, as well as the impact of the mining industry on Native American communities more broadly.

Fight Back explicitly builds on the long tradition of Native American resistance, as it was written for the Tricentennial celebration of the All Indian Pueblo Revolt of 1680, a movement that saw Indigenous peoples from across tribes united to revolt against Spanish colonizers. As Roxanne Dunbar-Ortiz writes in the collection's Preface, *Fight Back* "reminds us that the Revolt left a legacy of resistance."[19] Ortiz's collection vitally reframes Indigenous resistance in the twentieth century to be situated in opposition to extractive industries, specifically uranium mining on Indigenous territories. Writing about this topic in explicit relation to the 1680 Revolt clearly signals to the reader that settler colonialism is ongoing but, in this moment, looks quite different to how it did in the seventeenth century. Resistance, in the context of time in which the volume was written, "continues in the mines, in the fields, in the factories."[20] The collection's imperative title is a call to action, emphasizing the intrinsic relationality between the people and the land. With this comes the understanding that the survival of one depends on the other, an idea in which many North American Indigenous cultures are grounded. As Kim TallBear emphasizes, to understand genocide in its full meaning in the Americas "requires an understanding of the entangled genocide of humans and nonhumans here. Indigenous peoples cohere as peoples in relation to very specific places and nonhuman communities. Their/our decimation goes hand in hand."[21] This belief system sits in marked contrast to the notion of a fundamental and hierarchical separation between Humanity and Nature that, following Jason Moore, is foundational to capitalism and thus colonialism.[22]

Numerous Indigenous writers have documented the violence of settler colonial resource extraction. Within this body of literature, *Fight Back* is notable for the way that it represents Native Americans participating as workers in extraction, here in the mining industry. In doing so, it challenges exotic depictions of Indigenous peoples being "at one with nature" and the colonial trope of the Noble Savage, too "spiritual" to carry out hard labor or too "proud to work for a boss or master."[23] Instead, *Fight Back* depicts the necessity of participating in these industries as the reality for many tribal members who are faced with few income options: "A job was a job. / You were lucky to have one/ if you got one."[24] Colonial strategies of forced removal and forced environmental change meant that the survival of tribal nations was largely dependent on their participation in the capitalist economy. Settler colonialism, enabled by federal Indian law, disrupted previously existing economies and forms of social relation and left many tribes without the means for self-subsistence. Ortiz explores the impact of this process in the poem "Final Solution: Jobs, Leaving":

> We had to buy groceries,
> had to have clothes, homes, roofs,
> windows. Surrounded by the United States,
> we had come to need money.[25]

The title of the poem jarringly invokes the Nazis' Final Solution, implicitly marking Native Americans as survivors of genocide—in this case, one that is a combined product of settler colonialism and capitalism:

> The solution was to change,
> to leave, to go to jobs.
>   Utah.
> California.
>   Idaho.
>   Oregon.[26]

The solution referred to here is assimilation: an option that offered survival for some but at the price of irrevocable cultural disruption and geographical fragmentation, suggested here through the dispersed place-names and structure of the poem.

The most-cited poem from the collection, "It Was That Indian," evokes the ways that hegemonic narratives work to obfuscate colonial violence. The poem depicts the way that the US Government blamed a Native American, or "Indian" to quote Ortiz, for the discovery of uranium, rather locating responsibility with the settler colonial extractive economy:

> Well, later on,
> when some folks began to complain
> about chemical poisons flowing into the streams
> from the processing mills, carwrecks on Highway 53,
> lack of housing in Grants,
> cave-ins at Section 33,
> non-union support,
> high cost of living,
> and uranium radiation causing cancer,
> they – the Chamber of Commerce – pointed out
> that it was Martinez
> that Navajo Indian from over by Bluewater
> who discovered uranium,
> ...
> it was that Indian who started that boom.[27]

Ortiz lists the extensive consequences of uranium mining, which encompass environmental degradation—including chemical pollution and its health consequences for those living in proximity—as well as social issues, such as unfair labor conditions and economic inflation. These various concerns flow into one another with no clear distinction between them, suggesting that there is no line between the social and the environmental spheres. Rather, the slow violence that results from uranium mining is felt on multiple, intersecting scales and is not exclusively tied to environmental forms of harm. As the list of consequences grows, the Chamber of Commerce's blame of Martinez feels almost farcical in its attempt to point the finger at a singular individual instead of the systems that have created the various problems that are named. Ironically, its language also invokes the destructive Doctrine of Discovery, a concept used to legitimize the colonization of the United States, most notably in *Johnson v. M'Intosh* (1823).[28] The original Doctrine enabled Europeans to seize lands inhabited by Indigenous peoples under the guise of discovery. The Indigenous tribes who were present before the arrival of settlers had no property rights and instead merely held a right of occupancy. Here, we see the Chamber of Commerce using this rhetoric as a way to evade responsibility for the environmental and social fallout of uranium extraction. But ironically, this time, it is "that Navajo Indian" credited with the all-important discovery. In recalling the history of uranium mining in the Southwest—and, crucially, the complex place of those Native Americans who worked in and thus participated in the development of the industry—Ortiz's collection can be understood as a counternarrative that serves to challenge the hegemonic narratives about Native Americans and their experiences. Further, it explicitly names extractive capitalism as foundational to settler colonialism and the wide-ranging forms of harm it reaps.

Chickasaw author Linda Hogan builds on this tradition of Indigenous literary resistance in her 1994 novel *Solar Storms*. Though set in a fictionalized location spanning the US–Canada border, the novel was inspired by the resistance movement that developed in response to the James Bay Project in Quebec. The novel is set in 1972 and follows the narrator and protagonist Angela Jensen as she returns to her family, having been raised in foster care outside of her culture. Upon returning to the town of Adam's Rib, Angela (who later changes her name to Angel) becomes embroiled in a movement to resist the building of a hydroelectric dam, which would flood the lands of her ancestors. Like *Fight Back*, Hogan's novel directly invokes the history of the 1680 Pueblo Revolt, as Angela compares the leader of their group, Arlie, to the Pueblo leader Popé: "a man who led a successful revolt against the Spanish." Like Popé, Arlie "always made two plans of action. One he gave to them, the other he passed onto the rest of us, so the informants were always confused."[29] This point is not a coincidence, though it is interesting that both Ortiz and Hogan invoke this historic rebellion in order to advocate for a community-led environmental justice movement. The resonance of the Pueblo-led, pan-tribal revolt across twentieth century and contemporary Native American literatures emphasizes the renewed political emphasis on collaboration and trans-Indigenous solidarity in the present. This ethic carries particular weight in Hogan's novel, which, though set in the northern reaches of the United States and across the Canadian border, unusually does not name any specific Indigenous nations or cultures. This ambiguity as to which tribal nation(s) the characters belong creates a narrative that is not exclusive to any singular nation's experience.

While Angela is the primary narrator, the narrative includes vignettes that share the perspectives of the matriarchs in Angela's family: Bush, Agnes, and Dora-Rouge. These overlapping perspectives do not include the names of the narrators, which makes it difficult at times to ascertain exactly which character is speaking. The effect is that the vignettes take on the familial quality of the oral tradition— stories that have been spoken so many times, they do not have a singular voice. With all women narrators, the novel specifically charts the long impact of settler colonialism on generations of Indigenous women, which include accounts of sexual violence, forced adoption, and child abuse. However, *Solar Storms* is not only concerned with the violence done to (and by) women. Instead, it highlights the critical role that women play in advocating for environmental justice. In contrast to the masculine presence of the dam corporation and their workers, referred to repeatedly as "young men," the resistance movement is largely led by women elders. The eldest of the group, "Miss Nett and Dora-Rouge became an awe-inspiring pair." Their age, in fact, affords them advantages over the other protestors: "As older women, Miss Nett and Dora-Rouge were able to do what the rest of us couldn't."[30] These women are valued within their community for the knowledges they carry. As such, the men are a marked contrast to the young men who are valued for their physical strength and comparative lack of knowledge. Indeed, the men are portrayed as dangerous because of their ignorance: "look at those boys. They are so young. They don't even know history. They thought this place was barren. Now they are here. They will do as they are told. They don't have the courage not to."[31]

Solar Storm's positioning of women as powerful figures in the resistance is a recovery of the matrilineal traditions that characterize many Indigenous cultures. The enduring nature of these sociopolitical structures is reflected in the leadership positions that women have historically held, and continue to hold, in Indigenous resistance movements, from Idle No More, a transnational movement started in 2012 by four women in Saskatchewan, to the numerous female-led anti-extractive protests that are currently taking place across Latin America. The motto of Women of All Red Nations (WARN) sums up this tradition, stating: "Indian women have always been in the front lines in the defense of our nations."[32] Through colonialism, however, Indigenous women were removed from positions of power, as traditionally matriarchal societies were restructured. As Huhndorf and Cheryl Suzack highlight:

> [The consequences of colonialism are] always shaped by gender and the historic imposition of Western values and practices continues to structure conditions of inequality in distinctly gendered ways: For Indigenous women, colonization has involved their removal from positions of power, the replacement of traditional gender roles with Western patriarchal practices, the exertion of colonial control over Indigenous communities through the management of women's bodies, and sexual violence.[33]

The undoing of gendered oppression, which is intrinsically a part of the capitalist system, is necessary to dismantling the structures of settler colonialism. Hogan's repositioning of women at the center of political processes is explicitly decolonial, then, as it rejects colonially enforced patriarchal social norms.

At the heart of Indigenous literary engagements with environmental justice, there is often an emphasis on the resurgence of Indigenous worldviews. Such processes of resurgence exemplify *biskaaybiiyang*, an Anishinaabe word meaning "returning to ourselves," which Grace L. Dillon understands as vital to decoloniality.[34] The question of a return to Indigenous ways of knowing is central to Hogan's novel—and not only in its recovery of matrilineal gender norms. The concept of return provides the impetus for Angela's journey throughout, whose physical return to her ancestral lands is accompanied by the gradual relearning of forgotten cultural knowledge. Through foregrounding Indigenous ways of knowing, Hogan emphasizes the belief that environmental justice is grounded in the need to make kin by building reciprocal relations with human and nonhuman others. While deeply and intimately material, the struggle for the lands and waters on which Angela's family reside can be understood as a fundamental conflict between opposing interpretations of the landscape. On the one hand, the novel conveys the ways that local Indigenous communities understand the land that they have lived on and with since time immemorial: "The people at Adam's Rib believed everything was alive, that we were surrounded by the faces and lovings of gods ... Even the shadows light threw down had meaning, had stories and depth."[35] On the other side, the views held by most Euro-Americans in the novel are rooted in a logic of extraction, informed by historic colonial interpretations that view the land and water as inanimate resources for human consumption. In depicting these different perspectives, Hogan demonstrates how "the disruption of Indigenous relationships to land represents a profound epistemic, ontological, cosmological violence."[36]

The enduring impact of this simultaneously physical and epistemic violence is depicted through the smell of cyanide that Angel's mother and grandmother carry in their skin. The smell of "something sweet, an almond odor" is the result of Angela's grandmother, Loretta, having eaten poisoned meat that had been left by settlers as a trap. Loretta "was from the Elk Islanders, the people who became so hungry they ate the poisoned carcasses of deer that the settlers left out for the wolves." Her daughter Hannah inherits this scent, the "blood-deep" legacy of the "settlers' deeds."[37] While the scent can be read as a symbol for intergenerational trauma that is a consequence of colonialism, it too can be read quite literally as an example of how settler colonialism situates itself by carrying out combined violence against nonhuman environments/animals and Indigenous peoples. The attempted eradication of wolves here is just one example of how settlers asserted control over the landscapes that they came to inhabit: an attempt to reconfigure ecosystems rooted in a logic of human superiority. This process is exemplary of settler colonialism and, as Tuck and Yang observe, clearly distinguishes settlers from immigrants: "Settlers are not immigrants. Immigrants are beholden to the Indigenous laws and epistemologies of the lands they migrate to. Settlers become the law, supplanting Indigenous laws and epistemologies."[38] Unlike the Euro-American settlers, the majority of Indigenous characters understand human and nonhuman environments as intertwined through complex sets of kinship relations. As Angela asserts: "the division between humans and animals was a false one."[39] The only character who fails to understand this is LaRue: an example of an Indigenous person who fails to "respect the bond" between humans and animals.[40] The novel evokes an awareness of the relationality between humans, animals, and their ecosystems through a marked parallel between the histories of colonial and capitalist violence affected on human and nonhuman creatures. This framing is necessary to fully comprehend the possibility of environmental justice, as an imperative that not only requires material, physical transformation but also epistemic decolonization.

Ortiz's *Fight Back* and Hogan's *Solar Storms* each take distinct approaches to questions of environmental racism and environmental justice. Yet, both invoke this sense of relationality that exists between human and nonhuman forms as being integral to building a future world that is more just for all. Further, they also speak to the relationality that exists between different generations, each locating the inspiration for the environmental justice movements they depict with the 1680 Pueblo Revolt. The enduring image of this historic anticolonial, trans-Indigenous movement carries into these texts. It carries into the twenty-first century, too, if we are to consider the recent movements to oppose extractive projects on Indigenous lands that build on historic struggles through trans-Indigenous forms of solidarity. As Lakota historian Nick Estes has argued in relation to the 2016–2017 #NoDAPL movement, "What happened at Standing Rock was the most recent iteration of an Indian war that never ends."[41] While the potential of literature to highlight conditions of injustice is always complicated by the material realities of capitalism, which include questions of privilege, accessibility, and readership, it nevertheless provides a vital means by which Indigenous authors are able to advocate for specific struggles and imagine the possibility of more just futures. *Fight Back* and *Solar Storms* each is clear in its message: the need for anticolonial resistance continues, and it is, at its heart, a struggle for environmental justice.

Notes

1 Throughout this chapter, I use the word "Indigenous" to refer to the Native peoples of North America, specifically Native Americans in the United States and First Nations, Inuit, and Métis populations in Canada. Following dominant conventions in Indigenous studies, I capitalize the word "Indigenous" when referring to specific populations in order to mark the word as a proper noun.
2 Kathryn Yusoff, *A Billion Black Anthropocenes or None* (Minneapolis: University of Minnesota Press, 2018), xiii.
3 Heather Davis and Zoe Todd, "On the Importance of a Date, or, Decolonizing the Anthropocene," *ACME: An International Journal for Critical Geographies* 16, no. 4 (2017): 763.
4 Ingrid R.G. Waldron, *There's Something in the Water: Environmental Racism in Indigenous & Black Communities* (Nova Scotia: Fernwood Publishing, 2018), 2.
5 Eve Tuck and K. Wayne Yang, "Decolonization Is Not a Metaphor," *Decolonization: Indigeneity, Education, and Society* 1, no. 2 (2012): 5.
6 Patrick Wolfe, "Settler Colonialism and the Elimination of the Native," *Journal of Genocide Research* 8, no. 4 (2006): 387.
7 Traci Brynne Voyles, *Wastelanding: Legacies of Uranium Mining in Navajo Country* (Minneapolis: University of Minnesota Press, 2015), 7.
8 Ibid., 4.

9 The term "two-spirit" is the preferred term among many Native American cultures that names individuals who embody a nonbinary gender or a mixture of feminine and masculine spirits. Traditionally, two-spirit people occupy specific spiritual roles within their societies.
10 *Reclaiming Power and Place: The Final Report of the National Inquiry into Missing and Murdered Indigenous Women and Girls* (2019), www.mmiwg-ffada.ca/final-report/.
11 See Rob Nixon, *Slow Violence and the Environmentalism of the Poor* (Cambridge: Harvard University Press, 2011).
12 Billy-Ray Belcourt, *A History of My Brief Body* (Columbus: Two Dollar Radio, 2020), 5.
13 Lori Gruen and Greta Gaard, "Ecofeminism: Toward Global Justice and Planetary Health," *Society and Nature* 2, no. 1 (1993): 247.
14 Yusoff, xiii.
15 Ibid., 2.
16 Nixon, 2, 8, 14.
17 Sharae Deckard, "Mapping the World-Ecology: Conjectures on World-Ecological Literature," *Academia* (2014): 4. Retrieved 23 March 2021.
18 Daniel Heath Justice, *Why Indigenous Literatures Matter* (Waterloo: Wilfrid Laurier University Press, 2018), xix.
19 Roxanne Dunbar-Ortiz, "Preface," in *Fight Back: For the Sake of the People, for the Sake of the Land* (Albuquerque: University of New Mexico, Institute for Native American Development, 1980), ix.
20 Ibid.
21 Kim TallBear, "Beyond the Life/Not-Life Binary: A Feminist-Indigenous Reading of Cryopreservation, Interspecies Thinking, and the New Materialisms," in *Cryopolitics: Frozen Life in a Melting World*, ed. Joanna Radin and Emma Kowal (Cambridge: MIT Press, 2017), 198.
22 Jason Moore, "The Rise of Cheap Nature," in *Anthropocene or Capitalocene? Nature, History, and the Crisis of Capitalism*, ed. Jason Moore (Oakland: PM Press, 2016), 78.
23 Dunbar-Ortiz, xiii.
24 Simon J. Ortiz, "Starting at the Bottom," in *Woven Stone* (Tuscon: University of Arizona Press, 1992), 297.
25 Simon J. Ortiz, "Final Solution: Jobs, Leaving," in *Woven Stone*, 318.
26 Ibid., 28.
27 Simon J. Ortiz, "It Was That Indian," in *Woven Stone*, 295.
28 For a detailed discussion of the Doctrine of Discovery and its enduring relevance to federal Indian law, see Eric Cheyfitz, ed., *The Columbia Guide to American Indian Literatures of the United States since 1945* (New York: Columbia University Press, 2006).
29 Linda Hogan, *Solar Storms* (New York: Simon and Schuster, 1997), 310.
30 Ibid., 306.
31 Ibid., 307.
32 Nick Estes, *Our History Is the Future: Standing Rock Versus the Dakota Access Pipeline, and the Long Tradition of Indigenous Resistance* (London: Verso, 2019), 181.
33 Cheryl Suzack, Shari M. Huhndorf, Jeanne Perreault, and Jean Barman, eds., *Indigenous Women and Feminism: Politics, Activism, Culture* (Vancouver: University of British Columbia Press, 2011), 1.
34 Grace L. Dillon, *Walking the Clouds: An Anthology of Indigenous Science Fiction* (Tucson: University of Arizona Press, 2012), 10.
35 Hogan, 81.

36 Tuck and Yang, 5.
37 Hogan, 38, 40.
38 Tuck and Yang, 6–7.
39 Hogan, 81–82.
40 Ibid., 82.
41 Estes, 10. The #NoDAPL movement developed in response to plans to build the Dakota Access Pipeline just north of the Standing Rock Sioux reservation in North Dakota. The movement spread internationally beyond the physical space of the camp, garnering expressions of solidarity and material manifestations of support from Indigenous nations and allied groups around the world.

References

Belcourt, Billy-Ray. *A History of My Brief Body*. Columbus: Two Dollar Radio, 2020.
Cheyfitz, Eric, ed. *The Columbia Guide to American Indian Literatures of the United States since 1945*. New York: Columbia University Press, 2006.
Davis, Heather, and Zoe Todd. "On the Importance of a Date, or, Decolonizing the Anthropocene." *ACME: An International Journal for Critical Geographies* 16, no. 4 (2017): 761–780.
Deckard, Sharae. "Mapping the World-Ecology: Conjectures on World-Ecological Literature." *Academia* (2014). Retrieved 23 March 2021.
Dillon, Grace L. *Walking the Clouds: An Anthology of Indigenous Science Fiction*. Tucson: University of Arizona Press, 2012.
Dunbar-Ortiz, Roxanne. "Preface." In *Fight Back: For the Sake of the People, for the Sake of the Land*. Albuquerque: University of New Mexico, Institute for Native American Development, 1980.
Estes, Nick. *Our History Is the Future: Standing Rock Versus the Dakota Access Pipeline, and the Long Tradition of Indigenous Resistance*. London: Verso, 2019.
Gruen, Lori, and Greta Gaard. "Ecofeminism: Toward Global Justice and Planetary Health." *Society and Nature* 2, no. 1 (1993): 1–35.
Hogan, Linda. *Solar Storms*. New York: Simon and Schuster, 1997.
Justice, Daniel Heath. *Why Indigenous Literatures Matter*. Waterloo: Wilfrid Laurier University Press, 2018.
Moore, Jason. "The Rise of Cheap Nature." In *Anthropocene or Capitalocene? Nature, History, and the Crisis of Capitalism*. Edited by Jason Moore. Oakland: PM Press, 2016. 78–115.
Nixon, Rob. *Slow Violence and the Environmentalism of the Poor*. Cambridge: Harvard University Press, 2011.
Ortiz, Simon J. *Fight Back: For the Sake of the People, for the Sake of the Land*. Albuquerque: University of New Mexico, Institute for Native American Development, 1980.
Ortiz, Simon J. *Woven Stone*. Tuscon: University of Arizona Press, 1992.
Reclaiming Power and Place: The Final Report of the National Inquiry into Missing and Murdered Indigenous Women and Girls. 2019. www.mmiwg-ffada.ca/final-report/.
Suzack, Cheryl, Shari M. Huhndorf, Jeanne Perreault, and Jean Barman, eds. *Indigenous Women and Feminism: Politics, Activism, Culture*. Vancouver: University of British Columbia Press, 2011.
TallBear, Kim. "Beyond the Life/Not-Life Binary: A Feminist-Indigenous Reading of Cryopreservation, Interspecies Thinking, and the New Materialisms." In

Cryopolitics: Frozen Life in a Melting World. Edited by Joanna Radin and Emma Kowal. Cambridge: MIT Press, 2017. 407–433.

Tuck, Eve, and K. Wayne Yang. "Decolonization Is Not a Metaphor." *Decolonization: Indigeneity, Education, and Society* 1, no. 2 (2012): 1–40.

Voyles, Traci Brynne. *Wastelanding: Legacies of Uranium Mining in Navajo Country.* Minneapolis: University of Minnesota Press, 2015.

Waldron, Ingrid R.G. *There's Something in the Water: Environmental Racism in Indigenous & Black Communities.* Nova Scotia: Fernwood Publishing, 2018.

Wolfe, Patrick. "Settler Colonialism and the Elimination of the Native." *Journal of Genocide Research* 8, no. 4 (2006): 387–409.

Yusoff, Kathryn. *A Billion Black Anthropocenes or None.* Minneapolis: University of Minnesota Press, 2018.

5

THE WORLD IS BURNING

Racialized Regimes of Eco-Terror and the Anthropocene as Eurocene

Nicolás Juárez

Introduction

It is imperative to begin without delay—time, despite its disturbing stillness, is always moving too quickly, and we are already behind before we even begin. Even by the time you finish this paragraph, around 60,000 tons of CO_2 will be emitted, and the earth will creep dangerously closer to a climatic disaster that escapes imagination.[1] Every day, it seems, it is another dozen or so species lost, a couple of hundred thousand acres of rainforest burned away, or a new record for some ecological catastrophe. Not to mention the human stories of climate change that proliferate across the news—a third of the global population subject to lethal heat at least 20 days a year, 100 million hungry as a direct result of climatic disaster, 10,000 dead a day from air pollution, and on and on—usually accompanied with some grim reminder that what we experience today, as horrific as it is, will quickly become mild, unspectacular, and common over the next couple of decades.[2] This is, of course, an intimately familiar feeling: too much, too big, too late. All the while, one is expected to continue to keep living, keep consuming, keep working as if there is still anything remotely resembling a future to come. No doubt this is what is behind the growing proliferation of terms such as "eco-anxiety," "ecological grief," "climate trauma," or "solastalgia." These are the feelings that accompany the material and libidinal existence of what has been called the Anthropocene, a geological era in which "human activity is now global and is the dominant cause of most contemporary environmental change."[3]

However, that definition, along with the anxious and grieving apathy produced from attempting to confront it, immediately brings to mind several questions: When did this start? What is human activity? What is to be done? I attempt to answer these questions in this chapter, arguing that the moniker of the Anthropocene

DOI: 10.4324/9781003095347-7

misdirects our attention toward a generic, global Anthropos, thereby mystifying and occluding our capacity to recognize the origin and structural maintenance of the libidinal and political economies fueling the current crisis. In order to investigate this, I utilize Jarius Grove's concept of the Eurocene, which he takes up in response to Sylvia Wynter's critique that the Anthropocene too readily universalizes blame despite the fact that millions, if not billions, globally are not part of the lifeways that produce it. In deploying the term, Grove wishes to link "climate change, species loss, slavery, the elimination of native peoples, and the globalization of extractive capitalism [as] all part of the same global ordering."[4] However, rather than using the Eurocene as another alternative term for the Anthropocene, I show that despite the proliferation of alternative terms—Capitalocene, Plantationocene, Chthulucene, etc.—what is always spoken about is the proliferation of a regime of violence wherein "the West ... brought the whole human species into its hegemonic ... model of being human."[5] As such, the terminological centering of Europe speaks to the ways in which it is precisely the West qua Europe that historically and violently formed the contemporary understanding of what human and human activity is. Said another way, Grove deploys the prefix Euro- in order to signify how European colonialism institutes a way of being through genocide and slavery that becomes synonymous with what it means to be human, and that such an ordering is directly linked to the phenomena characteristic of the Anthropocene, in whatever parlance is used. To that end, this chapter traces potential starting points for the Anthropocene to argue that racialized eco-terror initiates the Anthropocene and that such terror occurs because of an ontological structure that takes Black and Native people as non-Human.

Anthropocene, Eurocene as Race War

There are three main considerations for the beginning of the Anthropocene: The Columbian Exchange (1610), the Industrial Revolution (1784), and the "Great Acceleration" (1945). While each of these events take place in radically different times and involve multiple countries, they each are made possible by the violence of settler colonialism and antiblackness, which animate time and space itself. In order to illuminate this claim, I turn to each event in turn and examine how its material and libidinal economies were made directly possible by these power structures such that it is impossible to consider the Anthropocene at all without them.

The Columbian Exchange (1610)

The Columbian Exchange—or the widespread flow and movement of flora, fauna, peoples, and technologies between Europe, Africa, and the Americas during the fifteenth and sixteenth centuries—has the earliest claim to being a start to the Anthropocene. Geologists have identified the "Orbis spike" in 1610 because the literal mass death caused by European conquest produced a global drop in carbon emissions as millions of Indigenous people became ghosts through a depopulation of over 90 percent. This drop was sufficiently large that it likely contributed, in part, to the Little Ice Age's globalization. Beyond this, geologists point to the ways in which species jumped continents and ecologies massively intermixed, beginning a homogeneity in Earth's biosphere that is unparalleled in Earth's geological history. These massive shifts—in carbon emissions changing Earth's global climate and in the biome of Earth—mark this event as a particular candidate for the beginning of the Anthropocene.[6]

However, it is also necessary to note that such an "exchange" was anything but. Instead, it was both an act of unparalleled and unrivaled violence, the institution of a structure of death that was and is filled with torture, rape, enslavement, displacement, and murder. Such an approach was unusual not only in its scope but also in its raw brutality. Despite the history of warfare and land-grabbing in Earth's history, never before had an entire race of people been indelibly marked by their skin color for death. While ethnic conflicts proliferate throughout history, this racial schema that marked the Indian as inevitably dead, dying, and deserving of death was a new appearance. At the same time, the "exchange" also allows us to focus on the ecological violence of such an encounter. In the first instance, the introduction of various foreign flora and fauna from Europe disrupted Indigenous food systems, introducing famine and malnutrition as a common part of Indigenous life. Combined with being displaced onto unfamiliar lands, this form of environmental violence mirrors the ecological devastation of today—lands in which food will not grow, forced migration into unfamiliar places, and sickness and disease resulting from environmental factors. Such displacement created a toxic geography "whereby life is systematically destroyed or compromised," transforming genocide from a behavioral act to a geographic and climatic one.[7]

However, this "exchange" did not stop there. As Black populations were stolen off African coasts, enslaved, and shipped across the Atlantic, the European colonial plantation became the model for agriculture, combining exotic, imported labor with exotic, imported flora and fauna. This disrupted natural, ecological rhythms, destroying soil quality and creating a more brittle, unstable ecology.[8] Outside of the spectacular brutality necessary to maintain such a slave system, the plantation also functioned as its own toxic geography such that antiblackness became the "total climate."[9] Outside of the laborious heat and exposure to new diseases Black slaves were forced to encounter, sewage and spoilage often contaminated food and water, and living spaces were often prone to decay, instilling disease and debility throughout all who were forced to live in those spaces.[10] Such devastation not only killed millions of Black and Native people through environmental violence but also made possible the environment and lives of Europeans into today: "By itself, Europe's biodiversity was probably insufficient to sustain its subsequent population growth. Without the American crops, Europe might not have been able to carry such heavy populations as she later did."[11]

If the Eurocene is, as Grove remarks, the order which links "climate change, species loss, slavery, the elimination of native peoples, and the globalization of extractive capitalism," then it is already clear at this point that the Anthropocene is nothing but the Eurocene. The Eurocene infects the logic of the Anthropocene to its core such that all of Europe is a settler colony and every European a settler-master whose lives depended and depend on that continued violence. As Indigenous Hawaiian scholar Haunani-Kay Trask reminds us, "civil society is itself a creation of settler colonies."[12] In articulating this, Trask illuminates an essential feature of the Anthropocene qua Eurocene: for those whose racialized body is synonymous with Humanity, life itself is synonymous with death for those who are positioned as the antithesis to that Humanity (marked here with a capital-H to denote its ontological designation rather than how the term is colloquially used). In examining this "exchange" between the Old and New Worlds, it was not only that Europe introduce death as normative for Black and Native American populations, but it relied upon that very death in order to give life to itself either through the raw wealth extracted through slavery or the transportation of essential American crops to Europe in order to stave off starvation. In this way, the civil society constructed through such violence is itself a settler colony, no matter where it finds itself. The transformation of the world into the colony-plantation, and its ecological effects, is the beginning of the Eurocene as such.

The Industrial Revolution (1784)

The second possible date for the beginning of the Anthropocene is the Industrial Revolution, a starting point that is most popular with social scientists. The reasoning for such preference is clear. The Industrial Revolution began the burning of fossil fuels which have radically changed the entirety of Earth's landscapes and its geological processes.

In the seventeenth century, gold and silver mined from the Americas through Black and Indigenous slave labor fueled the global expansion of European markets, making global trade possible and enabling Europe to both industrialize and develop its growing financial sector. When Britain emancipated slaves in the British Caribbean in 1833, slave owners received a compensation for the loss of their slaves that enabled them to build the physical infrastructure of the Industrial Revolution throughout Britain.[13] Yet, the compensation to these slave owners was financed by Barings Bank, a bank that exactly three decades before had financed the Louisiana Purchase and used the resulting funds and status to invest heavily in the American slave trade and cotton production. Financing both of these would allow the bank to fund the completion of the Canadian-Pacific Railway that would establish Canada through its clearing of Indigenous peoples. Thus, in a perverse chain of events, Indigenous dispossession of land would revitalize the dying institution of slavery in the United States, which would, in turn, both line the pockets of British slave owners and fund the further clearing of Indigenous peoples in Canada.[14] This set of events allowed companies to invest in cotton, steel, iron, coal, and other key industries. And the factories such industries built would, in turn, be *modeled off of the plantation*. By the time slaves were emancipated in the United States, cotton was no longer the driving force of industrialization. As Kathryn Yusoff writes,

> Enslaved "free" African Americans predominately mined coal in the corporate use of black power ... The Alabama Iron Ore and Tennessee Coal and Iron companies were the largest convict labor companies and fed the coal mines of the U.S. Steel Corporation, which built the country.[15]

The environmental violence of this entire process is, quite literally, impossible to mention in full. The mining of gold and silver made death and debility every day for African and Indigenous slaves: they were held captive within the toxic geographies of the mines, and the environmental devastation collapsed Indigenous food economies and ruined ecosystems.[16] The spread of plantations throughout the United States and the clearing of Indigenous peoples from their lands following the Louisiana Purchase possesses innumerable examples ranging from the deliberate overhunting of Buffalo, which pushed Indians into starvation, to the slave trade reducing the population of Africa to half of what it would have been otherwise in 1850.[17] This is, of course, without even getting into the ways in which carbon dioxide has and will continue to destroy communities of color.

If the Industrial Revolution is the beginning of the Anthropocene, it is no less defined by the Eurocene because it is part of that very same ordering which requires slavery, genocide, and extractive capitalism in order to function. European industrialists would not have had access to the financial, material, or *biological* resources they needed if it were not for slavery and genocide. Likewise, neither Europe nor the Americas could have built their nations or empires without the devastation they wrought not only on the land but also on the bodies they sacrificed on their path toward industrialization. Without the violences characteristic of the Eurocene, the Industrial Revolution qua Anthropocene could not have come into being. Furthermore, the logic of empire-building, industrialization, and the commodification of the environment is forged in the blood of those bodies, and their ghosts continue to haunt such logics into the modern day. The only thing that can be industrialized in the Eurocene is the murderous project of the world itself, and that is precisely what the Industrial Revolution was.

The Great Acceleration (1945)

The final period for consideration is the Great Acceleration, which marks a "major expansion in human population, large changes in natural processes, and the development of novel materials from minerals to plastics to persistent organic pollutants and inorganic compounds."[18] Two events tend to define this period: a spike in global carbon emissions, as consumption increases globally, and the detonation of nuclear bombs, which release elemental compounds that are not naturally occurring. Both events have shaped the world in ways often unnoticed or unthought. Three quarters of all carbon emissions have occurred since 1945, and the body of every human now contains the nuclear byproduct strontium-90.

To begin with nuclearization, the uranium ore used in testing and building the American bombs used on Hiroshima and Nagasaki came from the Congo, as well as Indigenous territories in Northwest Canada and the Southwest United States. In the process of mining, Indigenous American and African communities were heavily exposed to radiation, subjecting them to massive increased risks to various cancers, infertility, or immune system disorders. Beyond the literal uranium ore, the Manhattan Project—the United States' name for the secret government project that developed the nuclear bombs used in World War II against Japan—not only relied upon the military occupation of Indigenous land for testing but also would not have been able to function without cheap Native labor. Postwar, as the United States engaged in an arms race with the Soviet Union, the United States relied more heavily upon uranium mining in the American southwest, primarily on Diné territories, and continued to test nuclear bombs on Indigenous land, infamously at Bikini Atoll on the Marshallese. In both places, Indigenous peoples would become "living laboratories" as the United States government knowingly exposed populations to radiation poisoning in order to study the effects, with one scientist describing them as a "cross section of happy, amenable savages."[19] In sum, without the production of toxic geographies in Black and Native communities, the United States could not have mined the uranium, become a nuclear power, or learned about the effects of radiation.

In contrast, the spike in carbon that defines the Great Acceleration relied more on deploying the technologies and paradigms developed throughout the planation and settler colony globally. By 1945, the West had cemented the model of the Human as ontologically synonymous with itself and its ways of life. Even as non-Western powers arose, they modeled themselves on the West. As Madina V. Tlostanova and Walter Mignolo point out, "it is clear that in the polycentric world order the colonial matrix of power is still at work. Only that now it also is at work outside its place of origin."[20] This drive toward Western living expressed itself particularly through industrialization because, as Eve Tuck and K. Wayne Yang remind us, the settler defines civilization as "production … in excess of the sustainable production already present in the Indigenous world."[21] Not only did the factory, itself based on the plantation, proliferate globally, but plantation ecology, developed under chattel slavery, became prominent globally. Furthermore, as oil was pursued globally, Indigenous peoples bore the brunt of its violence, with displacements and genocides of Indigenous people occurring throughout Canada, the United States, Ecuador, Peru, and Nigeria.[22] Today, Black and Native peoples continue to face the most extreme effects of climate change, even as they gained the least from these extractivist policies. Not only this, but the massive deforestation that has resulted from plantation ecology has decimated ecosystems, spurring extreme biodiversity loss and the disappearance of global carbon sinks, creating an unparalleled ecological crisis.[23]

Even here, in the latest possible marker for the Anthropocene, we see the ways the Eurocene inheres itself. It is not simply the West, but the world which owes its existence to slavery and genocide because such violences not only set the model of "the good life" spread the world over by Western superpowers but enabled those superpowers to exist in the first place. The very ordering of Europe now infects itself into the non-European world, ensuring its continual reproduction. As Tuck and Yang remind us, "settler colonialism fuels imperialism all around the globe ... Settler sovereignty over [the] earth, air, and water is what makes possible these imperialisms."[24] In this final stage, the Eurocene not only enables its possibility, but it spurs the desire for the Western model of living, ensuring that the move toward the Eurocene is not only driven by the political economy but by the libidinal economy as well.

The Antagonism of the Anthropocene

The Anthropocene proceeds through regimes of ecological violence against Black and Native American people. If that violence did not occur, there would be no Anthropocene. Such gratuitous violence, in turn, has created a political ontology in which Black and Native American people are non-Human. Political ontology names the "powers subjects have or lack, the constituent elements of subjects' structural position with which they are imbued or lack prior to the subjects' performance," and which, despite being non-metaphysical since it arises from politics, "functions as if it were a metaphysical property across the *longue durée* of the premodern, modern, and now postmodern era."[25] The ecological terror of the Anthropocene demonstrates how Black and Native American populations have become structurally consigned to the status of Black Slaves and Indian Savages, as the rest of the world obtains and struggles over its Humanity. As Dylan Rodriguez writes, who will be subject to the terrors of the plantation and the colony has changed over time, but "there's little mistaking the Black and Aboriginal common denominator in all of it."[26] The *longue durée* of such violence also displays its temporal stillness—from the Columbian Exchange to the Industrial Revolution to the Great Acceleration, the non-Humanity of Black and Native populations is sustained. One only needs to examine the ecological terror of events such as the Standing Rock protests or the continued poisoning of Flint, Michigan, alongside the continued police killings, imprisonment, and civilian murders of Black and Native peoples to see how such an ontological structure continues into the present. As such, an examination of the Anthropocene reveals a general antagonism between the Human qua Settler-Master and the Black and Red bodies who have been transformed into flesh and ectoplasm by slavery and genocide's regimes of terror, especially in their ecological registers. Furthermore, the necessity of such violence for the Anthropocene's existence and continued maintenance suggests that environmental struggles must ground themselves in abolition and settler decolonization, and that the struggle for abolition and settler decolonization is always already an environmental struggle. As Frank B. Wilderson III points out, "in this trio [of the Savage, Human, and Slave] we find the key to our world's creation as well as to its undoing."[27]

Likewise, since the Anthropocene arises from the creation and maintenance of the Human, it is clear that the global ordering signified by the Eurocene inheres itself in every single potential candidate and terminology for the beginning and meaning of the Anthropocene, no matter the internal debates within geology or the humanities. In this way, the fetishism for a "golden spike" in which the Anthropocene begins, or a perfect term to describe its processes, is pushed aside in order to recognize that "the marker is not the epoch."[28] Put another way, given the ways in which the gratuitous ecological violence necessary to the formation and maintenance of the Human persists without change throughout the entire "Age of Humans," a particular starting point for the Anthropocene is nil. This is so because if "origins configure and prefigure the possibility of narratives of the present" such that "nothing that can be found in the end is not already prefigured in the origin," then the Anthropocene itself was already prefigured in the formation of a global Anthropos that took European Man as model and ideal.[29] Thus, to debate the terminology of the Capitalocene versus the Plantationocene versus the Chthulucene versus anything else figures as little more than rhetorical posturing. Such a debate ignores that what each signify—the rise of world integrated capitalism, the global plantation system, or the messiness that pushes bodies into bodies—is simply not possible without the antiblackness of Black chattel slavery or the settler colonialism of Native American genocide. So, the Eurocene is not an attempt to propose an alternative term that should enter into this endless play, but rather functions as a critique of this very proliferation. It is not that the term "Anthropocene" is insufficient in its characterization or focus; rather, it is us who are insufficient in our analysis of the Human, too easily fooled by "the enacting of a uniquely secular liberal monohumanist conception of the human" that views capitalism, the plantation system, or the collision between bodies as anything more than the formation of the Human.[30]

Conclusion: The World Is Burning

It is difficult to conclude a chapter like this given both the scope of the issue across time and space and the indescribable direness of the situation. In lieu of such a cataclysm, one is often compelled to put forth some legible solution as an attempt to ward off feelings of despair or pessimism or tragedy. However, such a recuperative effort is unsupported by the arguments I've put forward, and, furthermore, it would be disingenuous, betraying the point of this chapter that the world is burning. The reason for the world's burning is as tragic as it is perverse in that the flames are fanned precisely because the world's deepest pleasures, both directly and indirectly, come from abusing, beating, torturing, raping, slaving, and killing Black and Native people. It is so committed to these pleasures that it is likely that several of us will live to watch the world enter a state of ecological collapse whose omnicidal intensity can hardly be fathomed today.

Such a reality is heartbreaking, and we often ignore it in favor of liberal ideals of incremental reform or of working out our differences in some multicultural project. Yet, the sad truth is that there is simply not enough time for such things any longer, if there ever was. Such liberal processes may, at best, make us more comfortable as we prepare our graves, but they do nothing about our inevitable deaths.

If there is any hope left—and uprisings from Haiti to Chiapas, among others, suggest there might be—it is in the complete destruction of this world. In destroying it, it might be possible to craft new joys and pleasures and forms of living that are not so reliant on the transmutation of bodies into flesh and ectoplasm or on the deputization of some into slave masters and settler-conquerors. The success of such a project is not guaranteed, but it is all we have, and so it is what we must do.

Notes

1 Caleb A. Scharf, "The Crazy Scale of Human Carbon Emission," *Scientific American*, 26 April 2017.
2 David Wallace-Wells, *The Uninhabitable Earth: Life After Warming* (New York: Tim Duggan Books, 2020), 52, 62, 110.
3 Simon L. Lewis and Mark A. Maslin, "Defining the Anthropocene," *Nature* 519 (2015): 171.
4 Jairus Victor Grove, *Savage Ecology: War and Geopolitics at the End of the World* (Durham: Duke University Press, 2019), 39.
5 Sylvia Wynter and Katherine McKittrick, "Unparalleled Catastrophe for Our Species? Or, to Give Humanness a Different Future: Conversations," in *Sylvia Wynter: On Being Human as Praxis*, ed. Katherine McKittrick (Durham: Duke University Press, 2014), 21.
6 See Churchill Ward, *A Little Matter of Genocide: Holocaust and Denial in the Americas 1492 to the Present* (San Francisco: City Lights Books, 1997); Sylvia Knight, "Did the European Conquest of the Americas Contribute to the Little Ice Age?" *Teaching Geography* 44 (2019): 68–71; and Lewis and Maslin.
7 Neil Nunn, "Toxic Encounters, Settler Logics of Elimination, and the Future of a Continent," *Antipode* 50, no. 5 (2018): 1331.
8 See Anna Tsing, *The Mushroom at the End of the World: On the Possibility of Life in Capitalist Ruins* (Princeton: Princeton University Press, 2015), 38–39.
9 Christina Sharpe, *In the Wake: On Blackness and Being* (Durham: Duke University Press, 2016), 21.

10 See Emily Waples, "Breathing Free: Environmental Violence and the Plantation Ecology in Hannah Crafts's *The Bondwoman's Narrative*," *Victorian Literature and Culture* 48, no. 1 (2020): 107.
11 Jason M. Moore, "The Modern World-System as Environmental History? Ecology and the Rise of Capitalism," *Theory and Society* 32, no. 3 (2003): 318.
12 Haunani-Kay Trask, *From a Native Daughter: Colonialism and Sovereignty in Hawai'i* (Honolulu: University of Hawai'i Press, 1999), 25.
13 Kathryn Yusoff, *A Billion Black Anthropocenes or None* (Minneapolis: University of Minnesota Press, 2018), 40–41.
14 Deborah Cowen, "Following the Infrastructures of Empire: Notes on Cities, Settler Colonialism, and Method," *Urban Geography* 41, no. 4 (2020): 470–471.
15 Yusoff, 43.
16 See Andrés Reséndez, *The Other Slavery: The Uncovered Story of Indian Enslavement in America* (Boston: Mariner Books, 2017), 107; and Daviken Studnicki-Gizbert and David Schecter, "The Environmental Dynamics of a Colonial Fuel-Rush: Silver Mining and Deforestation in New Spain, 1522 to 1810," *Environmental History* 15 (2010): 96.
17 See Tasha Hubbard, "Buffalo Genocide in Nineteenth-Century North America: 'Kill, Skin, and Sell,'" in *Colonial Genocide in Indigenous North America*, ed. Andrew Woolford, Jeff Benvenuto, and Alexander Laban Hinton (Durham: Duke University Press, 2014), 293; and Patrick Manning, *Slavery and African Life* (Cambridge: Cambridge University Press, 1990), 171.
18 Lewis and Maslin, 176.
19 Rafael Moure-Eraso, "Observational Studies as Human Experimentation: The Uranium Mining Experience in the Navajo Nation (1947–66)," *New Solutions* 9, no. 2 (1999): 164; Yusoff, 46. Here, I am indebted to Hortense Spillers's theorization of Black bodies as "living laboratories." For more on this concept, see Hortense J. Spillers, *Black, White, and In Color* (Chicago: Chicago University Press, 2003).
20 Madina Tlostanova and Walter Mignolo, "Global Coloniality and the Decolonial Option," *Kult* 6 (2009): 138.
21 Eve Tuck and K. Wayne Yang, "Decolonization Is Not a Metaphor," *Decolonization: Indigeneity, Education & Society* 1, no. 1 (2012): 6.
22 See J.R. McNeill and Peter Engelke, *The Great Acceleration: An Environmental History of the Anthropocene Since 1945* (Cambridge: Harvard University Press, 2014), 14–19.
23 See Florence Pendrill, et al., "Agricultural and Forestry Trade Drives Large Share of Tropical Deforestation Emissions," *Global Environmental Change* 56 (2019): 1–10.
24 Tuck and Yang, 31.
25 Frank B. Wilderson III, *Red, White, and Black: Cinema and the Structure of U.S. Antagonisms* (Durham: Duke University Press, 2010), 8; Jared Sexton, "People-of-Color-Blindness: Notes on the Afterlife of Slavery," *Social Text* 28, no. 2 (2010): 37.
26 Dylan Rodriguez, "Insult/Internal Debate/Echo," *Propter Nos* 3 (2019): 129.
27 Wilderson, 24.
28 Clive Hamilton, "Getting the Anthropocene So Wrong," *The Anthropocene Review* 2, no. 2 (2015): 105.
29 Yusoff, 25.
30 Wynter and McKittrick, 21.

References

Cowen, Deborah. "Following the Infrastructures of Empire: Notes on Cities, Settler Colonialism, and Method." *Urban Geography* 41, no. 4 (2020): 469–486.

David, Wallace-Wells. *The Uninhabitable Earth: Life After Warming*. New York: Tim Duggan Books, 2020.

Grove, Jairus Victor. *Savage Ecology: War and Geopolitics at the End of the World*. Durham: Duke University Press, 2019.

Hamilton, Clive. "Getting the Anthropocene So Wrong." *The Anthropocene Review* 2, no. 2 (2015): 102–107.

Hubbard, Tasha. "Buffalo Genocide in Nineteenth-Century North America: 'Kill, Skin, and Sell.'" In *Colonial Genocide in Indigenous North America*. Edited by Andrew Woolford, Jeff Benvenuto, and Alexander Laban Hinton. Durham: Duke University Press, 2014. 292–305.

Knight, Sylvia. "Did the European Conquest of the Americas Contribute to the Little Ice Age?" *Teaching Geography* 44 (2019): 68–71.

Lewis, Simon L., and Mark A. Maslin. "Defining the Anthropocene." *Nature* 519 (2015): 171–180.

Manning, Patrick. *Slavery and African Life*. Cambridge: Cambridge University Press, 1990.

McNeill, J.R., and Peter Engelke. *The Great Acceleration: An Environmental History of the Anthropocene Since 1945*. Cambridge: Harvard University Press, 2014.

Moore, Jason W. "The Modern World-System as Environmental History? Ecology and the Rise of Capitalism." *Theory and Society* 32, no. 3 (2003): 307–377.

Moure-Eraso, Rafael. "Observational Studies as Human Experimentation: The Uranium Mining Experience in the Navajo Nation (1947–66)." *New Solutions* 9, no. 2 (1999): 163–178.

Nunn, Neil. "Toxic Encounters, Settler Logics of Elimination, and the Future of a Continent." *Antipode* 50, no. 5 (2018): 1330–1348.

Pendrill, Florence, U. Martin Persson, Javier Godar, Thomas Kastner, Daniel Moran, Sarah Schmidt, and Richard Wood. "Agricultural and Forestry Trade Drives Large Share of Tropical Deforestation Emissions." *Global Environmental Change* 56 (2019): 1–10.

Reséndez, Andrés. *The Other Slavery: The Uncovered Story of Indian Enslavement in America*. Boston: Mariner Books, 2017.

Rodriguez, Dylan. "Insult/Internal Debate/Echo." *Propter Nos* 3 (2019): 125–131.

Sexton, Jared. "People-of-Color-Blindness: Notes on the Afterlife of Slavery." *Social Text* 28, no. 2 (2010): 31–56.

Sharpe, Christina. *In the Wake: On Blackness and Being*. Durham: Duke University Press, 2016.

Studnicki-Gizbert, Daviken, and David Schecter. "The Environmental Dynamics of a Colonial Fuel-Rush: Silver Mining and Deforestation in New Spain, 1522 to 1810." *Environmental History* 15 (2010): 94–119.

Tlostanova, Madina, and Walter Mignolo. "Global Coloniality and the Decolonial Option." *Kult* 6 (2009): 130–147.

Trask, Haunani-Kay. *From a Native Daughter: Colonialism and Sovereignty in Hawai'i*. Honolulu: University of Hawai'i Press, 1999.

Tsing, Anna. *The Mushroom at the End of the World: On the Possibility of Life in Capitalist Ruins*. Princeton: Princeton University Press, 2015.

Tuck, Eve, and K. Wayne Yang. "Decolonization Is Not a Metaphor." *Decolonization: Indigeneity, Education & Society* 1, no. 1 (2012): 1–40.

Wallace-Wells, David. *The Uninhabitable Earth: Life After Warming*. New York: Tim Duggan Books, 2020.
Waples, Emily. "Breathing Free: Environmental Violence and the Plantation Ecology in Hannah Crafts's *The Bondwoman's Narrative*." *Victorian Literature and Culture* 48, no. 1 (2020): 91–126.
Ward, Churchill. *A Little Matter of Genocide: Holocaust and Denial in the Americas 1492 to the Present*. San Francisco: City Lights Books, 1997.
Wilderson III, Frank B. *Red, White, and Black: Cinema and the Structure of U.S. Antagonisms*. Durham: Duke University Press, 2010.
Wynter, Sylvia, and Katherine McKittrick. "Unparalleled Catastrophe for Our Species? Or, to Give Humanness a Different Future: Conversations." In *Sylvia Wynter: On Being Human as Praxis*. Edited by Katherine McKittrick. Durham: Duke University Press, 2014.
Yusoff, Kathryn. *A Billion Black Anthropocenes or None*. Minneapolis: University of Minnesota Press, 2018.

6
TRANS*PLANTATIONOCENE

Nicholas Tyler Reich

Anthropocene can't fully describe the way of reading this chapter argues. Below, I emphasize what I take to be a critical gap in scholarship attending to the unevenly distributed ecocides of this newly named epoch, scholarship that emphasizes difference but nonetheless stops short of accounting for gender and sexuality as a central component of racialized environmental (non)belonging in the afterlives of a plantation economy. I end with a brief look at the film *Tangerine* (2015) as a useful example for how this way of reading can allow Anthropocene scholars to grapple with gender, sexuality, and racialized embodiment, which, given the manifold problems the Anthropocene thesis presents, should be a significant point of interest.[1]

The term *Anthropocene* fails to adequately stretch across lines of difference. This "Age of Man," in His mastery over Earth, indicates a universalizing semantic dodge. Nicholas Mirzoeff writes, "Given that the Anthropos in *Anthropocene* turns out to be our old friend the (imperialist) white male, my mantra has become, it's not the Anthropocene, it's the white supremacy scene."[2] Reading against the Anthropocene means paying attention to coterminous historical relations between the human-precipitated ecological disaster symptoms readers might already associate with that name (like climate change) and the ransacking of lands, Earth resources, and organisms (human and more-than-human) enacted by Euro-American colonizers over the last several centuries. Blanketing accountability across all *humans* would seem "to forget all the work that has been done to establish how and why so many people have been designated as *nonhuman* and bought and sold as material objects."[3] Anthropocene is a useful starting point, then, so long as that titular "Man" is always traced to his racialized imperial roots.

Other revisionary names prove more effective for answering Mirzoeff's pivotal question: "What does it mean to say #BlackLivesMatter in the context of

DOI: 10.4324/9781003095347-8

the Anthropocene?" Capitalocene is useful, since accumulation is a raced framework: "If universal history is the history of how capitalism has produced globalization, that history in turn is also the history of enslavement."[4] Plantationocene, more pointedly, seeks to describe the reiterative violences of the colonial plantation economy as both an agricultural terror on nonhuman ecosystems across colonized spaces, as well as the supposed *raison d'être* for the captivity, enslavement, and decimation *en masse* of Black, Indigenous, and people of color's lives for imperial gain, engendering a centuries-long emergency.[5] Kathryn Yusoff's Black Anthropocene likewise addresses what she calls "the racial blindness of the Anthropocene" by redressing each of the Anthropocene's hypothesized Golden Spikes, showing how these narratives (and they *are* narratives) not only (re)produce but are also built upon blackening. She writes, "The superimposition of colonialism was a shearing of subjects from geography and the reinstantiation of these subjects into a category of geology that recorded them as property." This "fungibility of Blackness and geologic resources," and its insidious legacies across the Black Diasporas, helps me articulate this chapter's inflected version of Mirzoeff's question: What does it mean to say that Black (trans) Lives (have always) Matter(ed) in the Plantationocene?[6]

Trans★Plantationocene fills in a pivotal gap in these revisions, reading for strategies of particularly gender and sexual resistance against the powers that chronically (re)produce Anthropocenic symptoms. What I appreciate most about counter-strategies of reading is the resounding idea that "it matters which stories tell stories, which concepts think concepts."[7] Trans★Plantationocene is an act of synthesis, because it must be to account for the multidirectional currents displacing Black trans lives in the diasporas of the Plantationocene and, more importantly, to notice how those lives resist fungibility.

Works in the Name

Trans names a collection of identities and processes, transgender being the most politically mobile in this time of #Black(Trans)LivesMatter. C. Riley Snorton writes, "There is no absolute distinction between black lives' mattering and trans lives' mattering within the rubrics of racialized gender."[8] *Trans★* signifies a broader assemblage of concepts, all with the morpheme trans as *across, through, between*, or *changing* (like *trans*ition, *trans*form, *trans*mogrify, *trans*atlantic, *trans*-temporal, and so on). This is not a standard use of this term but one I am deploying to read movement on several scales. Used in proximity, trans★ encompasses trans in ways that ask after how trans relates to other kinds of across- or between-ness. *Transplant*, used in Anthropocene discourse, might refer to enforced movements, like those of uprooted plants, animals, and people across the Middle Passage.[9] The transplanting of human and nonhuman bodies across ecosystems and organic material across space (into and out of the plantation) cohered a stratigraphy of race, a Chain of Being. In this way, *Trans★Plantation* can refer to those movements across space as well as, thinking in afterlives, movements across time—how spatial movements produce temporal rippling that carries violence on in new forms.[10] And so, if Plantationocene names a history of vexed human–environmental relations that attends more closely (than Anthropocene or Capitalocene) to the inextricable forces of colonialism and slavery foundational to that vexation, and if the Transplantation-ocene articulates diasporic ecological displacements resulting from that Plantationocenic vexation, then *Trans*Plantationocene* names those displacements as seated in sex and gender, as well as resistance strategies thereof. This is a way of considering racialized gender, trans*ness, and environment together through emergency time.

Fungible Fugitivity

What does "racialized gender" mean in the context of the Plantationocene? In her landmark essay "Mama's Baby, Papa's Maybe: An American Grammar Book," Hortense Spillers argues that, to understand how gender functions within our racialized present, one must look to the *un*gendering function of the Middle Passage. Spillers notices that in the "willful and violent … severing of the captive body from its motive will … we lose at least *gender* difference *in the outcome*, and the female body and the male body become a territory of cultural and political maneuver." This ungendering produced what she calls "the unmade," bodies-as-material (or "flesh") stripped of its gendered and human symbolics and then rewritten under different strictures.[11] After that transplantation to the New World(s), these bodies were *dis*gendered and (mal)humanized within a new system, according to mutable logics that "produce and maintain an androcentric European ethnoclass of Man as the pinnacle,"[12] figuring blackness as an "enforced state of breach."[13] Fungibility within plantation economies not only dehumanized, as it (re)appropriated Black(ened) bodies as either material or subhuman in a European stratigraphy of human-ness, alongside materials like coal and other chattel bodies like cattle, but it also disgendered, as *when* Black bodies were gendered in the plantation's radius they served to graph gender as a scale with white woman falling somewhere apart from Black woman, and so forth. These ongoing processes are constitutive of the Plantationocene, as Black bodies and their trans/gender trouble become a tool for distinguishing the slipperiness between categories of human, nonhuman animals, inorganic material, and nature. Again, the Anthropocene's (hu)Man is too convenient, given these processes that have not finished.

Trans*Plantationocenic reading not only names these displacements but also looks for examples of resistance to this racializing fleshy fungibility, particularly in relation to environment and both enforced and voluntary movements across land. Spillers ends "Mama's Baby" with an "*insurgent*" strategy for Black(ened) female social subjects "*claiming* [their] monstrosity" in an ideological space apart from white woman-ness or white feminist politics, leaning into racialized gender not as nourishing homespace but rather an opportunity toward fugitivity.[14] This is not unlike examples of racialized bodies escaped from the plantation leaning into their gender (and therefore racial) fungibility. Snorton explains:

> Gender indefiniteness would become a critical modality of political and cultural maneuvering within figurations of blackness, illustrated, for example, by the frequency with which narratives of fugitivity included cross-gendered modes of escape ... In this regard, captive flesh figures a critical genealogy for modern transness, as chattel persons gave rise to an understanding of gender as mutable and as an amenable form of being ... To suppose that one can identify fugitive moments in the hollow of fungibility's embrace is to focus on modes of escape, of wander, of flight that exist within violent conditions of exchange.[15]

In the context of global emergency, it is important to recognize that these antebellum records of "fungible fugitivity," documenting belowground instances of trans / gender resistance, represent vexed movements across geography as much as gender.[16] They are *already* Trans*Plantationocenic archives of panicked "human" relations to land, a diasporic cartography of racialized gender. Fungible fugitivity entails trans-spatial movements (like from the agrarian South to the industrial north), as well as recastings of self within certain spaces (like maneuvering gender as a mode of escape from countrysides to cityscapes and then again and always in those cities). This is partly what leads Snorton to claim, "To feel black in the diaspora, then, might be a trans experience."[17]

Understanding this kind of resistance as durational across the span of the Plantationocene is central to Trans*Plantationocenic reading. Racialized gender as a legacy of chattel fungibility, a product of both white power and white terror (which are the same), marks what Christina Sharpe calls "a past that is not past."[18] This is the *longue durée* of chattel slavery, which is also the *longue durée* of the so-called Anthropocene, an emergency that is "slow" not only in duration but also in the sense that it has taken a very long time for (white) scholars to understand the imbricated surveillance technologies of race, gender, and nature grafted by the colonizers. Ceaseless and unfettered contemporary media coverage of Black and trans death in the United States is a "dysgraphia of disaster" that has unfolded into "antiblackness as total climate," which is not unrelated to *climate change*, since environmental injustice registers differently in racialized bodies.[19] As much as diaspora charts the movement of bodies across the Earth, it also records "the wake of the unfinished project of emancipation."[20] In other words, the Plantationocene did not end with the Emancipation Proclamation in 1863, not nearly, so much as its theater covered new ground in the afterlives of that economy. This is not a metaphor but a monitoring of the trans-temporal effects of that original plantation system as it lives on, how long and intensely it lives on. Spillers exposes the "the semantic and iconic folds buried deep in the collective past, that come to surround and signify the captive person."[21] The modern white man progresses through time into new possibilities, while the Black woman remains in a chronotope of global emergency, an image and plot of Black death tied closely to the preventable abundance of more-than-human deaths that characterize this epoch, as Her apocalypse began many centuries ago. When Donna Haraway writes that "ongoingness is at stake" in this doom, one must wonder which type of ongoingness.[22] Will it be the ongoingness of all human life, or perhaps the afterlives of slavery that have prevented certain bodies from moving onward in time? Gender and sexual resistance may help shape the answer.

Tangerine Trans*Plantationocene

To unpack and synthesize some of these slippery ideas, I want to briefly practice what Trans★Plantationocenic reading can look like with a fairly recent film. *Tangerine* made a stir when first released for a number of reasons: it was shot entirely on iPhone cameras; it focuses on Black trans sex workers with a closeness rarely seen at major film festivals (like Sundance, where it premiered); and its critical success led to the first ever Academy Awards campaign for openly trans actors (though neither lead was nominated in the end). A rough-and-tumble summary of the plot might go something like this: Sin-Dee Rella (played by Kitana Kiki Rodriguez), fresh from a jail sentence for drug possession charges, reunites with her best friend, Alexandra (played by Mya Taylor). Without meaning to, Alexandra divulges to Sin-Dee that, while she was in jail, Sin-Dee's pimp/boyfriend has been cheating on her with an unknown cis-woman—a "real fish"—after which Sin-Dee dedicates her day to tracking down this paramour, bent on revenge. The film follows these two on Sin-Dee's plight around the neighborhoods between West and East Hollywood, orbiting the corner of Santa Monica and Highland, as Sin-Dee interrogates a motley collection of personalities for information. This film moves at hyper-speed between episodes increasingly raucous until the final, shattering confrontation between Sin-Dee and her boyfriend, when Alexandra is revealed to have had sex with him, as well.[23] While this description may not itself communicate how this film tells a deeply environmental story, Trans★Plantationocenic readings matter even and perhaps especially when a text does not *seem* thematically "environmental." Sin-Dee and Alexandra's nearly ceaseless pavement-stomping is a diasporic tell—visualized in wild cross-cuts, breakneck tracking shots, and frenetic shaky-cam work—a flurry of fugitive movement that helps show how this cityscape on the West Coast might be decolonized from within, like a method of "making home in no home."[24]

Cities often figure (perhaps surprisingly) in Anthropocene and climate change studies for the possibilities they hold for sustaining large populations with a relatively small environmental footprint, compared to what would be rural dispersion where energy and resources need to be moved across large spaces. Too, beginning in the late nineteenth century and then formalized in the twentieth century, urban-ness became a central characteristic, to the point of damaging stereotypes, of both queer/trans and Black life in the United States. Considering Black trans representation in the contemporary American filmic imaginary, there are almost no existing examples outside of some cityscape (or incarceration). In fact, it is urban environs which constitute the loci of Black trans death in this new century. This is part of the vexation of the Plantationocene and the Great Migration. As Bruno Latour writes: "Migrations, explosions of inequality, and New Climatic Regime: *these are one and the same threat*."[25] This brings up a pivotal question I can ask of a film like *Tangerine*. If in the age of human-induced climate change, people will be, as Latour puts it, "fighting to land on Earth," or struggling to carve out homes and refuge among the places and spaces of the planet, then what strategies can Black trans people use to exact this "landing" in spaces where they are both consigned and conflicted?[26] And how can film imagine those futures?

To distill my Trans*Plantationocenic reading, I'm going to focus on a couple of back-to-back sequences that come at this question from different angles. About halfway through the film, Sin-Dee's quest is interrupted by several diversions. In one such sequence, Razmik, cab driver and friend/customer of the leads, is looking to solicit. He finds an unfamiliar woman who calls herself Selena. Razmik is intrigued by Selena's newness to the area and eager to learn more about her life and body. "Does it really matter where I'm from?" she asks Razmik, annoyed by his invasive personal questions, hers a question that itself speaks to (non)belonging. "The block is hot over here," Selena tells him, asking that he drive to a more discreet location. In other words, the block is being surveilled by the police and they must find less scrutinized space. Selena's awareness of this surveillance is a decolonizing tool. Yet, there is more to this block than even she understands, as Razmik quickly reveals. He requests that Selena let him go down on her. "Is it tucked?" he asks in surprise at seeing her genitals, "What the fuck is that?" The shot is positioned over Razmik's shoulder as he scrutinizes Selena. "It's a pussy," she retorts. It's as he feared; her newness to the block means she doesn't understand. "That's not for pussies," he says of the block. "You shouldn't be there." And so, the encounter ends in a lesson on spatial sovereignty. Selena is seemingly unaware that the block she's trying to work is trans place, a space reappropriated by trans people for trans* work.

The Plantationocene is a story of (non)belonging and surveillance, environmental manipulation and control. In this way, as Yusoff points out, "there is a parallel between the languages of the dispossession of subjects and land within the context of the inhuman."[27] Los Angeles is a fitting example of how these dual systems work together. Though we don't see in this film the kinds of disaster spectacles that continually make the news, L.A. is still a disaster zone. This city is what L.A. scholar Mike Davis calls the "Apocalypse Theme Park," where "historic wildfire corridors have been turned into view-lot suburbs, wetland liquefaction zones into marinas, and floodplains into industrial districts and housing tracts."[28] This is the same expanse of Southern California that has "reaped flood, fire, and earthquake tragedies that were as avoidable, as unnatural, as the beating of Rodney King and the ensuing explosion in the streets."[29] And it is over this connection exactly, between preventable ecological and racialized emergencies, that *Tangerine*'s environmental ethic pivots. This film foregrounds questions of the racialized, gendered human rather than "nature," but the forces animating those human inequities are also the forces of ecological catastrophe characteristic of an apocalyptic L.A., an egotistical mismanagement of the city's investments by that same Anthropocenic Man.[30] The block is hot in *Tangerine* because Black trans sex workers are a threat to property values. Ironically, the block is also literally hot here in the December swelter, a constant reminder of rising global temperatures. Keeping the block hot is the only way to maintain control over the unruly decolonizers who might prevent gentrification, and so the neighborhood remains in stasis. When considering the naïve land ethics and racial capitalism of L.A. within the purview of global emergency, damage at the scale of certain bodies in certain spaces and how those bodies and spaces are each relegated as the objects of neoliberal capitalist surveillance graphs how the Plantationocene has and will unfold inequitably, as it was meant to. The city was never going to be a refuge for the disfavored, even if it was their only choice.

But *Tangerine*, for its part, imagines how some of the trans★ work enacted by trans sex workers on screen challenges this fickle stasis. They perform fugitive strategies that undermine ongoing "captivities of the Diaspora."[31] There is the cultivation of this space into place, for instance, where belonging can develop even as it is threatened by surveillance and violence. And, relatedly, this place allows for the expression of trans★ness and different ways of living inside the city so bent on surveillance and willful ignorance. Importantly, these strategies demand queer and trans (or normative-resistant) relations to the land, a kind of belonging situated within movement. L.H. Stallings writes that "sexually marginalized persons (the poor, sex workers, and queers) become a threat to imperialist and capitalist arrangements of land" precisely because "sexual resistance to sexual terror and violence requires this mobility and a different relationship to the land, one less based on homespace and possession."[32] The trans★ work in *Tangerine* is transgender, trans-temporal, and transient, a kind of anti-gentrification.

Right before Razmik and Selena's misunderstanding, Alexandra is involved in her own botched solicitation. Her john asks for a cost-effective reprieve from his marital stagnation, arguing with Alexandra over the price of a bareback blowjob. "I can suck your dick with a condom for $80," she settles impatiently. But, alas, the john only has $40. "I just gotta get off … come on, it's Christmas," he urges, as if this consumer's holiday carries enough magic to forego her boundaries and help him escape his presumably straight Anglo-Christian marriage. At last, Alexandra agrees to hold his balls while he masturbates. Like so many of the sequences in *Tangerine*, this bit initially plays as comedy before grounding out into a gritty melancholy. Alexandra pokes fun at his small penis, his desperation, and his inability to cum quickly. Having had enough of her commentary, the john eventually ends the exchange, grabbing back his money from the dashboard. Alexandra demands money for services rendered, but the john refuses, because: "I didn't cum … you didn't get paid," revealing a racialized capitalist logic of pleasure for the white man as the only stricture that matters. To even the argument, Alexandra takes his car keys as collateral until he hands over the cash. A fight ensues. The john wrestles the keys from her hands. And it is at this point that Alexandra makes a fascinating choice. She says, "You forget I got a dick, too," and then presumably wrestles and fights with this man in the alleyway, as the shot cuts away. What we don't see on screen (like those "natural" catastrophes kept far from view) matters as much as what we do.

At several points in this film, Alexandra and Sin-Dee, as well as their surrounding community, dialogue about the hierarchy of *fish*. Fishiness—woman-ness or "the real thing," as they put it—is an important aspect (economically, culturally, emotionally, affectively) of appearing femme for many of the trans characters in this film. Sex workers on the block taunt one another for their respective fishiness or lack thereof. For Alexandra to *lean out of* her fishiness, then, is a risky move, flirting with the nadir of her experience as a Black trans sex worker. Calling attention to her penis reminds this john that her body retains that normative sign of maleness and its deeply associated violent potential, the very body he fetishizes, while risking confirming the fungibility of racialized gender (that is, transness) and its inscrutability under the colonial gaze. Yet, consider how this unruly choice resonates across time with the instances of fungible fugitivity Snorton reads in escape narratives from the nineteenth century. Imagine how Alexandra formulates "an escape route" by leaning into fungibility.[33] After the cut, Alexandra and her embattled john run into police officers who are monitoring the block. The officers' use of deadnaming and misgendering verifies that they imagine Alexandra as gender fungible, at best, and their needlessly testing her for drug use verifies that they view her as abject and untrustworthy. These are the watchers who intimidate Alexandra with legal recourse and decide to send her away without her earned money. Who else can Alexandra call on for help?[34] Still, she has accomplished a kind of fungible fugitivity, showcasing her "capability to adapt to a different kind of environment, one in which she might flourish and find fulfillment."[35] Both the risk and the reward navigate the breach of environmental (non)belonging.

At the film's end, Alexandra again leans out of her fishiness to build fugitive community. Sin-Dee is assaulted by a group of white men driving by who fling a cup of their piss into her face. She is distraught from the violence but also because she can't afford to replace her wig, a vital part of her self-image. Watching Sin-Dee struggle to recover in the absence of her hair, Alexandra chooses to remove her own hair and transfer some of that fishiness to her friend. She sponsors community fugitivity with a lean toward fungibility, repurposing colonial structures of gender against themselves. These acts of fungible fugitivity are "queer modes of protest," belowground gender and sexual decolonizing enterprises which unsettle Plantationocenic land politics from within. This is how "an intimate or spiritual relationship with land beyond ownership matters for sexual [and gender] resistance."[36] Trans*ing the Plantationocene is, at least in this way, acting and thinking in registers outside the normative, watching for how the underground nonetheless shifts the aboveground—since it is ground, after all, figurative and literal, that is so crucial. Liberation comes with transitivity without excluding *staying*. These two scenes showcase a balancing act, keeping the block through trans★ potential.

Theories and histories of Black Diaspora, queerness, and trans★ness have *already* been doing the work of understanding Anthropocenic emergency, though maybe not by that name. Now is the time to listen to them harmonize. My reading of *Tangerine* is a necessarily incomplete taste for how Trans★Plantationocenic readings can go. The key is understanding that racialized gender, cis-hetero-normativity, anti-sex moralizing, racialized capitalism, environmental surveillance, and environmental racism/fascism are not minor notes in the Anthropocenic fugue, nor reactions to that fugue-state. They helped build these conditions. Reading against the universalizing Anthropocene narrative will require elevating these concerns up to the level of ecological fallout, precisely because they are part of that ecological fallout and parcel to its genesis.

Notes

1 *Tangerine*, dir. Sean Baker (Los Angeles: Magnolia Pictures, 2015).
2 Nicholas Mirzoeff, "It's Not the Anthropocene, It's the White Supremacy Scene; or, The Geological Color Line," in *After Extinction*, ed. Richard Grusin (Minneapolis: University of Minnesota Press, 2018), 123.
3 Ibid., 125, my emphasis.
4 Ibid., 123, 127.
5 Donna J. Haraway, *Staying with the Trouble: Making Kin in the Chthulucene* (Durham: Duke University Press, 2016), 206.
6 Kathryn Yusoff, *A Billion Black Anthropocenes or None* (Minneapolis: University of Minnesota Press, 2018), xiii, 30, 32.
7 Haraway, 101.
8 C. Riley Snorton, *Black on Both Sides: A Racial History of Trans Identity* (Minneapolis: University of Minnesota Press, 2017), x.
9 Haraway, 206.
10 For a related but different neologism "trans★plant," see: Dylan McCarthy Blackston, "Monkey Business: Trans★, Animacy, and the Boundaries of Kind," *Angelaki: Journal of the Theoretical Humanities* 22, no. 2 (2017): 119–133. Blackston tracks disruptions of species being and embodiment in movements across media and categoricals that resonate immediately with my treatment of Black trans★ness across space and human-ness.
11 Hortense J. Spillers, "Mama's Baby, Papa's Maybe: An American Grammar Book," *Diacritics* 17, no. 2 (1987): 67, 72.
12 Snorton, 6.
13 Spillers, 74.
14 Ibid., 80.
15 Snorton, 56–57.
16 Ibid., 69.
17 Ibid., 8.
18 Christina Sharpe, *In the Wake: On Blackness and Being* (Durham: Duke, 2016), 13.

19 Ibid., 21.
20 Ibid., 5.
21 Spillers, 69.
22 Haraway, 101.
23 In an aptly titled interview, Sean Baker (director) had this to say about his film's authenticity to the lives of Black trans sex workers in Hollywood:

> We didn't fabricate anything … every vignette and subplot in the movie—from the way the cops interfere with the girls to the hate crime at the end—is based on stories that we heard from Mya and the other girls.

Yet, Baker and Chris Bergoch (both white cis-men) are the only writers credited. This is a good example of how fictive ethnography can operate within the logics of racialized capitalism, when Baker reaps the critical and professional reward of a screenplay that is really the self-authored stories of women who were themselves sex workers. See Jeremy Kinser, "*Tangerine* Director Sean Baker May Be a Straight White Man, but He's Made a Terrific Movie about Transgender Women of Color," *Queerty*, 9 July 2015.
24 Yusoff, 65.
25 Bruno Latour, *Down to Earth: Politics in the New Climatic Regime* (Cambridge: Polity, 2018), 9.
26 Ibid., 89.
27 Yusoff, 67.
28 Mike Davis, *Ecology of Fear: Los Angeles and the Imagination of Disaster* (New York: Metropolitan Books, 1998), 6, 9. Though Davis is writing just before "Anthropocene" entered the scholarly lexicon, his book nonetheless captures the environmental hubris of L.A., where "monolithic public works have been substituted for regional planning and a responsible land ethic" (9). He shows how the predictable catastrophes resulting from the regrettable mixing of that hubris with a land already inclined to major environmental events will only exacerbate tragedy in the lives of the poor and disfavored through the often unpredictable symptoms of climate change: "What is most distinctive about Los Angeles is not simply its conjugation of earthquakes, wildfires, and floods, but its uniquely explosive mixture of natural hazards and socials contradictions" (54).
29 Ibid., 9.
30 For the preeminent treatment of the overrepresentation of Anthropocene Man, see Sylvia Wynter, "Unsettling the Coloniality of Being/Power/Truth/Freedom: Towards the Human, After Man, Its Overrepresentation—An Argument," *CR: The New Centennial Review* 3, no. 3 (2003): 257–337.
31 Spillers, 73.
32 L.H. Stallings, *A Dirty South Manifesto: Sexual Resistance and Imagination in the New South* (Oakland: University of California Press, 2020), 97, 94.
33 LaVelle Ridley, "Imagining Otherly: Performing Possible Black Trans Futures in *Tangerine*," *TSQ: Transgender Studies Quarterly* 6, no. 4 (2019): 485.
34 For a history of L.A.P.D. anti-Black-trans-sex-worker discrimination and Rule No. 9, see Treva Ellison, "The Labor of Werqing It: The Performance and Protest Strategies of Sir Lady Java," in *Trap Door: Trans Cultural Production and the Politics of Visibility*, ed. Tourmaline, Eric A. Stanley, and Johanna Burton (Cambridge: MIT Press, 2017). For a look at the ongoing criminalization of Black trans lives in the crucible of

racialized capitalism and sex work, see Kaniya Walker, "To Protect Black Trans Lives, Decriminalize Sex Work," *ACLU*, 20 November 2020.
35 Ridley, 487.
36 Stallings, 62, 37.

References

Baker, Sean, dir. *Tangerine*. Los Angeles: Magnolia Pictures, 2015.

Blackston, Dylan McCarthy. "Monkey Business: Trans*, Animacy, and the Boundaries of Kind." *Angelaki: Journal of the Theoretical Humanities* 22, no. 2 (2017): 119–133.

Davis, Mike. *Ecology of Fear: Los Angeles and the Imagination of Disaster*. New York: Metropolitan Books, 1998.

Ellison, Treva. "The Labor of Werqing It: The Performance and Protest Strategies of Sir Lady Java." In *Trap Door: Trans Cultural Production and the Politics of Visibility*. Edited by Tourmaline, Eric A. Stanley, and Johanna Burton. Cambridge: MIT Press, 2017. 1–22.

Haraway, Donna J. *Staying with the Trouble: Making Kin in the Chthulucene*. Durham: Duke University Press, 2016.

Kinser, Jeremy. "*Tangerine* Director Sean Baker May Be a Straight White Man, but He's Made a Terrific Movie about Transgender Women of Color." *Queerty*. 9 July 2015.

Latour, Bruno. *Down to Earth: Politics in the New Climatic Regime*. Cambridge: Polity, 2018.

Mirzoeff, Nicholas. "It's Not the Anthropocene, It's the White Supremacy Scene; or, The Geological Color Line." In *After Extinction*. Edited by Richard Grusin. Minneapolis: University of Minnesota Press, 2018. 123–149.

Ridley, LaVelle. "Imagining Otherly: Performing Possible Black Trans Futures in *Tangerine*." *TSQ: Transgender Studies Quarterly* 6, no. 4 (2019): 481–490.

Sharpe, Christina. *In the Wake: On Blackness and Being*. Durham: Duke University Press, 2016.

Snorton, C. Riley. *Black on Both Sides: A Racial History of Trans Identity*. Minneapolis: University of Minnesota Press, 2017.

Spillers, Hortense J. "Mama's Baby, Papa's Maybe: An American Grammar Book." *Diacritics* 17, no. 2 (1987): 64–81.

Stallings, L.H. *A Dirty South Manifesto: Sexual Resistance and Imagination in the New South*. Oakland: University of California Press, 2020.

Walker, Kaniya. "To Protect Black Trans Lives, Decriminalize Sex Work." *ACLU*, 20 November 2020.

Wynter, Sylvia. "Unsettling the Coloniality of Being/Power/Truth/Freedom: Towards the Human, After Man, Its Overrepresentation—An Argument." *CR: The New Centennial Review* 3, no. 3 (2003): 257–337.

Yusoff, Kathryn. *A Billion Black Anthropocenes or None*. Minneapolis: University of Minnesota Press, 2018.

7
THE ANTHROPOCENE AND CRITICAL METHOD

Stephen Tedeschi

Around the year 2000, a group of geologists began to argue that human activities were producing patterns of deposits in strata of rock distinctive enough to mark the end of the Holocene epoch and the beginning of a new epoch, which they called the Anthropocene. The concept of the Anthropocene quickly spread to other disciplines, and each discipline adjusted the concept to its methods and its methods to the concept. The Anthropocene concept has become so ubiquitous so quickly that it helps to mark what appears to be a new epoch in intellectual history. In this chapter, I survey how literary critics have adapted their methods to account for the concept and the conditions of the Anthropocene. I find that critics have adjusted several dimensions of their practice to this new conception of the relation between the human and the natural worlds, and I suggest not only that such adaptations are integral to the life of criticism but also that criticism may have an increasingly prominent role in adapting human life to changing conditions.

Literary criticism that addresses the Anthropocene typically confronts commonplace critiques of the concept and how it has been used. Skeptics argue that the Anthropocene concept has been defined in so many ways by so many different disciplines that it no longer defines a coherent object or provides any explanatory power. To the skeptics, the concept is less a tool of inquiry than a bauble of academic fashion. Proponents of the Anthropocene concept counter that the variety of definitions testifies to the concept's vitality and importance. That scholars from several disciplines take up the concept indicates that it describes a problem too broad to be claimed by any single discipline; that scholars can study the same object with mutually inconsistent methods is in keeping with the concept's acknowledgment of the inconceivable complexity of human and planetary systems; and that critics hurry along without hammering out rigorous consistency follows not from

DOI: 10.4324/9781003095347-9

the superficiality of fashion but from a pragmatic urge to find the best response to the intensifying catastrophe the concept describes.[1]

The way a literary critic works with the Anthropocene concept necessarily entails a specific notion of the relation between the knowledge projects of the natural sciences and of the humanities. Critics tend to treat these knowledge projects as cooperating and complementary, but the specific relations their works enact differ. On the one hand, literary critics interested in the Anthropocene adjust their studies to the terms of the natural sciences. They derive the outlines of their topic from the natural sciences, and changing the definition of a topic sets off a series of other changes. For instance, it changes the set of texts relevant to the inquiry, which changes the patterns critics see in texts, which changes models of genres and understandings of periods of literary history. The Anthropocene concept has encouraged some critics to study literature on a global rather than national scale and over millennia rather than centuries.[2] On the other hand, literary critics working in the subfield of literature and science analyze the literary elements of scientific writings—such as their figurative language, point of view, and narrative elements—and relate their language to that of their historical moment. Since the emergence of the Anthropocene concept, literary critics have studied the discourses on aspects of the planetary system transformed by human activity, including rocks, the climate, the atmosphere, and the oceans.[3] Literary critics have also analyzed the present discourse on the Anthropocene, explicating, for example, its tendency to imagine an observer in the distant future poring over the geological traces of the present, the challenge of thinking of the conjunction of the seemingly incommensurable scales of human lives and planetary processes, and various ways of describing the interconnectedness of all beings on the planet. This kind of criticism studies how the natural sciences arise out of and are received back into the history of human life and thought. In theory, by assimilating human history, and therefore literary history, into natural history, the Anthropocene concept allows critics to consider how literature influences the biogeochemical processes of the planet directly through its material production and indirectly through its effects on the minds and actions of humanity. From this critical perspective, a complete geological account of the Anthropocene would require a theory of the novel.[4]

Scholars pursuing critique—that is, those who closely analyze discourses, social systems, the representations those systems generate, and the values implicit within them—have debated the extent to which working with a concept from the natural sciences challenges the methods of critique or if the concept extends the reach of critique into the natural world. As a concept from the natural sciences, the Anthropocene putatively poses the objective data of empirical observation as a limit to the epistemological relativism that might follow from recognizing, as critique recognizes, that knowledge is socially constructed. In practice, however, critique rarely approaches this theoretical limit. Indeed, since the Anthropocene concept already accepts that the natural phenomena measured by empirical data are socially determined, it could be said to expand rather than restrict the scope of critique.[5] The deeper theoretical challenge that the Anthropocene concept puts to critique is the way it recasts the distinction between the human and nonhuman. In doing so, it calls for new perspectives on many of the central concepts of canonical critical theory, such as agency, intention, and the subject. In order to redescribe the world in terms consistent with the Anthropocene concept, critics have compiled a thick dictionary of neologisms.[6]

If the Anthropocene concept presses critical theorists to rethink some of their basic concepts, critics in turn have picked apart the abstract notion of humanity as a whole implied by the name of the Anthropocene. Critique analyzes the differences, tensions, and inequalities within and between societies; it transmutes the Anthropocene's focus on the global into an imperative to think through the relations between parts and wholes. It recognizes that different societies have contributed in different degrees to produce the conditions of the Anthropocene and studies how various social processes have cooperated to distribute unevenly the risks and costs of the changing planet. Capitalism, colonialism, and racism, for example, have shaped the social geography and global patterns of production that are hardening into patterns of planetary geology. While a geologist in the distant future would learn little about these systems from the strata of the Anthropocene, that geologist might nonetheless account for them by leaving room for the unknown functions that determined the uneven distribution of the epoch's identifying traces. Major events in the history of capital coincide with the leading candidates to mark the beginning of the Anthropocene: the Columbian exchange, the invention of the steam engine, and the Great Acceleration of the atomic age.[7] Each historical regime of accumulation has unevenly distributed wealth and environmental damage. On a local scale, the poorer communities in cities tend to bear the costs of air and water pollution, while wealthier, resource-intensive suburbs offer the illusion of a controlled environment. On a planetary scale, through colonialism, imperialism, and globalization, capitalism has exported the slow violence of heavily polluting industries, cash-crop agriculture, and resource extraction to the Global South. Racism, active both locally and globally, provides capital with a defense against rival systems of practices and values by refusing to acknowledge other knowledges and informs where societies concentrate their trash and toxic waste.[8] Because marginalized people already bear the concentrated costs of environmental degradation, their experience may foreshadow what an increasing share of the population will experience as these costs become more pervasive.

Literary critics participate in these critiques by studying how literary texts represent and reflect ways of thinking about the natural environment that arise from the interactions among these various unequal social systems. Literary texts can model these ways of thinking both in their representations and in their form and style. Critics might consider, for example, representations of the effects of ecological damage on communities, or they might identify the structures of feeling that register an undefined unease with environmental changes that can be felt before thought. Critics might study how literary works represent the consequences of mapping the planet onto the spatiotemporal coordinates of global capital. They might consider the logic of the generic narratives that inform ecological thinking, such as the capitalist's utopian fantasy of indefinitely compounding economic growth; or the tragic plot in which the planet stores up the supposed externalities of economic activity before revealing them to be fatal; or the romance that humans might find radical solidarity with forces in the nonhuman world in the struggle against unequal social systems and ecological collapse.[9] Literary critics might also study how literary works represent diverse ways of living or dwelling—each realizing different practical understandings of the human subject—and the effects of their being forced into relation by global social systems.[10] In doing so, critics might discover alternative ways of thinking, living, and being and new perspectives on dominant social systems.[11]

Critical inquiries into the experiences and conditions of historically marginalized groups have generated theoretical repertoires that have illuminated the origin, nature, and challenges of the Anthropocene. For instance, recovering the historically disregarded contributions of women to the critical tradition exposes and critiques the role of masculine instrumental reason in the economic calculations, natural sciences, and Promethean engineering that drove the production of the Anthropocene and reassesses the holistic and open perspectives, respect for incalculable loops of interconnections, and ethics of practical care that have been traditionally coded feminine.[12] Queer theory has developed ways of thinking about intimate interchanges that can help to describe close entanglements in ecosystems.[13] Debates within queer studies about the tension between non-reproductive queer sexuality and heterosexual reproduction can frame thinking about humanity's deeply uncertain future in the Anthropocene. Critics pursuing critique while working with the Anthropocene combine elements from these critical traditions with vibrant eclecticism.

In the last instance, these critiques analyze the inter-involvement of the natural and the social in social terms. Their object is ultimately human: they study human actions and systems and the effects of planetary changes on human life. Like those who pursue other approaches, critics who practice critique have to adjust their topic and scope and some of their key concepts when they address the Anthropocene, but they do not necessarily have to change how they read texts or conduct their analyses.

Critics can also analyze the human in natural terms—seeing human activity as an impersonal geological force comparable to a coral colony or asteroid impact—or in terms that seek to describe the human and the nonhuman without reducing one to the other. The effort to rethink the human without anthropocentrism drives the emerging intellectual epoch to which the Anthropocene concept belongs. In the field of affect studies, for example, scholars examine the intimate responsiveness between the embodied human subject and its surroundings, the way affect circulates as if with a life of its own, and the way affect registers emergent situations before the understanding can conceptualize them.[14] Literary critics have resituated the intricate complexity of human semiosis (anthroposemiosis) within a hierarchy that descends to the cognitive use of signs by animals (zoösemiosis), to the sign systems plants use without recognizable cognitive intention (phytosemiosis), and the virtual semiosis that lies in any object's potential to represent a system merely by participating in it (physiosemiosis), the semiotic condition that makes stratigraphic reading possible.[15] New materialism posits the power of matter to compose complex systems and forms by itself and branches into explorations of nonhuman semiosis and the poetics of nature.[16] Actor-network theory rethinks agency not as the realized will of an autonomous human subject but as an effect of a network of interacting elements and forces, whether involving humans or not.[17] In literary studies, actor-network theory provides a new perspective on how literature functions within assemblages of human thoughts and feelings, social situations, and the disposition of the material planet. For example, the geography of a region, policies governing embanking, diverting, or damming rivers, the means of producing and circulating literary texts, and literary representations of landscapes may all operate together in a single complex of distributed agency.

The methods of literary criticism surveyed so far have treated works of literature as documents that offer evidence about historical discourses or social and cultural processes; they take literary forms and techniques into account, but they do not study them as the object of inquiry or consider reading literature as an aesthetic experience. The question of how literature as a distinctive kind of writing—whether distinguished by genres and forms, by literariness, or by aesthetic qualities—relates to the Anthropocene can be approached along much the same lines, and fissured by the same debates, as the richly theorized question of the relation between literature and history more generally. One approach is to consider the history of literary forms. Literary forms emerge from and continue to relate to historical discursive situations. For instance, the implied significance of the lyrical "I" varies widely across different continents and over the last two and a half millennia. Over the last few centuries in the Western tradition, the lyrical "I" has been associated with the concept of a private, autonomous, empirical subject. Critics writing on the Anthropocene and lyric tend to associate this conception of the subject with historical ideologies that prioritize private economic gain over ecological care and to seek out new figures of lyrical subjectivity.[18] This method assumes that literary forms reproduce and alter historical ways of thinking, feeling, and perceiving. This approach shades into a theory of literature as a privileged realm for the operation of the imagination in and upon language. By changing the language, literature changes or reproduces the set of concepts that humans use to organize their perceptions of the world around them.[19] New literary forms help to produce new understandings of the cosmos, and new understandings of the cosmos, such as the conception imposed by the Anthropocene, implicitly require new literary forms. Alternatively, critics can begin from the supposed autonomy of aesthetics from history. In a Kantian aesthetic moment, one perceives the form of an object independent of the historical considerations of the object's purpose or of one's own concepts or interests. The unknowing and detached attitude of the aesthetic spectator—her will to control suspended and her reserve both a liberation and a bereavement—echoes in the situation of life in the Anthropocene—uncertain, unknowable, tragically beyond an individual's power to control, and calling for restraint.[20]

One of the claims of this survey has been that the Anthropocene concept warns of both a global ecological crisis and a crisis of human thought and feeling. The planetary system has broken its long-standing habits. The ecological consequences are apparent to empirical observation. The phenomenological consequences—the effects on how people think and feel—appear not only in the experiences of those who suffer increasingly unstable access to food and water or those who have experienced extreme storms, fires, and floods but also, perhaps for the first time on a truly global scale, in the experience of the COVID-19 pandemic. This pandemic has conjured new atmospheres of moods. Anxiety, faltering solidarity, and frustration have intensified. The fissures within humanity along the lines of race and class have become still more pressing. Widespread unemployment has directed ever more people's attention back to the task of securing the basic necessities of life; the materially insulated middle classes respond to the same felt pressures, as if in a process of sublimation, by baking, gardening, and repairing their homes. People have learned new words and concepts from the natural sciences, from public health, and from activists invested in social justice. They have learned to watch their surroundings with alarmed alertness. And they have changed their habits. Plunged into a condition of uncertainty and aware of the limits of their knowledge, people have resorted to acting upon the best available information and adjusting in the light of new information. The pandemic exposes that in the last instance the abilities traditionally cultivated in the liberal arts—careful attentiveness, critical thinking, and imagination grounded in practice—are survival skills.

Literature and literary criticism will bear in the Anthropocene the same responsibilities they bore in the Holocene. Indeed, the Anthropocene may correct the inversion that casts literature and literary criticism as superstructural luxuries and economic growth as a basic necessity. The imagination, the narratives that construct meaning for experience, and the figures that assign value are the seeds and fruits of literature. Literature is integral to the processes by which humans organize their experiences and adapt to changing conditions. Aesthetic perception is not only detached, disinterested, and mournful; it is at the same time immersive, intuitive, and animated by the pleasure of thinking, feeling, and living. In *Art as Experience* (1934), John Dewey describes aesthetic experience in terms not limited to the human:

> To grasp the sources of esthetic experience it is, therefore, necessary to have recourse to animal life below the human scale. The activities of the fox, the

dog, and the thrush may at least stand as reminders and symbols of that unity of experience which we so fractionize when work is labor, and thought withdraws us from the world. The live animal is fully present, all there, in all of its actions: in its wary glances, its sharp sniffings, its abrupt cocking of ears. All senses are equally on the *qui vive*. As you watch, you see motion merging into sense and sense into motion—constituting that animal grace so hard for man to rival.[21]

A human who passes through this state and communicates the experience to another produces a work of literature. In the Anthropocene, literary criticism will continue to negotiate which works of literature we choose to live with us and integrate into our schematisms, which we archive under the care of scholars like a seed vault for thought, and which we preserve in unread oblivion. It will share in the work of observing the forces and agencies animating systems. And it will study, correct, and train our intellectual, affective, and imaginative responsiveness to the universe of signs and signals, human and nonhuman. Literary criticism helps sustain—with the taut alertness of a watchful fox—intentional, attentive human life in the midst of a planetary catastrophe.

Notes

1 Tobias Menely and Jesse Oak Taylor argue that the concept requires from literary critics a "multiplicity of approaches," "belief in complexity," and "acceptance of inconsistency" in "Introduction," *Anthropocene Reading*, ed. Tobias Menely and Jesse Oak Taylor (University Park: Penn State University Press, 2017), 13.
2 Wai Chee Dimock, *Through Other Continents: American Literature across Deep Time* (Princeton: Princeton University Press, 2009).
3 Excellent models include Noah Heringman, *Romantic Rocks, Aesthetic Geology* (Ithaca: Cornell University Press, 2004) and Jayne Elizabeth Lewis, *Air's Appearance: Literary Atmosphere in British Fiction, 1660–1794* (Chicago: University of Chicago Press, 2012).
4 Devin Griffiths, "Romantic Planet: Science and Literature within the Anthropocene," *Literature Compass* 14, no. 1 (2017): 13.
5 Claire Colebrook, "What is the Anthropo-Political?" in *Twilight of the Anthropocene Idols*, ed. Tom Cohen, Claire Colebrook, and J. Hillis Miller (London: Open Humanities Press, 2016), 81–125.
6 For example, Timothy Morton has introduced terms that seek to defamiliarize human and nonhuman modes of being and identify how things might appear from a thoroughgoing ecological perspective. Some of these terms, such as "hyperobjects" and the "mesh," have become standard counters in the critical discourse on the Anthropocene. See Timothy Morton, *The Ecological Thought* (Cambridge: Harvard University Press, 2010), and *Hyperobjects: Philosophy and Ecology after the End of the World* (Minneapolis: University of Minnesota Press, 2013).
7 Jeremy Davies, *The Birth of the Anthropocene* (Berkeley: University of California Press, 2016), 91–108. The history of the Anthropocene more closely coincides with the history of capitalism than it does with the history of humanity, which lived through the

Pleistocene and Holocene before producing the Anthropocene. Jason W. Moore, ed., *Anthropocene or Capitalocene?* (Oakland: PM Press, 2016).
8 Françoise Vergès, "Racial Capitalocene," in *Futures of Black Radicalism*, ed. Gaye Theresa Johnson and Alex Lubin (London: Verso, 2017), 72–82; and Axelle Karera, "Blackness and the Pitfalls of Anthropocene Ethics," *Critical Philosophy of Race* (2019): 32–56.
9 McKenzie Wark proposes forging comradeship with nonhumans in *Molecular Red: Theory for the Anthropocene* (London: Verso, 2015).
10 Ian Baucom, "History 4°: Postcolonial Method and Anthropocene Time," *Cambridge Journal of Postcolonial Literary Inquiry* 1, no. 1 (2014): 123–142.
11 Dipesh Chakrabarty, "The Climate of History: Four Theses," *Critical Inquiry* 35, no. 2 (2009): 207–212.
12 Donna Haraway, *Staying with the Trouble* (Durham: Duke University Press, 2016); and Richard Grusin, ed., *Anthropocene Feminism* (Minneapolis: University of Minnesota Press, 2017).
13 Timothy Morton, "Queer Ecology," *PMLA* 125, no. 2 (2010): 273–282.
14 Lisa Ottum and Seth T. Reno, eds., *Wordsworth and the Green Romantics: Affect and Ecology in the Nineteenth Century* (Lebanon: University of New Hampshire Press, 2016); and Kyle Bladow and Jennifer Ladino, eds., *Affective Ecocriticism* (Lincoln: University of Nebraska Press, 2018).
15 John Deely, *Basics of Semiotics* (Bloomington: Indiana University Press, 1990). Scholars interested in natural semiosis turn from Ferdinand de Saussure to Charles Sanders Peirce.
16 Karen Barad, *Meeting the Universe Halfway: Quantum Physics and the Entanglement of Matter and Meaning* (Durham: Duke University Press, 2007); and Jane Bennett, *Vibrant Matter: A Political Economy of Things* (Durham: Duke University Press, 2010). Consider the introduction and second and third chapters of Amanda Jo Goldstein, *Sweet Science: Romantic Materialism and the New Logics of Life* (Chicago: University of Chicago Press, 2017).
17 Bruno Latour, "Agency at the Time of the Anthropocene," *NLH* 45, no. 1 (2014): 1–14; Rita Felski, *The Limits of Critique* (Chicago: University of Chicago Press, 2015); Yves Citton, "Fictional Attachments and Literary Weavings in the Anthropocene," *NLH* 47, nos. 2–3 (2016): 309–329; and Bruno Latour, *Facing Gaia*, trans. Catherine Porter (Cambridge: Polity, 2017).
18 Tom Bristow, *The Anthropocene Lyric* (Basingstoke: Palgrave, 2015); and David Farrier, *Anthropocene Poetics* (Minneapolis: University of Minnesota Press, 2019).
19 Bernard Stiegler reads the Anthropocene in terms of his theory of the historical schematism in *The Neganthropocene*, trans. Daniel Ross (London: Open Humanities Press, 2018).
20 Anahid Nersessian, "Two Gardens: An Experiment in Calamity Form," *MLQ* 74, no. 3 (2013): 307–329; and Anne-Lise François, *Open Secrets: The Literature of Uncounted Experience* (Stanford: Stanford University Press, 2008).
21 John Dewey, *Art as Experience* (New York: Penguin, 1934 [rpt. 2005]), 18.

References

Barad, Karen. *Meeting the Universe Halfway: Quantum Physics and the Entanglement of Matter and Meaning*. Durham: Duke University Press, 2007.

Baucom, Ian. "History 4°: Postcolonial Method and Anthropocene Time." *Cambridge Journal of Postcolonial Literary Inquiry* 1, no. 1 (2014): 123–142.
Bennett, Jane. *Vibrant Matter: A Political Economy of Things*. Durham: Duke University Press, 2010.
Bladow, Kyle, and Jennifer Ladino, eds. *Affective Ecocriticism*. Lincoln: University of Nebraska Press, 2018.
Bristow, Tom. *The Anthropocene Lyric*. Basingstoke: Palgrave, 2015.
Chakrabarty, Dipesh. "The Climate of History: Four Theses." *Critical Inquiry* 35, no. 2 (2009): 197–222.
Citton, Yves. "Fictional Attachments and Literary Weavings in the Anthropocene." *NLH* 47, nos. 2–3 (2016): 309–329.
Colebrook, Claire. "What is the Anthropo-Political?" In *Twilight of the Anthropocene Idols*. Edited by Tom Cohen, Claire Colebrook, and J. Hillis Miller. London: Open Humanities Press, 2016. 81–125.
Davies, Jeremy. *The Birth of the Anthropocene*. Berkeley: University of California Press, 2016.
Deely, John. *Basics of Semiotics*. Bloomington: Indiana University Press, 1990.
Dewey, John. *Art as Experience*. New York: Penguin, 2005.
Dimock, Wai Chee. *Through Other Continents: American Literature across Deep Time*. Princeton: Princeton University Press, 2009.
Farrier, David. *Anthropocene Poetics*. Minneapolis: University of Minnesota Press, 2019.
Felski, Rita. *The Limits of Critique*. Chicago: University of Chicago Press, 2015.
François, Anne-Lise. *Open Secrets: The Literature of Uncounted Experience*. Stanford: Stanford University Press, 2008.
Goldstein, Amanda Jo. *Sweet Science: Romantic Materialism and the New Logics of Life*. Chicago: University of Chicago Press, 2017.
Griffiths, Devin. "Romantic Planet: Science and Literature within the Anthropocene." *Literature Compass* 14, no. 1 (2017): 1–17.
Grusin, Richard, ed. *Anthropocene Feminism*. Minneapolis: University of Minnesota Press, 2017.
Haraway, Donna. *Staying with the Trouble*. Durham: Duke University Press, 2016.
Heringman, Noah. *Romantic Rocks, Aesthetic Geology*. Ithaca: Cornell University Press, 2004.
Karera, Axelle. "Blackness and the Pitfalls of Anthropocene Ethics." *Critical Philosophy of Race* 7, no. 1 (2019): 32–56.
Latour, Bruno. "Agency at the Time of the Anthropocene." *NLH* 45, no. 1 (2014): 1–14.
———. *Facing Gaia*. Translated by Catherine Porter. Cambridge: Polity, 2017.
Lewis, Jayne Elizabeth. *Air's Appearance: Literary Atmosphere in British Fiction, 1660–1794*. Chicago: University of Chicago Press, 2012.
Menely, Tobias, and Jesse Oak Taylor, eds. *Anthropocene Reading*. University Park: Penn State University Press, 2017.
Moore, Jason W., ed. *Anthropocene or Capitalocene?* Oakland: PM Press, 2016.
Morton, Timothy. *The Ecological Thought*. Cambridge: Harvard University Press, 2010.
———. *Hyperobjects: Philosophy and Ecology after the End of the World*. Minneapolis: University of Minnesota Press, 2013.
———. "Queer Ecology." *PMLA* 125, no. 2 (2010): 273–282.
Nersessian, Anahid. "Two Gardens: An Experiment in Calamity Form." *MLQ* 74, no. 3 (2013): 307–309.
Ottum, Lisa, and Seth T. Reno, eds. *Wordsworth and the Green Romantics: Affect and Ecology in the Nineteenth Century*. Lebanon: University of New Hampshire Press, 2016.

Stiegler, Bernard. *The Neganthropocene*. Translated by Daniel Ross. London: Open Humanities Press, 2018.
Vergès, Françoise. "Racial Capitalocene." In *Futures of Black Radicalism*. Edited by Gaye Theresa Johnson and Alex Lubin. London: Verso, 2017. 72–83.
Wark, McKenzie. *Molecular Red: Theory for the Anthropocene*. London: Verso, 2015.

PART 2
Contexts

8
"ONE LIFE" AND ONE DEATH

Mary Shelley's *The Last Man*

Matthew Rowney

> A sudden break was made in the routine of our lives. In vain our Protector and his partizans sought to conceal this truth; in vain, day after day, he appointed a period for the discussion of the new laws concerning hereditary rank and privilege; in vain he endeavoured to represent the evil as partial and temporary. These disasters came home to so many bosoms, and, through the various channels of commerce, were carried so entirely into every class and division of the community, that of necessity they became the first question in the state, the chief subjects to which we must turn our attention.
>
> Mary Shelley, The Last Man (1826)[1]

Plague threatens because of its physical effects, but also because it challenges deeply held cultural beliefs about the place and purpose of human life. We have evolved as a species into highly social animals, making up for our lack of physical prowess by grouping together, cooperating, and forming communities that protect individuals who would otherwise be exposed and vulnerable. Yet it is this very grouping and the very bonds at the basis of this community that plague exploits, calling into question the values formed on the basis of these bonds. Plague is a paradox because it demonstrates to us the ties that bind us together while at the same time using those bonds against us.

The paradoxical nature of plague has been employed for millennia by authors as a way of thinking about the human condition. In Sophocles' *Oedipus Rex* (c. 429 BCE), plague appears, as it does elsewhere in ancient Greek literature, as a punishment sent from the gods for bad leadership. Giovanni Boccaccio's *The Decameron* (1353) employs the space of quarantine to satirize the corruption and hypocrisy of the clergy, the most powerful organization of his day. Daniel Defoe's *Journal of the Plague Year* (1722), set in 1665 London, describes attempts by local government to

DOI: 10.4324/9781003095347-11

quarantine the infected and the resistance to these attempts. In each instance, these authors utilize plague as a way of responding to their own historical and cultural moment. Even though they deal with localized outbreaks, each of these works also offers telling commentary on the contemporary COVID-19 global pandemic, reminding us that plague has always been part of the human experience.

The first literary work to depict a global pandemic is Mary Shelley's *The Last Man* (1826). Like others before her, Shelley uses plague as a way to offer social commentary and to critique power. Unlike others, she does so as the British Empire and industrial capitalism were spreading around the world, forming the bases for what is now often referred to as the Anthropocene epoch.[2] When Paul Crutzen first popularized the term "Anthropocene" in 2000, he suggested James Watt's patent of the steam engine in 1784 as a possible start date for this new geological epoch. The dual development of capitalism and the Industrial Revolution in the late eighteenth century was so powerful that it brought into question fundamental assumptions about human life: "the various channels of commerce" the epigraph to this chapter describes become the various vectors of infection, just as today the ease and speed of global travel serves to boost the effectiveness of viral contagion.

The figure of plague in *The Last Man* offers a scathing critique of the effects of the global spread of British Empire and industrial capitalism, processes foundational to the creation of our current globalized world. In turn, the novel also offers insights into early conceptualizations of the Anthropocene. Shelley critiques the human- and male-centered worldview necessary to the progress of globalization and the so-called Age of Man. She not only demonstrates that worldview leads to inevitable destruction but constructs an alternate structure in the ashes of that destruction. This portrayal of the end of humanity also contemplates the end of a certain idea of the human, offering the possibility of new conceptualizations of being. Shelley does this, I argue, by establishing a matrilineal textual authority and inheritance through the figure of her mother, Mary Wollstonecraft.

In order to understand both the critique and the new possibilities that Shelley's figure of plague makes available, this chapter is divided into three parts. In the first section, "One Life/One Death," I situate Shelley's novel within broader Romantic theories of the relationship between the human and the natural world, demonstrating how Shelley offers a differing commentary on the global than her Romantic predecessors. In the second section, "These Sibylline Leaves," I show how Shelley aligns her work with a female tradition, establishing a locus of possibility from which to rethink social structures. The concluding section, "Our Viruses/Ourselves," looks at Shelley's identification with her mother, and how this relationship can be reread in the context of the recent discovery of retroviruses in the human genome. I see these sections related in the way they demonstrate Shelley's novel to critique a male-centered construction of the "human" at the heart of a Western exceptionalism that reduces both human and nonhuman others to "natural" resources.

One Life/One Death

Shelley's plague offers a commentary on the classical Romantic notion of a "One Life within us and abroad," which unifies the viewer and the environment. The poet and philosopher Samuel Taylor Coleridge coined this phrase in his 1816 poem "The Aeolian Harp," though it encapsulates a broader Romantic-era belief in the harmony between humans and the natural world. Shelley's novel presents rather a one death, not a negative reflection of the Romantic concept, but a dramatic transformation of the bonds between humans and the natural world through the agency of plague. While earlier Romantics had insisted on a common purpose in all living things as a cornerstone of their moral and aesthetic beliefs, Shelley's novel presents a nature that, while not without agency, is indifferent, if not hostile, to human existence. Her one death only applies to humans and does not attempt to make a value judgment as to the purposes of the natural world.[3]

This difference is most easily perceived through direct comparison. The following are the first two stanzas from William Wordsworth's poem "Lines Written in Early Spring," first published in *Lyrical Ballads* in 1798:

> I heard a thousand blended notes,
> While in a grove I sate reclined,
> In that sweet mood when pleasant thoughts
> Bring sad thoughts to the mind.
>
> To her fair works did Nature link
> The human soul that through me ran;
> And much it grieved my heart to think
> What man has made of man.[4]

The insistence on the "link" between nature's works and "the human soul" in the second stanza recalls the "blended notes" of the first stanza that link the birds' singing to that of the poet, establishing a parallel in terms of their effects on the listener. The grief attending the meditation on human failings is not separated from this contemplation of the link between humans and the natural world. The poet uses "And" to connect these two seemingly contrasting thoughts, not "but." What the poet develops here is a simultaneous faith in the linked purpose of humanity and other living things with the recognition that human actions often unnecessarily work against this harmony. There is an added implication that the realization of this deep interconnection might be the beginning of a solution to what is causing human unhappiness.

The next passage is from Mary Shelley's *The Last Man*:

> Where was pain and evil? Not in the calm air or weltering ocean; not in the woods or fertile fields, nor among the birds that made the woods resonant

> with song, nor the animals that in the midst of plenty basked in the sunshine. Our enemy, like the Calamity of Homer, trod our hearts, and no sound was echoed from her steps.[5]

The birds sing here too, and animals bask in the sun, but the essential link to human experience is tellingly absent. The indifference of the natural world appears to mock human-centered conceptions of history, a history that, with industrialized methods of production, becomes increasingly indifferent to the delicate individuality and agency of the natural world. That "no sound" issues from this calamity appropriately conveys this indifference.

While both passages figure an assumed pleasure within living things and contrast it with human suffering, Shelley's passage refuses the consolation, or the potential moral value, of a shared fate. Though it attempts to identify its enemy in relation to a cultural model (Homer), this model comes to partake in the soundless devastation. The question "Where?" distinctly separates human pain and evil from the natural world, and directly interrogates Romantic notions of a benign interconnection.

In Shelley's novel, the history of the human interrelation with the natural world becomes one that is disturbed by humans' perversion of nature's products for their own aggrandizement. The results of a shift from a notion of value based on land to one based on capital is something quite like the shift in Shelley's novel from a pre- and post-plague society. She uses the metaphor of stolen fire, much as she had in *Frankenstein* (1818),[6] to comment on this development: "Could we take integral parts of this power, and not be subject to its operation? Could we domesticate a cub of this wild beast, and not fear its growth and maturity?"[7] These rhetorical questions point to the effects of newly industrialized methods of production and the global reach of trade as a kind of monstrous force no longer in the control of its creator. Just as Karl Marx would later make explicit, the worker becomes "subject to" the "operation" of his product.[8] And we are now in a position to consider (and properly fear) the "growth and maturity" of the types of industry in their infancy in Shelley's day. The movement to fossil fuels, the employ of steam-powered engines to do an ever-increasing number of tasks, and the introduction of industrial methods of agricultural production, all contributed to a major shift in the human exploitation of the environment, one that has, due to an exponential increase in the human production of carbon in the last fifty years, transformed the biosphere in ways that may well be irreversible.

This notion of the surrender of human agency to the forces of the market is further born out in other passages in the novel that address commerce in relation to human suffering, such as this one: "Our own distresses, though they were occasioned by the fictitious reciprocity of commerce, encreased in due proportion. Bankers, merchants, and manufacturers, whose trade depended on exports and interchange of wealth, became bankrupt."[9] There is a sustained critique, throughout the novel, on the high value placed on property ownership and the amoral pursuit of wealth. At the time Shelley is writing, property was appealed to as the foundation for Western democratic institutions, and her novel offers a critique of ownership as a basis for social life and a prediction that this system is unsustainable. The contemporary outbreak of COVID-19 is more closely related to market forces than has been generally recognized. According to a recent study, "global changes in the mode and the intensity of land use are creating expanding hazardous interfaces between people, livestock and wildlife reservoirs of zoonotic disease."[10] The expansion of the human footprint through the growth of global capitalism has caused a drastic reduction in biodiversity, favoring species that are more likely to pass disease to humans. The pattern for this rampant environmental degradation was established in the forms of industrial practice engendered in the Romantic period.

Shelley's interrogation of the "One Life" extends beyond a mere denial of a benign connection between humans and nature and applies to the larger critique of the process of globalization underway as Shelley wrote. Because the business of empire and international trade was by and large a male one, that at the same time operated under assumptions about the natural, God-given right of Europeans to subdue the natural world, her depiction of plague deconstructs the notion of a Eurocentric, male-centered (or androcentric), and finally human-centered (or anthropocentric) worldview. And because she critiques property ownership as the basis for the construction of social meaning, she also necessarily critiques a capital-centered (or capitalocentric) ideology. The type of worldview she establishes instead, which ironically comes into closer focus as the plague progresses, is strictly egalitarian: one of mutual effort and mutual care, of selfless dedication to the betterment of the whole, and thus of maximum benefit to each member of the group. It valorizes feminine virtues of care in place of a traditionally masculine reliance on force. It replaces a focus on accumulation (which becomes associated with death) with one on human beings.

The depiction of a global pandemic in *The Last Man* comments not only on the "One Life"; it critiques a Western patriarchal tradition that places the human on a separate level from the natural environment, what Val Plumwood calls "an ecology-blind conceptual framework of rationality."[11] This blindness is itself a kind of plague, an insistence on a superior transcendent realm that relegates the natural world to the passive and passing, to a raw material for human use, devoid of identity or agency. The "one death" can be read, then, in terms of this life-denying tendency within patriarchal Western culture, as a commentary on a system which through its subjugation of life to the notion of a transcendent realm becomes a de facto cult of death.

These Sibylline Leaves

Shelley's departure from this male- and human-centered worldview is evident in a number of ways, perhaps most tellingly in the way she comments on a tradition of male literature in the introduction to the novel. This introduction narrates an excursion by the author and an unnamed (and ungendered) "friend" in Italy that results in the eventual discovery of the Sybil's cave, the presumed location from which the ancient Roman prophetess performed her divinations. In the cave they find text written in different languages on leaves and other organic matter scattered around the floor. This text is painstakingly pieced back together in order to form the narrative presented by the novel. The Sybil's cave is described in ancient Roman literature, most notably in Book Six of Virgil's *Aeneid*, a text with which Shelley was very familiar: "Deep in a cave the Sibyl makes abode; / Thence full of fate returns, and of the god."[12] Yet Shelley makes an important distinction: "it is not indeed exactly as Virgil describes it; but the whole of this land had been so convulsed by earthquake and volcano, that the change was not wonderful."[13] This un-wonderful difference, when taken together with the distinctly un-Virgilian description of "the dim hypaethric cavern,"[14] suggests that Shelley's divergence from her source, though subtle, is important. The "hypaethric" cavern is open to the sky, a reference to the function of the cave as a temple in which the movements of the heavens were an important part of the ceremonial rights performed therein. This change, in which the cave is open rather than closed, suggests a metaphor for the female reproductive system, another way this introduction establishes a female line of inheritance. What Timothy Ruppert argues about the appearance of sibylline leaves is also pertinent to how the novel interacts with its literary forbears: "By transferring vatic authority from the patriarchal Judeo-Christian scriptures to the matriarchal sibylline leaves, Shelley meaningfully questions the masculine bias in Romantic poetry."[15] Shelley would find another motivation for this symbolic transfer of power in the work of her mother, Mary Wollstonecraft.

In a fragment of 1787, titled "Cave of Fancy," Mary Wollstonecraft begins a tale that features a cave, a deadly plague, and a grieving child. Though just a few pages, the fragment is highly suggestive of elements of Shelley's novel. The cave is figured as the home of spirits that obey the command of an old sage, who visits the cave nightly:

> One side of the hut was supported by the rock, and at midnight, when the sage struck the inclosed part, it yawned wide, and admitted him into a cavern in the very bowels of the earth, where never human foot before had trod; and the various spirits, which inhabit the different regions of nature, were here obedient to his potent word. The cavern had been formed by the great inundation of waters, when the approach of a comet forced them from their source.[16]

The cave functions as both retreat and place where power is exercised, not unlike the retreat Wollstonecraft describes in her childhood days in Beverley.[17] It significantly combines both aspects of the Deluge and cosmological event as formative to its structure, both features which figure prominently in *The Last Man*.[18] When the sage returns at dawn from a visit to the cave, he finds an all-consuming disaster has struck down humanity:

> He found that death had been at work during his absence, and terrific marks of a furious storm still spread horror around. Though the day was serene, and threw bright rays on eyes for ever shut, it dawned not for the wretches who hung pendent on the craggy rocks, or were stretched lifeless on the sand. Some struggling, had dug themselves a grave; others had resigned their breath before the impetuous surge whirled them on shore. A few, in whom the vital spark was not so soon dislodged, had clung to loose fragments; it was the grasp of death; embracing the stone, they stiffened; and the head, no longer erect, rested on the mass which the arms encircled. It felt not the agonizing gripe, nor heard the sigh that broke the heart in twain.[19]

It is almost as if we are reading *The Last Man*, in the style, subject matter, and coloring of the passage, especially in terms of the contrast between the "serene" face of nature and the graphic depiction of human suffering. This vivid description of death and dying is exactly the type of thing to which Shelley's initial critics objected. If Shelley was, to some extent, creating a tribute to her mother, she is also, through the repositioning of vatic authority, creating a tribute to those principles that her mother, the founding feminist icon, was so famous for delineating.[20] As Wollstonecraft's fragment draws to a close, the sage finds one survivor, a young girl mourning over her dead mother. The description, and the girl's appeal "Wake her, ah! Wake her ... or the sea will catch us," must have been particularly striking to Shelley.[21] And, while the novel has long been recognized as a tribute to the recently fallen figure of her husband Percy, Shelley's introduction strongly invokes her mother's legacy and spirit.

The Sibyl's cave is also strongly suggestive of Shelley's feelings of loss, regret, and guilt over her mother's death shortly after giving birth to her. The "dim hypaethric cavern" of the introduction takes on a new significance in this context, as both a revision of the male literary depiction of the sibyl's cave and as a potential womb in which a female line of prophecy dwells. This further suggests a specific link between mother and daughter, especially in Shelley's circumstances, given the fragmented placenta involved in Shelley's birth that led to the infection of her mother and her subsequent death. This matrilineal link provides a counter to a patriarchal system of value that underlies the making of the Anthropocene.

Our Viruses/Ourselves

The introduction to *The Last Man*, in which the novel is pieced together like a jigsaw puzzle, can also be read in terms of the tale the novel tells; that is, the human race gradually fragments and disintegrates, leaving behind only fossilized fragments, like the pieces left behind in the Sibyl's cave. These fragments first appear as different types of organic matter, as a kind of refuse of nature, that on closer examination reveal themselves to be pieces of a text that tell a story of intimacy and irremediable loss, separated from their collector across various ages and distances.

Shelley's separation from her mother presents a similar case. She has nothing to connect herself to her mother but fragments of text, like "The Cave of Fancy" above, and so, in this context, the cavern becomes all the more a symbol for her mother's womb. It is difficult to underestimate the effect on Shelley of her mother's death shortly after giving birth to her. She would have read, likely many times, the following account in her father William Godwin's *Memoirs of the Author of a Vindication of the Rights of Women* (1798):

> The child was born at twenty minutes after eleven at night. Mary had requested that I would not come into the chamber till all was over ... I was sitting in a parlour; and it was not till after two o'clock on Thursday morning, that I received the alarming intelligence, that the placenta was not yet removed, and that the midwife dared not proceed any further, and gave her opinion for calling in a male practitioner. I accordingly went for Dr. Poignand, physician and man-midwife to the same hospital, who arrived between three and four hours after the birth of the child. He immediately proceeded to the extraction of the placenta, which he brought away in pieces, till he was satisfied that the whole was removed. In that point however it afterwards appeared that he was mistaken.[22]

The placenta, that organ which delivers nutrients to the embryo, forms the connection and point of exchange, through the umbilical cord, between mother and child. In this case, it was the source of an infection, likely due to the doctor's attempt at removal, which was the cause of Wollstonecraft's death. Shelley no doubt felt a profound sense of loss and guilt at her birth being the occasion of her mother's death, and the introduction to *The Last Man* offers a way of thinking about this process of grieving for a person one has never met, yet to whom one owes one's life. The fragments found in the Sibyl's cave are in this way related to the fragments of the placenta, organic matter that communicates a shared heritage. The text written upon the fragments of the cave then becomes a way to reconnect to a lost mother, to piece back together the prophetic voice of that sibyl and reclaim an inheritance through this work, which is also the writing of the novel.

The loss of her mother is something Shelley must carry with her like an inactive virus. The production of a text from fragments of many ages and in many languages is suggestive of the formation of human DNA, which includes a large amount of viral material, generally known as retroviruses. This genetic material represents "the remnants of ancestral retroviral infections that became fixed in the germline DNA," which "are thought to have played an important role in the evolution of mammalian genomes."[23] While this has a larger bearing on the treatment of plague in the novel, it is specifically important to Shelley's relationship with her mother because of the role of a specific retrovirus: "The best example of a [retrovirus] with a known function is HERV-W,"[24] a retrovirus involved in the formation and growth of the placenta.[25] The "foreign" contributor to mammalian evolution now being studied by scientists can be read, then, in the fragments, written mostly in foreign languages, studied by the author and her companion found on the sibyl's cavern floor.

The piecing together of fragments that figures the composition of the novel is also comparable to the novel method of comparative anatomy, developed by George Cuvier, used for creating accurate skeletons of long-extinct species. Shelley brings the fossils of her introduction full circle in the quotation of her mother at the end of the novel. She describes the bare stone of the Alps as "the bones of the world, waiting to be clothed with everything necessary to give life and beauty."[26] The fragments of bone and other natural material at the opening of the novel come back here, in a way that is suggestive of the building blocks of creation, or what today we would call DNA, with all its viral content.

The broad identification of the self with the natural world in early Romanticism becomes a narrow identification with the plague in *The Last Man*. Though direct knowledge of viruses was not available to Shelley, she nevertheless demonstrates an important aspect of their interaction with the human that challenges male- and human-centered ideologies. Shelley's plague not only offers a critique of the process of globalization underway in her day, but also rethinks the category of the "human" long before "posthuman" theory. Her novel offers a point of identification with the viral that recent findings in the sciences reinforce. Not only are we part virus, the virus has played an important role in our evolutionary development, best recognized today in the formation of the placenta. The paradox that plague presents in exploiting the community on which humanity depends becomes expressed in Shelley's knowledge of her mother's death in giving birth to her. Though the appearance of a "one death" appears hopelessly bleak, it provides a much-needed critique of ideologies that have produced increasingly violent environmental catastrophe in the Anthropocene, and offers, however precariously, a way of moving beyond predictable and confining notions of the human centuries before science would unravel our unexpected genomic ancestry.

Notes

1. Mary Shelley, *The Last Man* (Peterborough: Broadview, 1996), 184.
2. This term, first developed in the sciences came to be applied, sometimes in inherently problematic ways, in the humanities. Critics of the term often point to its false application to all of humanity (as implied by the root "anthropos"). As Donna Haraway explains, "It's not a 'species act'; we're not doing this as a 'species,'" and, as Lisa Ottum recently observes, "Prevailing narratives of the Anthropocene … downplay or ignore

their roots in colonialism and war." Wealthy Western nations have been by far the largest contributor to environmental degradation. Haraway and others have preferred the term "Capitalocene," coined by James Moore, as more accurately reflecting the historical dynamic of human-induced change to the environment. See Donna Haraway, *Manifestly Haraway* (Minneapolis: University of Minnesota Press, 2016), 237; and Lisa Ottum, "The 'Vast Prison' of the World: Counter Anthropocenes in the Works of Mary Shelley," in *Gendered Ecologies: New Materialist Interpretations of Women Writers in the Long Nineteenth Century*, ed. Dewey H. Hall and Jillmarie Murphy (Clemson: Clemson University Press, 2020), 27.

3 This is not, however, an insistence on a distinction between humans and the natural world—plague is, after all, a natural phenomenon, and Shelley's novel stresses human vulnerability rather than human exceptionalism.
4 William Wordsworth, "Lines Written in Early Spring," in *Lyrical Ballads: 1798 and 1802*, ed. Fiona Stafford (Oxford: Oxford University Press, 2013), 51.
5 Shelley, 251.
6 The subtitle of which reads: "or, the modern Prometheus." Prometheus is the figure in Greek mythology who steals fire from the gods and gives it to humanity.
7 Shelley, 182. As I write in 2020, California is suffering some of the worst forest fires in its history, their size contributed to by human-induced climate change.
8 As Marx writes, "the more the worker spends himself, the more powerful the alien objective world becomes which he creates over-against himself, the poorer he himself—his inner world—becomes, the less belongs to him as his own." See Karl Marx, *Economic and Philosophical Manuscripts of 1844*, trans. Martin Milligan (Amherst: Prometheus Books, 1988), 71–72.
9 Shelley, 185.
10 Rory Gibb, et al., "Zoonotic Host Diversity Increases in Human-Dominated Ecosystems," *Nature* 584 (2020): 398.
11 Val Plumwood, "Ecofeminist Analysis and the Culture of Ecological Denial," in *Feminist Ecologies*, eds. Laura Stevens, Peta Tait, and Denise Varney (Cham: Palgrave, 2018), 98.
12 Virgil, *Virgil's Aeneid*, trans. John Dryden (London: Penguin, 1997), book 6, lines 14–15.
13 Shelley, 3.
14 Ibid.
15 Timothy Ruppert, "Time and the Sibyl in Mary Shelley's *The Last Man*," *Studies in the Novel* 41, no. 2 (2009): 146.
16 Mary Wollstonecraft, "The Cave of Fancy," in *The Works of Mary Wollstonecraft*, vol. 1, eds. Janet Todd and Marilyn Butler (London: Pickering & Chatto, 1986), 192.
17 Described in the autobiographical *Mary: A Fiction* as a place "where human foot seldom trod." In her Scandinavian *Letters*, Wollstonecraft describes herself imaginatively inhabiting caves:

> I should rather chuse, did it admit of a choice, to sleep in some of the caves of these rocks; for I am become better reconciled to them since I climbed their craggy sides, last night, listening to the finest echoes I ever heard.

See Mary Wollstonecraft, *Mary, A Fiction and the Wrongs of Women, or Maria*, ed. Michelle Faubert (Peterborough: Broadview, 2012), 88; and *Letters Written During a Short Residence in Sweden, Norway, and Denmark* (Oxford: Oxford University Press, 2009), 106.
18 A comet visible around the time of Shelley's birth caused her to attach to it a particular significance.

19 Wollstonecraft, "The Cave of Fancy," 192–193.
20 It is also worth noting here that Wollstonecraft repeatedly used disease metaphor to describe France before the Revolution. She describes, for example, in *The Vindication of the Rights of Women*, the "baneful lurking gangrene ... spread by luxury and superstition," aligning plague metaphor with conspicuous consumption. See Mary Wollstonecraft, *The Vindication of the Rights of Women*, in *The Works of Mary Wollstonecraft*, vol. 5, ed. Janet Todd and Marilyn Butler (London: Pickering and Chatto, 1989), 87.
21 The figure of an approaching Deluge also famously appears in Book Five of Wordsworth's *The Prelude*.
22 William Godwin, *Memoirs of the Author of the Vindication of the Rights of Women*, eds. Gina Luria Walker and Pamela Clemit (Peterborough: Broadview, 2001), 113.
23 David J. Griffiths, "Endogenous Retroviruses in the Human Genome Sequence," *Genome Biology* 2, no. 6 (2001): no page.
24 Ibid.
25 According to Rote, Chakrabarti, and Stetzer, "the principal proposed roles for HERV Env proteins are mediation of intercellular fusion and suppression of maternal immune response against the placenta." See Rote, N.S., S. Chakrabarti, and B.P. Stetzer, "The Role of Endogenous Retroviruses in Trophoblast Differentiation and Placental Development," *Placenta* 25 (2004): 673.
26 Mary Wollstonecraft, *Letters Written During a Short Residence in Sweden, Norway, and Denmark* (Oxford: Oxford University Press, 2009), 331.

References

Gibb, Rory, et al. "Zoonotic Host Diversity Increases in Human-Dominated Ecosystems." *Nature* 584 (2020): 398–402.
Godwin, William. *Memoirs of the Author of the Vindication of the Rights of Women*. Edited by Gina Luria Walker and Pamela Clemit. Peterborough: Broadview, 2001.
Griffiths, David J. "Endogenous Retroviruses in the Human Genome Sequence." *Genome Biology* 2, no. 6 (2001): no page.
Haraway, Donna. *Manifestly Haraway*. Minneapolis: University of Minnesota Press, 2016.
Marx, Karl. *Economic and Philosophical Manuscripts of 1844*. Translated by Martin Milligan. Amherst: Prometheus Books, 1988.
Ottum, Lisa. "The 'Vast Prison' of the World: Counter Anthropocenes in the Works of Mary Shelley." In *Gendered Ecologies: New Materialist Interpretations of Women Writers in the Long Nineteenth Century*. Edited by Dewey H. Hall and Jillmarie Murphy. Clemson: Clemson University Press, 2020. 23–40.
Plumwood, Val. "Ecofeminist Analysis and the Culture of Ecological Denial." In *Feminist Ecologies: Changing Environments in the Anthropocene*. Edited by Lara Stevens, Peta Tait, and Denise Varney. Cham: Palgrave, 2018. 97–112.
Rote, N.S., S. Chakrabarti, and B.P. Stetzer. "The Role of Endogenous Retroviruses in Trophoblast Differentiation and Placental Development." *Placenta* 25 (2004): 673–683.
Ruppert, Timothy. "Time and the Sibyl in Mary Shelley's *The Last Man*." *Studies in the Novel* 41, no. 2 (2009): 141–156.
Shelley, Mary. *The Last Man*. Peterborough: Broadview, 1996.
Virgil. *Virgil's Aeneid*. Translated by John Dryden. London: Penguin, 1997.
Wollstonecraft, Mary. *Letters Written During a Short Residence in Sweden, Norway, and Denmark*. Oxford: Oxford University Press, 2009.

———. *Mary, a Fiction and the Wrongs of Women, or Maria*. Edited by Michelle Faubert. Peterborough: Broadview, 2012.

———. "The Cave of Fancy." In *The Works of Mary Wollstonecraft*. Vol. 1. Edited by Janet Todd and Marilyn Butler. London: Pickering and Chatto, 1986. 185–206.

———. *The Vindication of the Rights of Women*. In *The Works of Mary Wollstonecraft*. Vol. 5. Edited by Janet Todd and Marilyn Butler. London: Pickering and Chatto, 1989. 79–266.

Wordsworth, William. "Lines Written in Early Spring." In *Lyrical Ballads: 1798 and 1802*. Edited by Fiona Stafford. Oxford: Oxford University Press, 2013. 51.

9
HENRY DAVID THOREAU
A New Anthropocenic Persona

Robert Klevay

For contemporary readers working with Anthropocene scholarship, literary voices who were once seen as straightforward inspirations for environmental advocacy and preservation can be found wanting. Even a work as important as Henry David Thoreau's *Walden* (1854) can fail to reach the high expectations of this critical field. Thoreau's work could be seen as too positive in its view of humanity's relationship with nature to be read without critical commentary, especially in an era where nature as something "wild" has all but vanished—and the end of nature as a sustaining source for life on Earth can seem within reach. Thoreau was in many ways a conventionally romantic thinker who loved to dramatize the supposed "Order of Nature" beneath any threatening disorder. In *Walden*, as well as Thoreau's earlier book, *A Week on the Concord and Merrimack Rivers* (1849), the conception of a world in which nature is entirely overwhelmed by humanity's actions can seem beyond the author's imagination, as the transcendentalist frequently portrays nature as having the ability to outwait (or outwit) humanity.

However, recent scholarship treating Thoreau through the lenses of canon reassessment, the material sciences, and the Anthropocene has increasingly turned to the more scientifically focused and less commonly taught works from the close of his career, including finished lectures like "The Succession of Forest Trees" (1860) and "Wild Apples" (1862), incomplete manuscripts like his late natural history texts "The Dispersion of Seeds" and "Wild Fruits" (edited and finally published in 1993 by Brad Dean after over a century of neglect), and even his meticulous journals of natural data connected to his hometown of Concord, Massachusetts, in order to temper this strain of optimism in Thoreau's most famous self-representation. Thoreau's later passions for mapping, cataloguing, and interacting with material objects that straddle the natural and human worlds have

DOI: 10.4324/9781003095347-12

uncovered a writerly persona more useful to Anthropocene scholarship than the seemingly overconfident philosophical voice of *Walden*. Furthermore, reading this more materialistic and meticulous later voice back into *Walden* can uncover a less frequently stressed skepticism about humanity's designs on nature that balances Thoreau's more unworldly transcendental effusions and potentially makes the texts more palatable to a skeptical generation of environmentalist readers.

The "Anthropocene" summons up an explicit vision of environmental disasters attributed to human actions that began with the Industrial Revolution. It also emphasizes that we now live within a natural world that is utterly inextricable from past and continuing changes wrought by human beings: human influences have irrevocably changed nature, and accepting this is an important part of how humanity should approach the crises caused by climate change. Human beings are not somehow detached or removed from the natural world but are now, and always have been, imbedded in it and the changes that they have brought. Human dwellings, objects, and industrial processes are just as much a part of nature as flora, fauna, and geographical features—and the impact of the former on the latter is evident even as far as the geological record itself is concerned.

In a first glance at his two most familiar and commonly read books, *A Week on the Concord and Merrimack Rivers* and *Walden*, Thoreau seemingly cannot conceive of a world in which nature is entirely overwhelmed by humanity. At times, he also implies that Nature is a force that is sublimely invulnerable to any human violence at all. Humanity may occasionally change nature, but its hold on control only seems desperately tenuous from Thoreau's early romantic, transcendental perspective. For example, in the Saturday chapter early in *A Week on the Concord and Merrimack Rivers*, he writes with some concern about how recently introduced industrial and commercial changes to the Concord River have impacted its fish:

> Salmon, Shad, and Alewives were formerly abundant here, and taken in weirs by the Indians, who taught this method to the whites, by whom they were used as food and as manure, until the dam, and afterward the canal at Billerica, and the factories at Lowell, put an end to their migrations hitherward; though it is thought that a few more enterprising shad may still occasionally be seen in this part of the river. It is said, to account for the destruction of the fishery, that those who at that time represented the interests of the fishermen and the fishes, remembering between what dates they were accustomed to take the grown shad, stipulated, that the dams should be left open for that season only, and the fry, which go down a month later, were consequently stopped and destroyed by myriads. Others say that the fish-ways were not properly constructed.[1]

He is aware that the fishes' disappearance was caused by human beings by one mistake or another—either a misconception about seasonal timing or a design flaw in the dams' "fish-ways." And yet, he goes on to note:

> Perchance, after a few thousands of years, if the fishes will be patient, and pass their summers elsewhere, meanwhile, nature will have levelled the Billerica dam, and the Lowell factories, and the Grass-ground River run clear again, to be explored by new migratory shoals, even as far as the Hopkinton pond and Westborough swamp.[2]

He has quite a serene confidence that Nature's dominion will outlast that of human beings—Nature only has to bide its time until the works of humanity pass away. But it isn't the case that those fish can simply find a place to wait for human civilization to crumble. How differently those of us who live in the long wake of the Industrial Revolution see things from someone experiencing only its beginnings!

Thoreau betrays a different serenity in the face of the destruction when he celebrates death as a natural necessity in *Walden*'s penultimate chapter, "Spring":

> I love to see that Nature is so rife with life that myriads can be afforded to be sacrificed and suffered to prey on one another; that tender organizations can be so serenely squashed out of existence like pulp,—tadpoles which herons gobble up, and tortoises and toads run over in the road; and that sometimes it has rained flesh and blood! With the liability to accident, we must see how little account is to be made of it. The impression made on a wise man is that of universal innocence. Poison is not poisonous after all, nor are any wounds fatal. Compassion is a very untenable ground. It must be expeditious. Its pleadings will not bear to be stereotyped.[3]

The fact that Thoreau celebrates how nature is destructive within itself—not only allowing animals to eat one another for food but also encouraging them to reproduce to the point that accidental "roadkill" is no real loss—suggests not just that violence is "innocence" within the natural world but also could present an argument that human beings' own violence and over-reproduction are "natural" rather than harmful. Is this poison not poisonous, after all, from Thoreau's perspective? How can one argue for the preservation of the natural world from humanity if one doesn't acknowledge that it can be harmed in the first place? Or, even worse, that because animals eat one another and die all the time that "compassion" itself is open to question? Thoreau is welding the natural world to his own distrust of philanthropy as portrayed in the book's first chapter here:

> I do not value chiefly a man's uprightness and benevolence, which are, as it were his stem and leaves. Those plants of whose greenness withered we make herb tea for the sick, serve but a humble use, and are most often employed by quacks.[4]

Surely it is significant that this most "bloody" passage in *Walden* is meant only to show that life will ultimately triumph—we're far away from an apocalyptic vision that might be inspired by the Anthropocene here. As environmental activist Bill McKibben pithily writes, though Thoreau "could perhaps foresee the ruination that greed might cause ... he had no inkling we could damage the ozone or change the very climate with our great consumer flatulence."[5]

Perhaps for these reasons, Thoreau scholars (who tend to be, unsurprisingly, quite aware of contemporary ecocriticism and environmental science) are increasingly drawn to Thoreau's later, unfinished natural history works. Here, as Rochelle Johnson has argued, he seems interested in exploring nature as matter rather than as a metaphor for a human spiritual experiences, a celebration of the material that Johnson feels is even less common in his mentor Ralph Waldo Emerson's work than in Thoreau's.[6] Juliana Chow also points out how these later natural history writings serve as models for Anthropocene scholars who are interested in uncovering local and experiential changes brought about by the era in a more "bottom up way" than the frequently "top down" methods of academic literary theory.[7] Chow could not base her own project on *A Week* and *Walden* because they participate in the same kind of "top down" theoretical thinking in pushing their own transcendental ideas (and what Johnson might identify as an overwhelming spiritual metaphor shutting out actual, material nature) that she feels scholars of the Anthropocene should be wary of in their own work. Importantly, when looking at the history of how Thoreau has been used as an aspirational figure for those concerned with climate change, Scott Hess has noted how Thoreau scholars "have recently emphasized his deep lifelong implication in complex networks of social and economic relationship, even during his time at Walden."[8] Aware of the problems of how individual changes in behavior simply are not drastic enough to have an effect given the scale of the crisis (and often are not put into practice anyway), Hess calls for more climate activists and scholars to pursue this new critical emphasis. Doing so reveals a Thoreau who would "realize that climate change is not something he could simply withdraw from or address as an isolated individual, but [rather] the effect of complex and interdependent global systems, at once social, material, and ecological." This new Anthropocenic Thoreau would acknowledge the need for "wide-ranging and decisive collective political action."[9]

While I hope that Thoreau's earlier, complete, and perhaps overgeneralizing works will always receive their due in English courses, a teacher using an Anthropocenic approach might start a unit on Thoreau with less frequently taught texts like "The Succession of Forest Trees" and "Wild Apples" in order to emphasize Thoreau at his least abstract, theoretical, and transcendental. "The Succession of Forest Trees" poses an answer to a question that Thoreau had discussed with the members of the Middlesex Massachusetts Agricultural Society to whom the speech was first addressed: "how it happened that when a pine wood was cut down an oak one sprang up, and *vice versa*."[10] His answer involves an early account of forest succession that traces how seeds spread in clear patterns to make the cycle of pine and oak growth hold true—it is a much more proto-ecological than romantic view of nature, drawing closely on his own observations that were also present in his unfinished "Dispersion of Seeds" and "Wild Fruits" manuscripts.[11]

The essay "Wild Apples," on the other hand, starts with a summary of historical and mythological appearances of apples that might not seem out of place in an earlier text like *Walden*:

> The apple-tree has been celebrated by the Hebrews, Greeks, Romans, and Scandinavians. Some have thought that the first human pair were tempted by its fruit. Goddesses are fabled to have contended for it, dragons were set to watch it, and heroes were employed to pluck it.[12]

But as the essay progresses beyond its early paragraphs, Thoreau leaves behind myth for the physical world, which is a reversal of the transcendentalist trajectory of his more famous writing. He seeks to chart the varieties of the humble wild apple with its rude appearance instead of a more transcendental or ideal fruit. He goes so far as to note even the "gnarliest [wild apple] will have some redeeming traits even to the eye."[13] He closes the essay with an invocation of the consequences that the widespread cultivation of apples is likely to have for its wild varieties:

> Now that they have grafted trees, and pay a price for them, they collect them into a plat by their houses, and fence them in,—and the end of it all will be that we shall be compelled to look for our apples in a barrel.[14]

Thoreau wistfully acknowledges here that human interference with nature, however well intended, may put an end to wild apples for good, leaving the cultivated fruit in commercial barrels as the *only* apples left. As the cultivated apples enmesh themselves more deeply into the humanity surrounding them, the definition of the fruit and afterwards its natural manifestation will irrevocably change.

The same two texts could also be used to follow Chow's advice to emphasize the space between the different types of natural realizations and idealizations that Thoreau presents for his readers.[15] Indeed, given that Thoreau's records of "iceouts" on Walden Pond, flowering times in the spring, and the return of birds to Concord have inspired actual studies showing the local effects of climate change where he once lived, perhaps it makes sense to start with the aspects of Thoreau that are closest to the desperation of our current moment and then to work back to the more spiritual and transcendental viewpoint that he held earlier in this life.[16] As recently as the Spring of 2020, Primack and Caitlin McDonough MacKenzie announced that Thoreau's meticulous cataloguing of natural phenomena has allowed them to show that "ecological mismatches between wildflowers and trees ... leads to reduced carbon budgets in spring wildflowers," that "plants in northern Maine may be responding to climate change less dramatically than in

Concord [although] migratory birds in the north are similarly decoupled from local plant phrenology," and also to explore "how the loss of wildflower species in Concord compares to changes in the floras of other areas of the northeastern United States."[17]

The Anthropocene concept serves as a reminder to treat Thoreau's early works, in all their humorous irony and serious play, as literary works recreating the world in their own imperfect image—a process that invariably leaves out many other perspectives to focus on the "I" that Thoreau acknowledged we are always speaking through.[18] It opens up a new persona in Thoreau's work that steps away from this famous romantic "I," allowing us to more accurately address the feelings and challenges of our current environmental moment. Thoreau's later emphasis on physical materialism, ecological connectedness, and the implications of humanity and its actions within the natural world are the only notes to play in our current and conflicted world. Hess is right that asking how Thoreau would respond to climate change is "ultimately a misleading and pyhrric question," but he's also right when he shows that we can embrace a new persona for Thoreau that uses the latest in transcendentalist scholarship to make him more useful to the cause of the Anthropocene.[19]

Notes

1 Henry David Thoreau, *A Week on the Concord and Merrimack Rivers, Walden, the Maine Woods, Cape Cod*, ed. Robert F. Sayre (New York: Library of America, 1985), 28–29.
2 Thoreau, *Week*, 29.
3 Thoreau, *Walden*, 576.
4 Ibid., 383.
5 Bill McKibben, "What Would Thoreau Think of Climate Change?" *The New Republic* (12 July 2017).
6 Rochelle Johnson, *Passions for Nature: Nineteenth Century America's Aesthetics of Alienation* (Athens: University of Georgia Press, 2009), 3.
7 Juliana Chow, "Partial Readings: Thoreau's Studies as Natural History's Casualties," in *Anthropocene Reading: Literary History in Geologic Times*, ed. Tobias Menely and Jesse Oak Taylor (University Park: Pennsylvania State University Press, 2017), 129.
8 Scott Hess, "Thoreau's Legacy for Climate Change," *The Concord Saunterer* 28 (2020): 156.
9 Ibid., 175.
10 Henry David Thoreau, *Collected Essays and Poems*, ed. Elizabeth Hall Witherell (New York: Library of America, 2001), 430.
11 Henry David Thoreau, *Faith in a Seed: The Dispersion of Seeds and Other Late Natural History Writings*, ed. Bradley P. Dean (Washington, DC: Island Press, 1993).
12 Thoreau, *Collected Essays*, 44.
13 Ibid., 461.
14 Ibid., 467.
15 Chow, 129.

16 Richard B. Primack, *Walden Warming: Climate Change Comes to Thoreau's Woods* (Chicago: University of Chicago Press, 2014), 5.
17 Richard B. Primack and Caitlin McDonough MacKenzie "Thoreau's Continuing Contributions to Climate Change Science," *Thoreau Society Bulletin* 309 (2020): 1.
18 Thoreau, *Walden*, 325.
19 Hess, 156.

References

Chow, Juliana. "Partial Readings: Thoreau's Studies as Natural History's Casualties." In *Anthropocene Reading: Literary History in Geologic Times*. Edited by Tobias Menely and Jesse Oak Taylor. University Park: Pennsylvania State University Press, 2017. 117–131.

Hess, Scott "Thoreau's Legacy for Climate Change." *The Concord Saunterer* 28 (2020): 151–184.

Johnson, Rochelle. *Passions for Nature: Nineteenth Century America's Aesthetics of Alienation*. Athens: University of Georgia Press, 2009.

McKibben, Bill. "What Would Thoreau Think of Climate Change?" *The New Republic*, 12 July 2017.

Primack, Richard B. *Walden Warming: Climate Change Comes to Thoreau's Woods*. Chicago: University of Chicago Press, 2014.

Primack, Richard B., and Caitlin McDonough MacKenzie. "Thoreau's Continuing Contributions to Climate Change Science." *Thoreau Society Bulletin* 309 (2020): 1–4.

Thoreau, Henry David. *A Week on the Concord and Merrimack Rivers, Walden, the Maine Woods, Cape Cod*. Edited by Robert F. Sayre. New York: Library of America, 1985.

———. *Collected Essays and Poems*. Edited by Elizabeth Hall Witherell. New York: Library of America, 2001.

———. *Faith in a Seed: The Dispersion of Seeds and Other Late Natural History Writings*. Edited by Bradley P. Dean. Washington, DC: Island Press, 1993.

10

IT'S THE END OF THE WORLD

Can We Know It?

Tobias Wilson-Bates

In *The Birth of the Anthropocene* (2016), Jeremy Davies argues that deploying the term "Anthropocene … provides both the motive and means of taking a very, very long view of the environmental crisis."[1] However, as he details throughout his study, the term contends with political, scientific, and ethical discourses that make it difficult to settle on a single accepted use or definition. Another stumbling block to the dissemination and acceptance of the term is that it also competes with a set of narratives that occupy the conceptual space it seeks to fill. Gillian Beer writes that early theory has a tendency toward the fictive: "The awkwardness of fit between the natural world as it is currently perceived and as it is hypothetically imagined holds the theory itself for a time within a provisional scope akin to that of fiction."[2] In theorizing the Anthropocene, scholars have drawn repeatedly on the tool of fictional narrative to communicate fully the scale and stakes of the topic, but those stories also come with their own narrative histories and complications. The clearest expression of this narrative activity is the time machine, a story trope that sharpened a long-standing tradition of artistic explorations attempting to imagine both the world without humans and also how to capture conceptually the cumulative effect of all human existence. In order to engage with this additional dimension of Anthropocenic discourse, scholars like Davies must recognize that they themselves have also grounded their thinking in a kind of time travel fantasy.

Paul Crutzen, one of the foundational thinkers of the Anthropocene, describes the concept as already existing in the late nineteenth century, when Italian geologist Antonio Stoppani coined the expression "Anthropozoic era."[3] Crutzen's interest in historicizing the idea attempts to place it outside of the current debates about the Anthropocene's place among a slew of similar but separate terms that seek to contextualize the unique environmental circumstances of the industrial

DOI: 10.4324/9781003095347-13

era. Davies also draws on Stoppani in describing how the Italian's central thought experiment—an alien race arriving at the planet in a distant post-human future—compounds Crutzen's initial claim: "Let us admit," Stoppani writes, "though eccentric it might be, the supposition that a strange intelligence should come to study the Earth in a day when human progeny ... has disappeared completely."[4] At stake in this speculative fiction is the possibility that considering whether the Anthropocene is indeed a new geological period may not be fully understood without an extra-human actor to perceive it as such. What the thought experiment illustrates is the difficulty of conceptualizing an expanse of time necessarily devoid of human perception but nonetheless still possessing an observational consciousness that does not render the entire discussion moot. While Crutzen and Davies both allow that the particular parameters of the period allow for some debate, the objective existence of the future geological record offers present thinkers a firm foundation in theorizing the Anthropocene.

Historian Dipesh Chakrabarty approaches the Anthropocene as a historical conundrum that collapses distinctions between "natural" and "human" history, refiguring concepts like globalism and capital as necessarily integrated into the web of geological and biological systems that constitute natural history.[5] In initiating his study, Chakrabarty draws on Alan Weisman's *The World Without Us* (2007), an experimental text that seeks to imagine what enduring mark would be left on the universe should humans suddenly go extinct. While shifting the disciplinary conversation from geology to history, Chakrabarty nonetheless grounds his exploration in essentially the same story.

Stoppani and Weisman are hardly alone in their fantasies of a world after the fall of humanity. In fact, beginning in the nineteenth century, there has been a consistent stream of speculative stories that forecast the end of current political regimes or all of civilization more generally. Mary Shelley's *The Last Man* (1826), Edward Bellamy's *Looking Backward: 2000–1887* (1888), William Morris' *News from Nowhere* (1890), and M.P. Shiel's *The Purple Cloud* (1901), just to name a few early examples, all perform imaginative leaps into hypothetical futures. Despite this proliferation of stories that navigate time and humankind as pivotal concepts, none have had quite the cultural footprint of H.G. Wells' first novel, *The Time Machine* (1895). Among the many reasons the story has remained in the cultural imaginary for so long is that it does not simply transport its central protagonist to the future but also theorizes heavily about the conceptual stakes of reimagining humans in relationship to objective scientific time as a means of treating deep time as a narrative concept.

The eighteenth and nineteenth centuries were witness to a proliferation of theories attempting to historicize human existence within the context of expanding time frames and scientific expertise.[6] Charles Darwin's *Origin of Species* (1859) accelerated this tendency to rethink the present moment as part of unimaginably vast time scales. As a scholarship student learning science at the Normal School in South Kensington, Wells studied directly under Thomas Henry Huxley, known as Darwin's bulldog, and became enamored of the idea of scientific objectivity capable of thinking a world beyond the human world, a concept that would characterize much of his work. Alongside Darwin, William Thompson (later Lord Kelvin) sparked a fascination with the passage of time in physics by theorizing that since all mechanical systems lose energy over time, the universe itself must be running down. In *The Unseen Universe* (1875), prominent thermodynamic scientists Peter Guthrie Tait and Balfour Stewart fashioned a natural-theological vision from this premise, imagining a universe dying and reborn via God's grace. As a student, teacher, and writer of science during this period, Wells was at the forefront of a cultural awakening to the narrative possibilities of a newly expansive sense of Time.

The Time Machine's engagement with Time is partitioned into four different machine transportations. The initial mechanical experiment with temporality actually occurs before the story itself even begins. Wells subtitles his story "An Invention," and this subtle choice signals his larger project of reimagining narrative as itself a form of mechanistic inquiry. All of the machines that come after the subtitle are wheels within wheels of that initial temporal manipulation. Every claim to objective knowledge or theoretical reality, many of which were grounded in prevailing hypotheses of the period, is a production of narrative play even as the story itself proposes the opposite. After the Time Traveler's explanation of time as a fourth spatial dimension, the nameless narrator observes "a glittering metallic framework, scarcely larger than a small clock," that turns out to be a time machine prototype.[7] In short order, this clockwork device is activated and disappears as a proof of concept. As readers, we must pause to consider where the device potentially goes in such a moment. Backward, forward, upward, inside, beyond, through, or any other preposition seems inadequate to communicate what happens to the prototype. Without coordinates, it does not arrive at another moment in time but instead seems to become a new form of narrative temporality. A proof of concept that exists outside of the narrative as soon as its existence is initiated. Like Stoppani and Weisman's post-human perspectives, the reader is offered a non-human engagement with time. This initial mechanistic trigger splits Wells' novel from every speculative fiction that came before and most that have come since in that no consciousness, human or otherwise, is required for the machine to travel through time. The human becomes dispensable, little more than a recording device to give the reader temporary access to deep time.

While the third journey through time involving the Morlocks is generally how the story is reproduced in film and popular culture, the fourth and final journey reconnects Wells' work to the concept of deep time and offers a complex parallel to modern attempts to think the Anthropocene. Despite its popularity, the third journey is largely unremarkable as an iteration of the Incredible Journey genre that has existed in various oral and written traditions as far back as stories themselves have existed. However, the fourth journey is much more illustrative of Wells' engagements with deep time. After spinning through thousands of years and having a near-fatal encounter with giant crabs, the Traveler finds himself at the entropic conclusion of life in the universe:

> At last, more than thirty million years hence, the huge red-hot dome of the sun had come to obscure nearly a tenth part of the darkling heavens ... I saw the black central shadow of the eclipse sweeping towards me. In another moment the pale stars alone were visible. All else was rayless obscurity. The sky was absolutely black.[8]

Wells drew this vignette from the new science of energy that was emerging in the nineteenth century. A group of British natural philosophers (James Prescott Joule, William Thompson, Macquorn Rankine, James Clerk Maxwell, and Peter Guthrie Tait) revised the older term, energy, "to supersede the older notion of mechanical force and, in the process, to secure broader cultural authority."[9] Perhaps the most culturally resonant products of this new science were the laws of thermodynamics, universal principles concerning the tendencies of matter and energy. William Thompson's paper "On the Universal Tendency in Nature to the Dissipation of Mechanical Energy" (1852) was crucial to this era of classical thermodynamics. In his work, Thompson predicted that in something like thirty million years (clearly the influence for Wells), "the solar system is fated to exhaust its energic resources and enter into a terminal state of heat death."[10] The Time Traveler, witness to the logical conclusion of the second law of thermodynamics, arrives at a "death." Thompson's contention that the universe would arrive at a state of heat death personifies the physical process and couches the arc of universal expansion as a lifespan. The Time Traveler does not invest deep time with a story, so much as arrive to verify a story that had already been put into place to understand and disseminate the concept. When the Traveler (who never bears a proper name) returns to the present perspective of the narrator, it is only to report his journeys before immediately beginning to lose his memory of the events he has just related. Far from delegitimizing his experiences, the Traveler's sudden loss of memory seems to further remove him from the particular domain of his consciousness. He has acted as another machine, merely recording and reporting the "truth" of deep time to the assembled spectators. George Levine describes this impulse as an intellectual enterprise that displaced church and religion in favor of a scientific institution that depended upon a proclaimed willingness "to suffer the consequences of finding out that the world is not only not made for us, but that it may well be without intention, meaning, or direction."[11] Scientific suffering like the Traveler's sacrifice of his own memory was imagined as a validation of real scientific knowledge. The Traveler's desperate return to the machine models a form of engagement not bent on self-benefit but on a self-annihilating search for truth.

Alongside early conversations about the thermodynamic implications of deep time, the English public, and the quickly globalizing world in general during the period, were also participating in debates concerning Time that had immediate environmental and economic impacts. Wells had been working on the time machine idea since at least 1888, when he began publishing an earlier version titled "The Chronic Argonauts," making his publication very nearly contemporaneous with The International Meridian Conference of 1884. The Conference's central tension was between England and the United States, who were determined to locate the Prime Meridian at Greenwich, and France, whose delegates argued that the Meridian must be located at a neutral site without clear national ownership or identity. The French delegates sought aid, not from another world power, but from the world powers that would inevitably succeed the industrial age in a future world:

> When France, at the end of the last century, instituted the metre, did she proceed thus? Did she, as a measure of economy and in order to change nothing in her customs, propose to the world the "Pied de Roi" as a unit of measure? You know the facts. The truth is, everything with us was overthrown—both the established methods and instruments for measurement; and the measure adopted being proportioned only to the dimensions of the earth, is so entirely detached from everything French that in future centuries the traveller who may search the ruins of our cities may inquire what people invented the metrical measure that chance may bring under his eyes. Permit me to say that it is thus a reform should be made and becomes acceptable. It is by setting the example of self-sacrifice; it is by complete self-effacement in any undertaking, that opposition is disarmed and true love of progress is proved.[12]

The speculative forecast of a postapocalyptic traveler discovering the remains of modern civilization is the delegate's premier description of French neutrality. Beyond any agreements formed by the participants in the conference, this repeating pattern of the subject being removed from a position of desire or action is the central product of the discussion. Such a removal also speaks to what is lost to the traveler of the future—namely, an ability to historicize a future archaeology. In this fantasy, the postapocalyptic individual is faced with an object that bears no identification to explain its logic, which is purely relational to the naturally occurring structure of the planet. Not only has civilization forgotten the industrial era, but the scientific logics of the period, in the ideal, foreclose the possibility of any such remembrance. In the place of a historical context or national paradigm is a system that services economics and science specifically by erasing all of the human except for the human impulse to construct a system that erases it.

The International Meridian Conference did not yield any major shifts in national policy. The agreements signed by most of the nations attending were ceremonial and nonbinding. What the conference did produce was a story about consensus that proved useful after World War I when many telecommunications were part of a push toward further standardization. French arguments about neutrality proved less convincing than the combined pressure of English/American imperial power and the received notion that "something" had been agreed on.

Wells' *Time Machine* is a foundational work of the many scientific fantasies of a world without humans but still perceived by an alien intelligence or personified as a cosmic lifecycle. The novel established a mode of conceiving the Anthropocene and coming to terms with the complicated narrative propositions that make such a conception difficult. As scholars negotiate the particular historical parameters, or atmospheric and geologic markers, that should define the Anthropocene, they should also consider what stories each choice conveys about Time and the Human.

Notes

1 Jeremy Davies, *The Birth of the Anthropocene* (Oakland: University of California Press, 2016), 2.
2 Gillian Beer, *Darwin's Plots: Evolutionary Narrative in Darwin, George Eliot and Nineteenth-Century Fiction* (Cambridge: Cambridge University Press, 2000), 1.
3 Paul J. Crutzen, "Geology of Mankind," *Nature* 415 (2002): 23.
4 Qtd. in Davies, 77.
5 See Dipesh Chakrabarty, "The Climate of History: Four Theses," *Critical Inquiry* 35, no. 2 (2009): 197–222.
6 See Efram Sera-Shriar, *Historicizing Humans: Deep Time, Evolution, and Race in Nineteenth-Century British Sciences* (Pittsburgh: University of Pittsburgh Press, 2018).
7 H.G. Wells, *The Time Machine: An Invention* (Peterborough: Broadview Press, 2001), 65.
8 Ibid., 147–148.
9 Bruce Clarke, *Energy Forms: Allegory and Science in the Era of Classical Thermodynamics* (Ann Arbor: University of Michigan Press, 2001), 18.
10 Ibid., 3.
11 George Levine, *Dying to Know: Scientific Epistemology and Narrative in Victorian England* (Chicago: University of Chicago Press, 2002), 4.
12 *International Conference Held at Washington for the Purpose of Fixing a Prime Meridian and a Universal Day* (Washington, DC: Gibson Bros., 1884), 29.

References

Beer, Gillian. *Darwin's Plots: Evolutionary Narrative in Darwin, George Eliot and Nineteenth-Century Fiction*. Cambridge: Cambridge University Press, 2000.
Chakrabarty, Dipesh. "The Climate of History: Four Theses." *Critical Inquiry* 35, no. 2 (2009): 197–222.
Clarke, Bruce. *Energy Forms: Allegory and Science in the Era of Classical Thermodynamics*. Ann Arbor: University of Michigan Press, 2001.
Crutzen, Paul J. "Geology of Mankind." *Nature* 415 (2002): 23.
Davies, Jeremy. *The Birth of the Anthropocene*. Oakland: University of California Press, 2016.
International Conference Held at Washington for the Purpose of Fixing a Prime Meridian and a Universal Day. Washington, DC: Gibson Bros., 1884.

Levine, George. *Dying to Know: Scientific Epistemology and Narrative in Victorian England.* Chicago: University of Chicago Press, 2002.

Sera-Shriar, Efram. *Historicizing Humans: Deep Time, Evolution, and Race in Nineteenth-Century British Sciences.* Pittsburgh: University of Pittsburgh Press, 2018.

Wells, H.G. *The Time Machine: An Invention.* Peterborough: Broadview Press, 2001.

11

ORLANDO IN THE ANTHROPOCENE

Climate Change and Changing Times

Naomi Perez

In her novel *Orlando* (1928), Virginia Woolf challenges commonly held beliefs about gender, sexuality, and literary form, all while satirizing English history and culture. The novel's titular character lives a supernatural life spanning nearly 400 years, from the English Renaissance to the early twentieth century, first as a man, and then as a woman—fantastical plot points that don't really cause much of a stir in the world of the novel. The novel is also deeply personal: the character of Orlando is based on Woolf's lover and fellow writer Vita Sackville-West, whose son wrote that *Orlando* was "the longest and most charming love letter in literature."[1] Scholars have written extensively on these topics, and the novel is often taught in classrooms as a feminist classic.

But there's much more to *Orlando* than gender and sexuality; it's also a novel about climate. Woolf provides an early history of climate change through her novel, in part as a symbolic tool to reflect England's changing social, political, and cultural landscapes, as well as to represent the physical effects of climate change in the wake of the British Industrial Revolution. In fact, *Orlando* is structured around three major climatic events: the Great Frost of 1608, the Industrial Revolution, and World War I, which coincided with globalized industrialization. By foregrounding the novel's engagements with climate, a slightly different narrative emerges: Orlando lives through the birth of the Anthropocene, and Woolf shows how this new geological epoch upends everything, from climate to gender to architecture.

In his 2002 essay "Geology of Mankind," Paul Crutzen proposed that the Anthropocene began with the Industrial Revolution, citing James Watt's patent of the steam engine in 1784 as a possible start date. While he and other scientists have since put their support behind a twentieth-century start date, the Industrial Revolution remains a key event in many histories of the Anthropocene.[2] The

DOI: 10.4324/9781003095347-14

rapid development of industrial technology, agricultural reforms, and mechanized travel forever changed the landscapes of England and Earth itself. Industrial capitalism, formed in eighteenth-century Britain, would eventually spread throughout the world, creating the globalized world of the twenty-first century in which we live today. Nineteenth-century scientists and writers were keenly aware of these changes: climatologists, geologists, and poets collaborated in documenting and theorizing what would become known as "global warming" in the twentieth century.[3] Modernist writers such as Woolf continued this tradition, responding to climate change and the subsequent sociocultural changes wrought by the Industrial Revolution.

Woolf's *Orlando*, while not an overtly Anthropocene novel, draws upon an existing body of Victorian climate literature. Numerous industrial poets had traced England's transformation from a largely agrarian nation to an industrial superpower in the nineteenth century. Writers such as John Ruskin and William Delisle Hay described a new England of the nineteenth century defined by smoke, pollution, and demonized mega-factories. In *The Doom of the Great City* (1880), Hay imagines a future London in which residents perished in poisonous smog. In Ruskin's famous lectures on *The Storm-Cloud of the Nineteenth Century* (1884), with which Woolf was quite familiar, Ruskin traces the transformation of England's atmosphere from the 1830s through the 1870s, arguably presenting the first sustained case for what we now call global warming. Only a few years later in 1896, the Swedish chemist Svante Arrhenius proved the link between carbon dioxide emissions and Earth's global temperature.[4]

Woolf draws from this tradition of climate writing in *Orlando*. Importantly, the disruptions caused by climate change, which now typify life in the Anthropocene, relate directly to disruptions in received notions of gender and sexuality. Woolf deconstructs commonly accepted binaries like male/female and human/nature. In this way, *Orlando* can be read as an ecofeminist novel. Ecocritic Greg Garrard explains:

> Deep ecology identifies the anthropocentric dualism humanity/nature as the ultimate source of anti-ecological beliefs and practices, but ecofeminism also blames the androcentric dualism man/woman. The first distinguishes humans from nature on the grounds of some alleged quality such as possession of an immortal soul or rationality, and then assumes that this distinction confers superiority on humans. The second distinguishes men from women ... and then assumes that this distinction confers superiority upon men.[5]

In Woolf's narrative, she ultimately argues that interconnectedness defines the human experience more than separateness. In her play with the ever-shifting nature of gender, as explored in characters like Orlando, Harriet/Harry, and Shel, Woolf breaks down the traditionally reinforced boundaries that were commonly held during the time about what it means to be a man or a woman. She also suggests that our humanity is directly linked to the natural world. Orlando often feels more a part of nature than humanity, and the narrative is regularly interrupted with reflections on the beauty of the landscape. For Garrard and for Woolf, humanity's notion of separateness is tied to anthropogenic change and to a disconnectedness from our true selves and each other. Garrard goes on to claim,

> merely differentiating men from women, humans from nature, or reason from emotion, does not itself constitute problematic anthropo- or androcentrism. Rather, the underlying model of mastery shared by these forms of oppression is based upon alienated differentiation and denied dependency.[6]

That is to say, if humans continue hierarchical thinking based on gender, and continue to see themselves as different from and superior to nonhumans, they will continue to perpetuate the kinds of ecological catastrophe that coincide with the Anthropocene. In order to create a different future—a different Anthropocene—humans must dismantle these models of mastery. Woolf attempts this kind of thinking in *Orlando*, directly challenging divisions of gender—a distinction Woolf depicts as primarily performative—and the separation of humans from the natural world. She creates a narrative that brings the Anthropocene to the forefront, where, over centuries, humankind has become what Dipesh Chakrabarty terms "a geological force."[7] As Orlando moves through time, he/she questions what it means to be a man, then a woman, and, at the same time, reflects on humans' role in a new geological epoch.

In the first chapter of *Orlando*, Woolf details the Great Frost of 1608, when the River Thames in London was completely frozen over for two months. Londoners held the first recorded "frost fair," which became a recurring event when the Thames froze over in subsequent years: a marketplace and carnival were set up on the Thames, and something of a citywide celebration ensued. Yet, Woolf describes the Great Frost as particularly harsh, akin to an ecological disaster:

> The Great Frost was, historians tell us, the most severe that has ever visited these islands. Birds froze mid-air and fell like stones to the ground … The mortality among sheep and cattle was enormous … The severity of the frost was so extraordinary that a kind of petrification sometimes ensued … the solidification of unfortunate wayfarers who had been literally turned to stone where they stood.[8]

The poor suffer greatly, while only the wealthy courtiers and royalty enjoy the fair, cordoned off from the general public. Climate here serves to distinguish the ruling classes from the rest of society. Orlando recalls, "For the frost continued unbroken; the nights were of perfect stillness; the moon and stars blazed with the hard fixity of diamonds, and to the fine music of flute and trumpet the courtiers danced."[9]

While the wealthy dance in this new winter, the poor freeze and perish. But Woolf makes clear that the climate, both cultural and physical, was of a different era:

> The age was the Elizabethan; their morals were not ours; nor their poets; nor their climate; nor their vegetables even. Everything was different. The weather itself, the heat and cold of summer and winter, was, we may believe, of another temper altogether.[10]

Climate, she suggests, is central to a culture's morals, literature, and food. She also suggests climate change here: it's much warmer in twentieth-century England when Woolf is writing the novel. The last frost fair was held in 1814, and it is highly unlikely that the Thames will freeze over again in the next 1,000 years. Woolf emphasizes just how much England's climate has changed over the span of 400 years.

Woolf also uses the Great Frost to introduce one of her many challenges to ideas of gender in her depiction of Orlando's first impressions of Sasha, an androgynous Russian princess with whom he falls deeply in love. Orlando, perplexed, recalls his first meeting of Sasha:

> He called her a melon, a pineapple, an olive tree, an emerald, and a fox in the snow all in the space of three seconds ... When the boy, for alas, a boy it must be—no woman could skate with such speed and vigor—swept almost on tiptoe past him, Orlando was ready to tear his hair with vexation that the person was of his own sex, and thus all embraces were out of the question.[11]

Distinction in gender is complicated and challenged in the same way that distinctions of class are critiqued, all in the backdrop of a changing natural landscape. At the same time, Orlando's tumultuous relationship with Sasha is aligned with the thawing of the Thames, a climatic event which helps to drive the plot forward and mirrors the instability of Orlando's fixed ideas of love and desire. Woolf reflects the interconnectedness between Orlando's romance and the natural world in Orlando's ruminations on Sasha: "he heard the waters flowing and the birds singing; spring broke over the hard wintry landscape; his manhood woke."[12] Sasha's betrayal and departure with her Russian lover on the newly thawed Thames coincides with Orlando's rage, heartbreak, and dismissal from court. Orlando notes:

> In the summer of that disastrous winter which saw the frost, the flood, the deaths of many thousands [a result of the thawing], and the complete downfall of Orlando's hopes ... Orlando retired to his great house in the county and there lived in complete solitude.[13]

Orlando's first questioning of gender and courtly romance are inextricably tied to the natural landscape that he lives in, one that is defined by instability and great climatic change.

The second major climatic event in *Orlando* is the Industrial Revolution, symbolized by what Woolf calls the "great cloud" of the nineteenth century. This great cloud is accompanied by strong winds, dark shadows, dimmed sunlight, and an encroaching muddied and dampened climate. Woolf makes clear that industrialization changes every aspect of life in England, from the construction and layout of cities to the interior design of homes to the nature of human relationships. Moreover, Woolf's image of the "great cloud" is a clear adaptation of Ruskin's storm cloud of the nineteenth century. The similarities between Woolf's description of nineteenth-century England and Ruskin's 1884 lectures are unmistakable.[14] Ruskin writes at length on the new "plague winds" and "plague clouds" of the nineteenth century, so-called because of their ominous appearance and virus-like takeover of the skies throughout the nineteenth century. Here, he links these new clouds directly to industrialization:

> The first time I recognized the clouds brought by the plague-wind as distinct in character was in walking back from Oxford, after a hard day's work, to Abingdon, in the early spring of 1871 … It looks partly as if it were made of poisonous smoke; very possibly it may be: there are at least two hundred furnace chimneys in a square of two miles on every side of me.[15]

Woolf devotes several pages to the great cloud in *Orlando*, emphasizing that it appeared exactly at the turn of the nineteenth century:

> This great cloud which hung, not only over London, but over the whole of the British Isles on the first day of the nineteenth century stayed, or rather, did not stay, for it was buffeted about constantly by blustering gales, long enough to have extraordinary consequences upon those who lived beneath its shadow. A change seemed to have come over the climate of England. Rain fell frequently, but only in fitful gusts, which were no sooner over than they began again. The sun shone, of course, but it was so girt about with clouds and the air was so saturated with water, that its beams were discoloured and purples, oranges, and reds of a dull sort took the place of the more positive landscapes of the eighteenth century.[16]

Similar to her comments on the climate of the Elizabethan era, the lengthy description of the great cloud attributes nearly every cultural change in England to climate change: "Thus, stealthily, and imperceptibly, none marking the exact day or hour of the change, the constitution of England was altered and nobody knew it."[17]

Woolf's adaptation of Ruskin's storm cloud is both satirical and insightful. She reveals how the drastic change in climate resulting from the Industrial Revolution directly affects both the literal climate and the sociocultural climate. On the one hand, with the great cloud comes industrial pollution, altered weather patterns, and a permeating "damp" that depletes the health, alters the diet, and fosters the growth of invasive species on the homes of the English. On the other hand, climate change affects the inward lives of the people. Woolf explains:

> The damp struck within. Men felt the chill in their hearts; the damp in their minds. In a desperate effort to snuggle their feelings into some sort of warmth one subterfuge was tried after another. Love, birth, and death were all swaddled in a variety of fine phrases. The sexes drew further and further apart. No open conversation was tolerated.[18]

As modernity encroaches, so too is ecological decline and cultural distance/disconnect between individuals, especially between men and women.

Yet, in the backdrop of this great cloud, Woolf continues to challenge the male/female binary when Orlando finds her match in Marmaduke Bonthrop Shelmerdine. After centuries of romances and affairs with both men and women, Orlando bemoans the lack of a mate. She begins to consider the benefits of adhering to the expected institution of marriage, which would offer her the traditional helpmeet and protection that a man offers a woman as her husband. But Woolf doesn't quite allow Orlando to succumb to tradition. At first, Orlando is distracted by the beauty of nature while ruminating on marriage. She follows a trail of feathers to a silvery lake, and decides, "I have found my mate ... I am nature's bride ... I shall dream wild dreams. My hands shall wear no wedding rings ... The roots shall twine about them."[19] Shel interrupts this interlude and rescues her from a broken ankle. Their romance is one defined by intensity and mutual admiration, as well as gender fluidity, both of them later exclaiming: "'You're a woman, Shel!' she cried. 'You're a man, Orlando!' he cried."[20] Unsurprisingly, Shel's departure from Orlando's life is reflected in the natural world, in the falling of leaves and a change in the winds. The winds are so strong, their marriage vows could not be heard, confused for "the jaws of death."[21] For Woolf, just as nature is unpredictable and difficult to define, so too is the performance of gender and humans' role in a changing world.

As the novel spills into the twentieth century, Orlando remarks on the ecological decline of London, while also taking note of the isolation and disconnect that seems to define modern English society. Woolf writes, "Behold, meanwhile, the factory chimneys, and their smoke ... The clouds had shrunk to a thin gauze; the sky seemed made of metal ... People were much gayer ... there was a distraction, a desperation."[22] In the wake of global industrialization and the aftereffects of the world's first fully industrialized war, Orlando sees a disconnect between life and technology. She continues to remark on the crowds of people, some in the throes of sadness, some jolly in their excess, but all moving past each other in a hurry to get about their business, with no time to consider each other or the world around them. She tellingly reflects on the prominence of railway trains, airplanes, automobiles, and radios, all modern inventions that seem fantastical:

> The very fabric of life now, she thought as she rose, is magic. In the eighteenth century, we knew how everything was done; but here I rise through the air; I listen to voices in America; I see men flying—but how it's done, I can't even begin to wonder.[23]

Orlando does not recognize the world around her—she was born a man in the Elizabethan era, but now she's a married woman in 1928—in the Anthropocene. She experiences was Glenn Albrecht calls "solastalgia," a particular emotion specific to the Anthropocene: "the lived experience of negative environmental change ... the homesickness you have when you are still at home."[24] What does it feel like when your home is no longer recognizable? Disorienting, terrifying, sorrowful, unreal—all of which Orlando experiences at the end of the novel.

The novel closes with time collapsing on itself in a parallel to the collapse of geological and human histories that characterizes the Anthropocene. Orlando wonders what it all was for, the sociocultural norms, progress, the seeking of fame and success, human relationships:

> She had thought then of the oak tree on its hill, and what has that got to do with this ... An eagle soared above her. The raucous voice of old Rustum, the gypsy croaked in her ears, "What is your antiquity and your race, and your possessions compared with this [i.e., Nature]?"[25]

This question echoes that of Garrard, as well as Woolf's own anxiety and growing uncertainty of the modern Anthropocene age wherein upholding binaries like man/woman and culture/nature were obstacles to enacting meaningful change. Garrard explains that in order to change Earth for the better as both human citizens and geophysical agents, "We need to understand and affirm both otherness and our community with Earth."[26] There is no arguing, according to Woolf, that humanity shapes the climate, and the climate has a hand in shaping and reflecting humankind. A dependence on ideas of separateness and destructive hierarchies between man and woman, humans and nature, can only lead to an isolating disassociation with truth and with the world around us—a natural world that may continue to change for the worse if we refuse to see that we are a part of it and it with us.

Notes

1. Nigel Nicolson, *Portrait of a Marriage* (New York: Athenaeum, 1973), 202.
2. See Paul J. Crutzen, "Geology of Mankind," *Nature* 415 (2002): 23.
3. See, for example, Jesse Oak Taylor, *The Sky of Our Manufacture: The London Fog in British Fiction from Dickens to Woolf* (Charlottesville: University of Virginia Press, 2016); and Seth T. Reno, *Early Anthropocene Literature in Britain, 1750–1884* (London: Palgrave Macmillan, 2020).
4. See Heidi Scott, *Chaos and Cosmos: Literary Roots of Modern Ecology in the British Nineteenth Century* (University Park: Pennsylvania State University Press, 2014); Taylor; and Reno.
5. Greg Garrard, *Ecocriticism* (London: Routledge, 2012), 26.
6. Ibid., 228.
7. Dipesh Chakrabarty, "The Climate of History: Four Theses," *Critical Inquiry* 35 (2009): 206.
8. Virginia Woolf, *Orlando* (Orlando: Harcourt, 2006), 25–26.
9. Ibid., 27.
10. Ibid., 20.
11. Ibid., 28.
12. Ibid., 30.
13. Ibid., 49
14. See Diane R. Leonard, "Proust and Virginia Woolf, Ruskin and Roger Fry: Modernist Visual Dynamics," *Comparative Literature Studies* 18, no. 3 (1981): 333–343; Gillian Beer, "The Victorians in Virginia Woolf: 1832–1941," in *Dickens and Other Victorians: Essays in Honour of Philip Collins*, ed. Joanne Shattuck (New York: Macmillan, 1988), 214–235; and John Coyle, "Ruskin, Proust, and the Art of Failure," *Essays in Criticism* 56, no. 1 (2006): 28–49.
15. John Ruskin, *The Storm-Cloud of the Nineteenth Century*, in *The Complete Works of John Ruskin*, vol. 34, ed. E.T. Cook and Alexander Wedderburn (London: George Allen, 1908), 33.
16. Woolf, 167.
17. Ibid.
18. Ibid.
19. Ibid., 182.
20. Ibid., 184.
21. Ibid., 192–193.
22. Ibid., 215, 217–218.
23. Ibid., 220.
24. See Glenn Albrecht, *Earth Emotions: New Words for a New World* (Ithaca: Cornell University Press, 2019), 200.
25. Woolf, 238–239.
26. Garrard, 29.

References

Beer, Gillian. "The Victorians in Virginia Woolf: 1832–1941." In *Dickens and Other Victorians: Essays in Honour of Philip Collins*. Edited by Joanne Shattuck. New York: Macmillan, 1988.

Chakrabarty, Dipesh. "The Climate of History: Four Theses." *Critical Inquiry* 35 (2009): 197–222.
Coyle, John. "Ruskin, Proust, and the Art of Failure." *Essays in Criticism* 56, no. 1 (2006): 28–49.
Crutzen, Paul J. "Geology of Mankind." *Nature* 415 (2002): 23.
Garrard, Greg. *Ecocriticism*. London: Routledge, 2012.
Leonard, Diane R. "Proust and Virginia Woolf, Ruskin and Roger Fry: Modernist Visual Dynamics." *Comparative Literature Studies* 18, no. 3 (1981): 333–343.
Nicolson, Nigel. *Portrait of a Marriage*. New York: Athenaeum, 1973.
Reno, Seth T. *Early Anthropocene Literature in Britain, 1750–1884*. London: Palgrave Macmillan, 2020.
Ruskin, John. *The Storm-Cloud of the Nineteenth Century*. In *The Complete Works of John Ruskin*. Vol. 34. Edited by E.T. Cook and Alexander Wedderburn. London: George Allen, 1908.
Scott, Heidi. *Chaos and Cosmos: Literary Roots of Modern Ecology in the British Nineteenth Century*. University Park: Pennsylvania State University Press, 2014.
Taylor, Jesse Oak. *The Sky of Our Manufacture: The London Fog in British Fiction from Dickens to Woolf*. Charlottesville: University of Virginia Press, 2016.
Woolf, Virginia. *Orlando*. Orlando: Harcourt, 2006.

12

CORPOREAL MATTERS

J.P. Clark's *The Wives' Revolt* and the Embodied Politics of the Anthropocene

Kimberly Skye Richards

While the Anthropocene concept has been helpful for describing the impacts of extractive practices on Earth systems, its universalizing claim under the sign of the "anthropos" has generated much critique. Scholars from disciplines like Indigenous studies and Black studies, and from vantages in the Global South, have pointed out that only white, Western, modern, able-bodied, heterosexual men have been able to act on such a vast scale. As Kathryn Yusoff writes, the Anthropocene implicates all humans in actions and decisions only taken by, and available to, "an exclusive notion of humanity (coded white)."[1] This is also why Nicholas Mirzoeff has adopted the mantra, "it's not the Anthropocene, it's the white supremacy scene."[2] Rather than abandoning the term, Heather Davis and Zoe Todd (Métis/otipemisiw) suggest approaching the Anthropocene as a performative utterance. They ask, "If the Anthropocene is already here … what can we do with it as a conceptual apparatus that may serve to undermine the conditions that it names?"[3] Davis and Todd argue that we peg the start date of the Anthropocene to coincide with the colonization of the Americas, thereby coupling the literal transformation of the environment with practices of dispossession and genocide "that have been at work for the last five hundred years."[4] Yusoff uses this approach, contending that coloniality and anti-Blackness are "materially inscribed" in the Anthropocene.[5] As geology organizes and categorizes materiality into life and non-life, it functions as "a regime for producing both subjects and material worlds."[6] As such, geology is a praxis of colonialism that produces a taxonomy of race and extends racial logics through and beyond minerology. "Geo-logics" were historically and intentionally constituted to displace and eradicate Indigenous peoples to enable mining, which also led to the dispossession of African people for slavery, which Yusoff explains was "driven by an indifferent extractive geo-logic that is motivated by the desire for inhuman properties."[7] The geo-logic formation of anti-Blackness has consequences in the afterlives of slavery from

DOI: 10.4324/9781003095347-15

the chain gangs that laid the railroad and worked the coal mines [in the New World] through to the establishment of new forms of energy, in which, Stephanie LeMenager ... comments, "oil literally was conceived as a replacement for slave labor."[8]

Submerged within the idea of the Anthropocene are violent histories and stories of the making of modern world.

By making explicit the relations between the Anthropocene, colonialism, and the exploitation and death of Black and Brown bodies, we can better understand the current climate crisis, take steps to counter the modes of geopolitical mattering that have dominated this epoch, and begin the project of "decolonizing the Anthropocene."[9] To challenge the "racial blindness of the Anthropocene," and to resist the geo-logics of whiteness that recenter Eurocentric and White narratives as neutral, global perspectives that forget histories of oppression and dispossession, I turn to *The Wives' Revolt* (1991), a play written by the prolific Nigerian poet and playwright John Pepper (J.P.) Clark.[10] While Clark's writing has been the subject of scholarly attention within Nigerian literature and African literary studies, his significant contributions to the development of postcolonial theater deserves broader recognition.[11] *The Wives' Revolt* tells the story of a community in the oil-rich Niger Delta region that received a payout from an oil firm drilling on its land. In accordance with customary law, the money was shared three ways—to elders, men, and women—but as all the elders are men, they accrued twice as much rent. The women of the town demand equal pay and walkout when their request is dismissed. While the play champions gender equality, the toxic repercussions of living in the "extractive zone" compromise the notion of women's bodies as a site of agency when they become diseased from exposure to contaminated water during their walkout.[12] The embodied politics of race, coloniality, gender, and sexuality in *The Wives' Revolt* draw attention to the making of the Anthropocene as a material fact in bodies and environments, and provide an occasion to consider: What are the conditions of possibility for liberation if coloniality, anti-Blackness, and heteropatriarchy are materially inscribed within the Anthropocene?

To appreciate Clark's political commentary in *The Wives' Revolt*, it is first necessary to understand the postcolonial situation of Nigeria. As a unified territory, Nigeria was created in 1914 through the amalgamation of Britain's colonial possessions in the region. The Federation of Nigeria was granted independence on 1 October 1960, amidst the movement toward decolonization sweeping the continent. As large amounts of high-quality oil reserves had been discovered in 1958, Nigeria was considered one of Africa's most promising postcolonial states; the potential for development and economic integration into the global market seemed boundless for a nation born into "natural" wealth.[13] Yet the territorial borders that marked Nigerian society under colonial rule remained in place, and discord among ethnic groups impaired the evolution of a stable political system. When Nigeria was established as a centrally governed federal state, it was split into three regions, each dominated by an ethnic majority: the Hausa-Fulani in the north, Yoruba in the west, and Igbos in the east (and south). More than 300 other ethnic minorities made up the rest of the population, including the Urhobo of Erhuwaren, who are represented in the play.

There were only a few years of harmony between the states, as the three semi-autonomous regions competed for power at the center, creating three political parties founded on platforms that capitalized on ethnic affiliation. By the mid-1960s, optimism about decolonization had begun to crumble. A deepening rift between the northern and southern regions led to the creation of an independent state of Biafra subsumed within Eastern Nigeria and gave rise to the Nigerian Civil War (1967–1970). After Biafra surrendered, minorities living within oil-producing areas, who had been absorbed into a Nigeria created by the British, and who had never ceded their sovereignty or been conquered, were again subjected to internal colonialism and indirect rule by the ethnic majorities who were more interested in their own welfare than establishing a fair and just state. Although communities directly affected by oil infrastructure were to receive "community benefits" (rent), oil companies made alliances and cut deals with powerful chiefs, and corruption operated with impunity. Nigeria's centralized state consolidated control of the country through oil rents and revenues acquired from companies like Shell-BP, Elf, Mobil, Texaco, Agip, and Chevron. The federal government swindled local communities of wealth and ignored the deleterious activities of the oil companies.[14] Although Nigeria quickly became one of the biggest oil producers in the world, most of the population did not significantly benefit from it through jobs or infrastructural development in the form of schools, hospitals, roads, potable water, or electricity. This situation is represented by Erhuwaren in Clark's play, which is an agrarian rural community with no modern amenities or infrastructural facilities. As Oyeh Otu and Obumneme F. Anasi point out, "oil exploration and spillage [have] degrade[d] the environment so much that fishing and farming are no longer productive."[15]

Much of this context of national development, and the marginalization and neglect of the people of the Niger Delta on the basis of tribe or ethnicity, is merely background for Clark's play. And yet, we see the post-independence era repeat the colonial past as the men benefit from a corrupt system of allocation that reinstalls their power to make, change, and enforce the law. There is no illusion of "sweet surplus" to mask the harm of extraction, only the contradictions of state wealth and regional poverty, and the stark reality of oil's failure to produce "wealth without work" and progress without the passage of time.[16]

The Wives' Revolt begins with Okoro, the town-crier of the Erhuwaren, announcing a proclamation resulting from dissatisfaction over the division of money from an unnamed oil firm payout. While Okoro and his peers deem it a "fair and reasonable distribution of the money," the women demand the money should be divided equally.[17] To the make their point, they are refusing to perform their civic duties, which has resulted in goats roaming the streets and public spaces to become filled with "rank excrement" and stench.[18] Angered by the women's behavior, three male elders decree that all goats, which are conventionally kept by the women, be removed. The conflict escalates in a domestic setting when Koko, Okoro's wife, calls for the "obnoxious law" to be repealed.[19] She points out that although pigs tear the land into pits and mounds as they roam, they are tolerated because the men hold swine in common trust and sell them at inflated prices. In so doing, she challenges the system in which men inherit money, money begets land titles, and land titles position men to acquire political power and pass discriminatory laws. Okoro purports the women should stay in the kitchen and with the children, while the affairs of the state should be left to men.

The next morning, while preparing to roast a goat he has just captured, Okoro admits to his friend Idama that the law has presented a golden opportunity for wealth acquisition. Assuming Koko is lazy and still in bed, he is surprised when he learns that all the wives have walked out of town in protest. While Idama believes they should repeal the law and call back the women before they go too far, Okoro, the defender of patriarchy, suggests the women be arrested, tried, and punished, even though they have not broken any law. By expelling themselves, the women allow the law to have full sway, giving Okoro and his supporters every opportunity to impound their goats, all the while communicating their own grievance. Their self-exile draws attention to their contributions at home and in the community: in their absence, the men struggle to tend the farm, collect milk, haul water, prepare food, care for the children, *and* sell goods in the market. Idama reports that the women traveled to Iyara, indebting Erhuwaren to their "enemies," who offered the women hospitality during the walkout, thus bringing shame on Erhuwaren. The women will come back if they are paid, and Iyarans are compensated—an act that would, perhaps, help to unify communities in the region, an essential step toward self-determination and resource control.

When Koko returns, she complains of a burning in the crotch, and Okoro accuses her of adultery, beats her, and threatens to kill her or throw her out and ask her parents to return his dowry. He claims she has title to nothing—not cloths, pots, pans, or gold trinkets. Idama interferes when he explains that all the women are similarly afflicted. In Iyara, a local intentionally infected the women through shared toilet usage, presumably because the people of Erhuwaren and Iyara are hostile to each other as a result of ethnic conflicts exacerbated during colonial rule. Fed up with Okoro's arrogance, Koko announces she will not stay with a man who no longer wants her and rejoins the women, who are marching outside, singing and shouting their demands: the return of all goats, a fat cow, 100 heads of yams, 10 barrels of palm oil, and relief from the affliction brought upon them when the men forced them to migrate to Iyara.

By the end of the day, Okoro makes a proclamation announcing all factions of the town have reconciled:

> The unfortunate incidents of the last few days have shown how an idea, meant for the common good, if not debated in public and adopted by consensus, can give rise to dissension, and create havoc in a community, right down to the family level, even to the nuclear unit of one man, one wife.

He declares the law banning goats from the city and its precincts is revoked, and any citizens who have suffered loss are entitled to compensation. He admits women's "insight into these matters passes the understanding of all men" and announces all of the women's demands will be met. He reports the money will be set aside to open a school because "in education lies equity; lies equality."[20] The play concludes with Okoro pledging that husbands will share whatever fortune comes their way.

While the resolution to the conflict is abrupt, its message is clear: dismantling the hierarchal systems installed during the colonial period is essential for the betterment of society. Clark was among a class of writers from the Niger Delta committed to finding solutions to contemporary problems, including the devastating social and environmental impacts of oil extraction and petro-imperialism on the oil-rich region where particularly damaging strategies of extraction were deployed.[21] In *The Wives' Revolt*, Clark pinpoints the source of conflict to the system of rent allocation from fossil fuel companies: in his final proclamation, Okoro acknowledges that it was the original matter of the oil company money that started the dispute. However, Clark allows a complicated history of gendered petroleum politics to emerge by focusing on the communal and domestic impacts that arise from the oil firm's presence in the region to recommend solutions to those conflicts. Doing so locates the colonial tendency of male chauvinism as the problem as much as the unjust legal system installed to perpetuate the colonial logics that serve new imperial interests. Moreover, it draws attention to what Heather Turcotte has coined "petro-sexual politics"—the ways in which conditions of petro-violence are embedded within larger structures of gender violence and international oppressions.[22]

Koko draws attention to the intersectional nature of the women's disenfranchisement when she complains, "You rigged the whole thing to do us out of our fair share of the money that the white men paid us."[23] Although women attempted to present their complaint to the general assembly (the governing body of the town), the president fell asleep, and dismissed them. While technically satisfying the principle of freedom of expression, the law perpetuates inequality.[24] This point is further enforced when Okoro suggests that Koko and the women turn their anger upon the centralized government, and she retorts, "It's you men who should take up the fight for our common rights."[25] Thus, rather than trying to eliminate the problem and challenge the colonial system, the men try to improve their situation within the colonized world by exploiting the women.[26]

In addition to the issue of rent distribution, the women's revolt is about wives standing up to husbands who give them black eyes and broken limbs. Koko believes that the men's story about women changing into goats to wreak havoc on the community arose when one of the men—whose vision was blurred from drunkenness—spotted his wife trying to escape his beating by hiding with the herd. The association of women with witchcraft is merely an old patriarchal tactic of dehumanizing and stigmatizing women who threaten the patriarchal power by associating their defiance as "evil" and a threat to the community's safety. In this instance, Okoro defines the women's so-called transfiguration by power of witchcraft an "unpatriotic practice," form of harassment, and terrorism that threatens the state and rule of law and community safety:

> now that we know they [goats] also provide refuge for forces of evil ... that wherever there is a herd of goats there is a coven of witches, our immediate and mandatory duty to the community is to see them safely out of town.[27]

We can thereby understand the wives' revolt as the result of the intersecting dynamics of colonial and patriarchal power as they play out alongside extractive imperial activities, especially if we treat domestic violence as a quotidian form of colonial violence. Equal voting, the empowerment of oppressed communities—namely, women and girls—and the investment in education are the path forward.

Clark celebrates feminist activism and peaceful protest as tactics for social progress. In this misogynist culture, women's agency is through their bodies—a core concept in post-structural feminist understandings of the human body as a site of power and control, and one that is accessible to women like Koko who never acquired literacy. In both the colonial and postcolonial period, Nigerian women routinely engaged in women's marches and public displays of nudity to draw attention to their disenchantment with the prevailing social order. In 1929, hundreds of women stripped naked in the towns of Owerri, Calabar, and Aba to protest harsh colonial tax laws, declining palm oil prices, and the complicity of community male elders and elites with colonial authorities. In the 1930s, members of the Abeokuta Women's Union in SW Nigeria walked half-naked to protest the Alake of Abeokuta's actions. The undressing tactic was often effective, as it would have been an abomination for policemen and soldiers to see their mothers and grandmothers naked. Bright Alozie explains that naked protest represents a deep-seated traditional curse imbued in every woman's reproductive and generative power:

> by stripping naked in front of men old enough to be her children or grandchildren, a mother is symbolically taking back the life she gave, so in a way,

pronouncing death on them, unless of course, something is done about the situation at hand.[28]

Nakedness for these women is "an instrument of power, rather than shame as they contest and negotiate their rights and privileges."[29] Moreover, naked protests disrupt the idea of women as being passive, powerless, sexual objects, and they challenge the masculinist and patriarchal urge to proclaim "mankind" or "the human" as the agent of major change.

Clark similarly approaches the body as a material and political entity, a medium of communication and interaction, in his use of the theatrical form and in the embodied politics of the play. Power is inscribed in the female body as rural women march to protest the lack of equitable representation and equal wages, as well as to undermine the hegemony of repressive regimes. Like women's naked protest, Koko subverts and resists dominant scripts—scripts of subordination, passivity, sexuality, subservience, and vulnerability—engraved on her body by her husband and patriarchal power. In the penultimate scene, when Koko hears the women in the streets, Clark writes in stage directions that she dashes into her room and out again instantly,

> She has a blouse over her into which she is struggling at the same time that she is trying to turn her top wrapper into a girdle to belt the lower one about her waist. She rushes out right without stopping to finish.[30]

While the actress is not asked to expose herself, this stage direction could be interpreted in various ways in production to signal Koko's consideration of using nakedness in this phase of the protest. Something remarkable happens between the end of act five and Okoro's second proclamation in act six, and it would be logical to deduce it has to do with the shaming of the men, especially when the undressing tactic has been discussed by Okoro and Koko in an earlier scene.[31]

The Wives' Revolt reveals the possibilities and limitations of embodied politics in challenging the logics that created the Anthropocene, especially the grammars of possession that have come to have material consequences. Koko complains about "my husband who owns me," and Idama acknowledges, "it's a slave life for you women."[32] Okoro's treatment of Koko as his possession highlights the exchangeability between human thing, subject, and matter that Yusoff addresses when she highlights how the language of geology enabled "the exchange of a person as a material object of property and properties," which led to slavery in the Americas and anti-Blackness worldwide.[33] To act politically, the women of Erhuwaren are forced to sever relationships between body and land, mother and child—a world-ending violence if not quickly repaired. Thus, Clark's play takes Yusoff's argument one step further in terms of intersectionality by foregrounding the experience of Black women from the Global South.

It is telling that the women are punished with an STI for demanding equality, their bodies subjected to polluted waters and physical violence because of domestic and civic dispute and unjust law rather than exposure to toxic oil substances. The STI contagion will impact hierarchical sexual norms—as Koko previously complained, "All you want to do is get on top of us women."[34] But as much as *The Wives' Revolt* celebrates gender equality, the toxic repercussions of living in the "extractive zone" compromise the notion of women's bodies as a site of agency; only by becoming diseased do the women gain political progress. Despite Okoro's effort to destigmatize the women when he assures the citizens no one should be afraid or ashamed of the venereal disease, the women's sexual relations with other kin are negatively affected. This twist illustrates Yusoff's point that "while Blackness is the energy and flesh of the Anthropocene, it is excluded from the wealth of its accumulation. Rather, Blackness must absorb the excess of that surplus as toxicity, pollution, and intensification of storms. Again, and again."[35] The community's proximity to harm, resulting from historical geographies of extraction, grammars of geology, imperial global geographies, and contemporary environmental racism, represents what Yusoff calls the "Black Anthropocene" wherein Black Anthropocenes are "predicated on the presumed absorbent qualities of black and brown bodies to take up the body burdens of exposure to toxicities and to buffer the violence of the earth."[36]

The Wives' Revolt renders a history of Black Anthropocene Feminism that productively unsettles White Anthropocenic thoughts through its depiction of the brutal experience of a community enmeshed in anti-Black, heteropatriarchal, and colonial structures. It gives visibility to the corporeal matters that bring the Anthropocene into being; it illuminates the structural and interpersonal histories of gender, sexual, and racial violence; and it reflects the conditions and limitations of agency within the Niger Delta's extractive zone. The point is not to claim that women can or would offer an essentially different, non-contaminating, less violent, "natural," or attuned relation to the earth; as Claire Colebrook points out, such an argument would "entail choosing sexual difference at the expense of the question of how gendered sexual being emerges from a history that is ecological bound up with violence and depletion."[37] Likewise, the point of reading *The Wives' Revolt* is not to claim space for Blackness within or outside the Anthropocene. *Rather, the point is to illuminate the structures of thought, racializing assemblages, and colonial histories from which a Black Anthropocene emerged.* If, as Yusoff argues, "Anthropocenic discourse enacts a foundational global inscription of race in the conception of humanity that is put forth as an object of concern in the Anthropocene," Clark's play reveals the Blackness of the Anthropocene is not a metaphor but is its material, embodied form.[38]

The naming of the Anthropocene presents an opportunity to study race as a building block and anchor of the modern world system and its extractive and dispossessive modalities, as well as to acknowledge the role of Africa—and specifically its mines and oil enclaves—in the making of the modern world.[39] In choosing who, or what, we study, read, remember, and learn from in and about the Anthropocene, we are, again, negotiating properties of value and belonging, making judgments about whose lives matter—and how *Black lives matter*—on a planetary and geologic scale. The stories we tell about the afterlives of invasion, genocide, slavery, and colonialism determine how we understand how we got here, and what we need to do. We must listen to those voices of "a billion Black Anthropocenes" to contemplate the consequences of declarations that an epoch is over, and a new one has begun.[40]

Notes

1 Kathryn Yusoff, *A Billion Black Anthropocenes or None* (Minneapolis: University of Minnesota Press, 2018), 3.
2 Nicholas Mirzoeff, "It's Not the Anthropocene, It's the White Supremacy Scene; or, The Geological Color Line," in *After Extinction*, ed. Richard Grusin (Minneapolis: University of Minnesota Press, 2018), 123.
3 Heather Davis and Zoe Todd, "On the Importance of a Date, or Decolonizing the Anthropocene," *ACME: An International Journal for Critical Geographies* 16, no. 2 (2017): 763.
4 Ibid., 761. Origin dates range from the birth of agriculture, to the first steam engine, to the "great acceleration" of the mid-twentieth century at which time measurable anthropogenic changes, such as carbon dioxide levels and mass extinctions, became observable.
5 Yusoff, 19. Here I am using the term "coloniality" as opposed to "colonialism" to refer to "long-standing patterns of power that emerged as a result of colonialism, but that define culture, labor, intersubjective relations, and knowledge production well beyond the strict limits of colonial administrations." See Nelson Maldonado-Torres, "On the Coloniality of Being: Contributions to the Development of a Concept," *Cultural Studies* (2007) 21, nos. 2–3: 243.
6 Yusoff, 4.
7 Ibid., 16.
8 Ibid., 6. See also Andrew Baldwin and Bruce Erickson, "Introduction: Whiteness, Coloniality, and the Anthropocene," *Environment and Planning D: Society and Space* 38, no. 1 (2020): 3–11.
9 Davis and Todd, 763. Relatedly, on Indigenizing the Anthropocene, see Zoe Todd, "Indigenizing the Anthropocene," in *Art in the Anthropocene: Encounters among Aesthetics, Politics, Environments and Epistemologies*, ed. Heather Davis and Etienne Turpin (London: Open Humanities Press, 2015), 241–254; Kyle Powys Whyte, "Our Ancestors' Dystopia Now: Indigenous Conservation and the Anthropocene," in *Routledge Companion to the Environmental Humanities*, ed. Ursula Heise, Jon Christense, and Michelle Niemann (London: Routledge, 2016), 206–218; and Macarena Gómez-Barris, "The Colonial Anthropocene: Damage, Remapping, and Resurgent Resources," *Antipode: A Radical Journal of Geography*, 19 March 2019.
10 Yusoff, xiii.
11 Clark is one of the first generations of playwrights of Africa whose works were widely read and given scholarly attention. He is better known for his poems that relayed pungent messages about issues such as the causes and effects of violence and protests,

corruption in government, pride in African values, and the evils of neo-colonialism. He is regarded as one of four literary giants who pioneered modern African literature in Nigeria: poet Christopher Okigbo, novelist Chinua Achebe, and Wole Soyinka, the first Black African winner of the Nobel Prize for Literature. Other plays by Clark include *The Song of a Goat* (1961), *The Masquerade* (1964), *The Raft* (1964), *Ozidi* (1966), *The Boat* (1981), and *All for Oil* (2009). He also published as J.P. Clark and J.P. Clark-Bekederemo.

12 See Macarena Gomez-Barris, *The Extractive Zone: Social Ecologies and Decolonial Perspectives* (Durham: Duke University Press, 2017).
13 See Ukoha Ukiwo, "Empire of Commodities," in *Curse of the Black Gold: 50 Years of Oil in the Niger Delta*, ed. Michael Watts (Brooklyn: PowerHouse Books, 2008), 73.
14 Michael Watts writes,

> Over 80 percent of oil revenues accrue to 1 percent of the population. According to former World Bank President Paul Wolfowitz, around $300 billion of oil revenues accrued since 1960 have simply "gone missing." Between 1970 and 2000, the number of income poor grew from 19 million to a staggering 90 million. Over the last decade, GDP per capita and life expectancy have, according to World Bank estimates, both fallen. Oil, in sum, has lubricated—it is a medium for—a catastrophic failure of secular national development.

See Michael Watts, "Oil Frontiers," in *Oil Culture*, ed. Ross Barrett and Daniel Worden (Minneapolis: University of Minnesota Press, 2014), 198.

15 Oyeh O. Otu and Obumneme F. Anasi, "Oil Politics and Violence in Postcolonial Niger Delta Drama," *African Research Review* 11, no. 45 (2017): 173.
16 Jennifer Wenzel, "Petro-Magic-Realism: Toward a Political Ecology of Nigerian Literature." *Postcolonial Studies* 9, no. 4 (2016): 451.
17 J.P. Clark, *The Wives' Revolt* (Alexandria: Alexander Street Press, 1985), 2.
18 Ibid., 2.
19 Ibid., 4.
20 Ibid., 59.
21 Wastewater was dumped directly into rivers, streams, and the sea; canals from the ocean were dug in ways that turned freshwater sources salty; pipelines were left exposed and unmaintained, contributing to thousands of spills; and gas was flared which sends the gas into the atmosphere in great pillars of polluting fire. Among Clark's peers was Ogoni writer and activist Ken Saro-Wiwa who became internationally recognized for broadcasting the plight of the Ogoni people. In the early 1990s, Saro-Wiwa led the Movement of the Survival of the Ogoni People (MOSOP) and presented *The Ogoni Bill of Rights* to the federal government to gain political and economic autonomy of Ogoniland for the Ogoni people. MOSOP threatened mass action if their demand for $6 billion of reparations and reallocated revenues for forty years of oil exploitation was not met. When their demands were dismissed, the Ogoni staged a historic rally, and a youth wing of the organization radicalized and began to sabotage pipelines and oil installations. Violence escalated until Shell pulled out of the region—one of the most significant achievements of grassroots activism anywhere in the world. As a result of his opposition and the threat of a united Delta front, the government seized and executed Saro-Wiwa and eight of other MOSOP leaders for trumped up charges of incitement to murder. One of the witnesses during the trial in October 1995 confessed he, like

other witnesses, had been offered bribes of 300 pounds by Shell to make statements incriminating Saro-Wiwa. See Paul Lewis, "In Nigeria's Oil Wars, Shell Denies it Had a Role," *New York Times*, 13 February 1996.
22 Heather Turcotte, "Contextualizing Petro-Sexual Politics," *Alternatives: Global, Local, Political* 36, no. 3 (2011): 201. See also Cecily Devereux, "Made for Mankind: Cars, Cosmetics, and the Petrocultural Feminine," in *Petrocultures: Oil, Politics, Culture*, ed. Sheena Wilson, Adam Carlson, and Sheena Wilson (Montreal and Kingston: McGill-Queen's University Press, 2017), 162–185.
23 Clark, 6.
24 A parallel logic is seen in the "duty to consult" Indigenous communities in settler colonial states, like Canada and the United States.
25 Clark, 15.
26 This plotline aligns with other postcolonial Niger Delta plays in which

> most of the chiefs do not fight to wrest power from Federal Government or oil companies that exploit the oil resources of their land and ruin the lives and environment of their people. Their business or stock in trade is to betray their people in their unbridled quest for wealth. They are in league with "other people" against their own people, a situation that makes the struggles of the well-meaning masses of the Niger Delta over resource control and self-determination almost impossible to win. This is the tragedy of the Niger Delta.

See Otu and Anasi, 177.
27 Clark, 2, 6.
28 Bright Alozie, "Undressing to Redress: The Sexual Politics of Protests in Colonial and Postcolonial Southeastern Nigeria," in *Women and the Nigeria-Biafra War: Reframing Gender and Conflict in Africa*, ed. Gloria Chuku and Sussie U. Aham-Okoro (Lanham: Lexington Books, 2020), 26.
29 Ibid., 34. On naked protest, see also Naminata Diabate, *Naked Agency: Genital Cursing and Biopolitics in Africa* (Durham: Duke University Press, 2020).
30 Clark, 56.
31 Binebai Benedict and Christine Odi support this idea when they point to the prophetic quality of Clark's play, which premiered in 1985, and the women in the Niger Delta who occupied pipeline terminals and threatened to strip naked if their demands were not met by oil companies in the 2000s. See Binebai Benedict and Christine Odi, "Drama and Prophecy: The J.P. Clark Paradigm," *UJAH: Unizik Journal of Arts and Humanities* 10, no. 2 (2009): 77–85.
32 Clark, 16, 52.
33 Yusoff, 7.
34 Ibid.
35 Ibid., 82.
36 Ibid, xii.
37 Claire Colebrook, "We Have Always Been Post-Anthropocene: the Anthropocene Counterfactual," in *Anthropocene Feminism*, ed. Richard Grusin (Minneapolis: University of Minnesota Press, 2017), 19. Colebrook points out what we know *narrowly* as feminism relies on hyper-consumption; abolition and suffrage movements developed when industrialized economies were able to extract more energy with less violent subjection of humans for labor. Human enslavement would have been worse had developments in

mining and resource extraction, and the burning of coal and carbon, that have resulted in the Anthropocene not occurred:

> When Wollstonecraft called for the rights of women and extended the trope of slavery and abolition to the liberation of women, she was relying on technological developments that allowed the greater freedom of humans precisely because industry was now extracting energy from the earth, in the form of coal and other ultimately polluting and depleting resources. Women could start to demand equality precisely because of an industrial capitalism in a certain portion of the world that extended the leisure time once reserved for the very few.
> (15–16)

As Koko and the women who revolt are not educated women, or a reading elite liberated from domestic labor, capable of thinking about the freedom of thought and reason, blessed with favorable conditions of personhood, their activism reflects a different woman-of-color feminism, one submerged within the "extractive zone."

38 Yusoff, 61.
39 On Afropolitanism, see Achille Mbembe and Sarah Balakrishnan, "Pan-African Legacies, Afropolitan Futures," *Transition* 120 (2016): 28–37.
40 Yusoff, xiv.

References

Alozie, Bright. "Undressing to Redress: The Sexual Politics of Protests in Colonial and Postcolonial Southeastern Nigeria." *Women and the Nigeria-Biafra War: Reframing Gender and Conflict in Africa*. Edited by Gloria Chuku and Sussie U. Aham-Okoro. Lanham: Lexington Books, 2020. 23–48.

Baldwin, Andrew, and Bruce Erickson. "Introduction: Whiteness, Coloniality, and the Anthropocene." *Environment and Planning D: Society and Space* 38, no. 1 (2020): 3–11.

Benedict, Binebai, and Christine Odi. "Drama and Prophecy: The J.P. Clark Paradigm." *UJAH: Unizik Journal of Arts and Humanities* 10, no. 2 (2009): 77–85.

Clark, J.P. *The Wives' Revolt*. Alexandria: Alexander Street Press, 1985.

Colebrook, Claire. "We Have Always Been Post-Anthropocene: The Anthropocene Counterfactual." In *Anthropocene Feminism*. Edited by Richard Grusin. Minneapolis: University of Minnesota Press, 2017. 1–20.

Davis, Heather, and Zoe Todd. "On the Importance of a Date, or Decolonizing the Anthropocene." *ACME: An International Journal for Critical Geographies* 16, no. 2 (2017): 761–780.

Devereux, Cecily. "Made for Mankind: Cars, Cosmetics, and the Petrocultural Feminine." In *Petrocultures: Oil, Politics, Culture*. Edited by Sheena Wilson, Adam Carlson, and Sheena Wilson. Montreal and Kingston: McGill-Queen's University Press, 2017. 162–185.

Diabate, Naminata. *Naked Agency: Genital Cursing and Biopolitics in Africa*. Durham: Duke University Press, 2020.

Gomez-Barris, Macarena. *The Extractive Zone: Social Ecologies and Decolonial Perspectives*. Durham: Duke University Press, 2017.

Lewis, Paul. "In Nigeria's Oil Wars, Shell Denies It Had a Role." *New York Times*, 13 February 1996.

Maldonado-Torres, Nelson. "On the Coloniality of Being: Contributions to the Development of a Concept." *Cultural Studies* 21, nos. 2–3 (2007): 240–270.

Mirzoeff, Nicholas. "It's Not the Anthropocene, It's the White Supremacy Scene; or, The Geological Color Line." In *After Extinction*. Edited by Richard Grusin. Minneapolis: University of Minnesota Press, 2018. 123–150.

Otu, Oyeh O., and Obumneme F. Anasi. "Oil Politics and Violence in Postcolonial Niger Delta Drama." *African Research Review* 11, no. 45 (2017): 171–181.

Todd, Zoe. "Indigenizing the Anthropocene." In *Art in the Anthropocene: Encounters among Aesthetics, Politics, Environments and Epistemologies*. Edited by Heather Davis and Etienne Turpin. London: Open Humanities Press, 2015. 241–254.

Turcotte, Heather. "Contextualizing Petro-Sexual Politics." *Alternatives: Global, Local, Political* 36, no. 3 (2011): 200–220.

Ukiwo, Ukoha. "Empire of Commodities." In *Curse of the Black Gold: 50 Years of Oil in the Niger Delta*. Edited by Michael Watts. Brooklyn: PowerHouse Books, 2008. 69–91.

Watts, Michael. "Oil Frontiers." In *Oil Culture*. Edited by Ross Barrett and Daniel Worden. Minneapolis: University of Minnesota Press, 2014. 189–210.

Wenzel, Jennifer. "Petro-Magic-Realism: Toward a Political Ecology of Nigerian Literature." *Postcolonial Studies* 9, no. 4 (2016): 449–464.

Whyte, Kyle Powys. "Our Ancestors' Dystopia Now: Indigenous Conservation and the Anthropocene." In *Routledge Companion to the Environmental Humanities*. Edited by Ursula Heise, Jon Christense, and Michelle Niemann. London: Routledge, 2016. 206–218.

Yusoff, Kathryn. *A Billion Black Anthropocenes or None*. Minneapolis: University of Minnesota Press, 2018.

13
WHAT GLOBAL SOUTH CRITICS DO

Antonette Talaue-Arogo

There has long been an agonistic relationship between theory and literary studies. Is theory a supplement to literary studies, understood as an analytic lens or interpretative framework for the appreciation of literature, or is it an autonomous discipline with its own fields of application and engagement? The oft-invoked claim that "theory is dead" arises from the latter understanding of theory. The "theoretical turn" in the 1960s signaled a shift from theory of literature to theory of culture, a movement toward identity politics that has become ever more contentious with social media and digitally driven movements in the twenty-first century. The most relevant of these movements at the time of writing this chapter is #WashTheHate against anti-Asian sentiment, as the world is learning how to live with COVID-19. The rise of cyberactivism is a form of resistance against cultural elitism through a democratization of the public sphere where amateurs, so to speak, can contribute to important and consequential discussions. It is also a sign of the resistance to theory, for theory's commitment to the politics of identity is undermined by the language it deploys, which is full of jargon narrowing its communicative reach and transformative effect. Heightening such resistance is the predictability of theory's line of argumentation, where it is applied in literary and cultural studies with the conclusion being either the critique of power and ideology or the co-optation by the very same. How can theory be made more relevant in these times of urgency when racism, capitalism, patriarchy, and anthropocentrism are experienced in increasingly proximate and intimate ways?

In *The End of the Cognitive Empire: The Coming of Age of Epistemologies of the South* (2018), Boaventura de Sousa Santos argues for interpretation as a response to the challenge of translating theory into politics: "we must change the world while constantly reinterpreting it."[1] The relentless work of interpretation is the persistent presence of literature *in* theory even as theory has made the turn from reading

DOI: 10.4324/9781003095347-16

literary texts to reading everything that makes up a society as text. Indeed, theory through its various movements enables a deeper understanding of literature, what is written and the way it is written in relation to its biographical, social, and linguistic contexts of production and reception, but it is equally true that literature develops theory, and from literary texts can be derived conceptual categories and ways of thinking the world anew. We see this most compellingly in how the novel participates in the ongoing theorization of the Global South.

Broadly, the Global South refers to regions in Latin America, Africa, Asia, and Oceania, as opposed to the Eurocentric Global North. However, the Global South is not a geographical marker: it is among the confluence of critical terms that scholars utilize to interrogate the history and experiences of colonialism and imperialism; modernity and modernization; the intersection of race, sex/gender/sexuality, and class in identity and nation-formation; nationalism and citizenship; and migration and diaspora. This theoretical vocabulary includes the Third World, postcolonialism, subaltern studies, decoloniality, cosmopolitanism, planetarity, and world literature. Making appearances since the 1970s and entering public discourse through the 2003 United Nations Development Program titled "Forging a Global South," it supplanted the designation of Third World, which refers to formerly colonized and developing nations adopted by the participating Asian and African countries in the 1955 Bandung Conference. Delegates from Asia and Africa met in Bandung, Indonesia, under President Sukarno to confer about international relations in the time of decolonization. The transnationalism of the Bandung Conference makes it the harbinger of the Global South. However, its unifying and resistant energy resonated beyond the region, for example, providing inspiration to the civil rights movement in the United States. The Filipino delegate Carlos P. Romulo argued for an even wider scale of affiliation beyond Asian and African nations to encompass the whole of humanity, a cosmopolitan viewpoint expressed by his reading from Rabindranath Tagore's poem, "Where The Mind Is Without Fear." Prescient was that call through literature, for border-crossings have only intensified since then, the movement of people, money, technology, and ideas within South-to-South but also from South-to-North and North-to-South. In light of this fluidity, the capacious nature of the Global South can be better understood as a term that "refers simultaneously to a geopolitical area, a global economic process, a collective actor, a discursive event, and a body of theories, paradigms, and texts."[2]

The convergences and divergences between these critical terms generate a more precise understanding of the Global South. The Bandung Conference envisioned the Third World differently from the developmental narrative toward capitalist modernity, seeing in national liberation movements the promise of a transnational revolution against the problems created by socialism and capitalism. But globalization troubled this ideal and instead brought to light the disparities among and within nations seeking a place in the global economy.[3] Threading through the Third World and the Global South is the theme of belatedness that characterizes developing countries and formerly colonized peoples, an enduring colonial judgment of "not yet."[4] They are not yet developed, not yet capable of self-rule, not yet mature or enlightened, not yet modern. The danger is how easily this rhetoric devolves into "not ever," attested by persistent structures of inequality in the neocolonial period.

This time lag distancing the Global North from the Global South features as a central concern for the Anthropocene, referring to the current geological epoch in which environmental destruction is primarily driven by human activity. Ever since the Industrial Revolution, human beings have come to possess "geological agency."[5] Initially in the domain of the geological sciences, the Anthropocene has now entered the humanities as an inquiry into the "new contexts and demands—cultural, ethical, aesthetic, philosophical and political—of environmental issues that are truly planetary in scale."[6] Yet, Anthropocene studies have had a tentative dialogue with postcolonialism and the Global South, explained by diverging theoretical positions "over the politics of purity, place, nation, and history."[7] The "ecocritical belatedness"[8] in postcolonial theory is significant considering that the Global South houses most of the planet's natural resources, yet they do not have the sufficient means to offset the environmental costs of neoliberalism. In contrast, the Global North has already gone green because they can afford to, having the capacity to meet their material needs by sourcing raw materials from developing countries while displacing environmental impacts onto them, a phenomenon that can be traced back to new imperialism in the latter half of the nineteenth century propelled by the second Industrial Revolution. This situation has spurred environmental activism in the Third World called "environmentalism of the poor" or "popular environmentalism."[9] It is important to interrogate this conjunction of colonialism and anthropocentrism and the invisibility of the Global South in Anthropocene studies.

What is ethically and politically at stake in the deliberate deployment of the Global South? And how can the critical interpretation of literature help to address this question? In this chapter, I analyze Gina Apostol's novel *Insurrecto* (2018) within the theoretical framework of the Global South. *Insurrecto* relives the 1901 Balangiga Massacre, the most violent episode in the "unremembered" Philippine–American War.[10] Known as America's "first Vietnam War,"[11] the Philippine–American War began after the 1898 Treaty of Paris in which Spain ceded the Philippines to the United States for $20 million and lasted until 1902, the onset of American colonial rule over the country. This was a struggle between a new imperial power and an emerging nation-state that had just staged "the first anticolonial revolution in Asia."[12] Balangiga, a municipality in Samar, was turned into a "howling wilderness" upon the orders of General Jacob H. Smith—an overturning of the wilderness trope in ecocriticism that sees the wild as a sanctuary from economic interests and a place for authenticity based on proximity to nature, recalling instead the religious representations of the wilderness as terror-inducing—as American soldiers carried out a scorched-earth policy in the province.[13]

One year before the Philippine–American War began, Samar, along with nearby Leyte, had been ravaged by a typhoon that "claimed about 1500 human victims." In a devastating historical repetition of this 1897 typhoon, Samar and Leyte were once again directly hit in 2013 by the Category 5 Super Typhoon Haiyan, or Yolanda as locally named, that took more than 6,000 lives among other losses. Filipino environmentalist Naderev "Yeb" Saño considers Haiyan and other typhoons in the recent past as manifestations of worsening climate change, the consequences of which are mostly suffered by developing countries.[14] The wide temporal horizon invoked by *Insurrecto* both as a text made meaningful by its form and content and as a text arising from its context of production—the colonial past and postcolonial present of the Philippines—foregrounds the violent recurrences of history and the tragedies of war and climate change. The novel examines personal and national trauma as constitutive of Philippine history and contemporaneity, offering sharp insights into the violence and inequality that characterize a globalized world, while also displaying cautious optimism for the possibility of societal transformation.

Insurrecto moves across various locations, from New York to Las Vegas to Hong Kong to Metro Manila and to Samar. The story is told from the viewpoints of multiple characters, namely Magsalin, a *balikbayan* from New York who is back home to write a mystery novel, and Chiara Brasi, an American who travels to the Philippines to make a film about the Balangiga Massacre. Her voyage, too, is a return, having spent time in the country as a young girl with her parents, Ludo and Virginie. An acclaimed director, Ludo Brasi was in the Philippines to shoot a film about the Vietnam War, believed to rival Francis Ford Coppola's *Apocalypse Now*, although Brasi's *The Unintended* appears to have drawn from the largely forgotten tragedy at the turn of the twentieth century. Chiara asks Magsalin to work with her as a translator—the *nom de plume* Magsalin in Tagalog means to translate—and to accompany her to Samar. What was intended to be a work of translation becomes a work in uneasy collaboration as Magsalin writes her own version of the script, leading to a revealing exchange between the characters:

"You are replacing the story. It's not a version. It's an invasion."

"Oh no. That is not my intention. A mirror, perhaps?" asks Magsalin.[15]

This trope of mirroring, what we may also call doubleness, underlines the novel both as narrative technique and thematic feature. The book is divided into two parts, mapping the movement of the main characters from the city to the province paralleled by the deeper journey into their internal lives. This is Magsalin's true homecoming, we learn, having come from Tacloban, the capital of Leyte. She left after her husband's death—Stig Alyosha Virkelig was a writer whom she met while in graduate school at Cornell University and who lived with her in her hometown—not returning even after the passing of her mother. While the temporal progression from Part I to Part II is linearly ordered, both sections contain shifts in plot time signaled by the achronological sequence of chapters. The nonlinear storytelling enables the presentation of the competing versions of the movie script, the novels within the novel as it were.

Each script centers on female protagonists. In Magsalin's rewriting, we meet the American photographer Cassandra Chase and the native trader and heroine Casiana Nacionales, the insurrecto, or "revolutionary," based on the historical "Geronima of Balangiga." She was the only woman to have participated in the plotting of the Balangiga uprising that killed "forty-eight Americans" and against which the colonizers retaliated, leaving "thirty thousand Filipinos" dead. Chiara's work features an imagined Virginie and the schoolteacher and mystery writer Caz, Virginie's "alter-native."[16] Caz is Ludo's lover to whom the director's manuscript about the Balangiga Massacre was given after he committed suicide, leaving the film unfinished. Chiara's manuscript is a film about reality, an exemplification of *Insurrecto*'s metafictional quality reinforced by various elements, such as the intrusive narrator or the sudden appearance of a first-person speaking subject commenting on the exchange between the main characters, foregrounding more powerfully questions of representation and textuality.

Put another way, the novel incites us to ask: whose narration of events are we reading? Furthermore, how do we understand actions that are pervasively mediated by writing and other forms of technology, like photography and the Internet, especially if what is represented is as formative as the violence of colonialism and its historical legacies? While on the ferry and passing by Allen, Samar, Magsalin explains to Chiara how this town was named after the American General Henry T. Allen. General Allen headed the Philippine Constabulary and established a system of policing and counterinsurgency inherited and practiced by Filipinos from the time of Ferdinand Marcos to the present under President Rodrigo Duterte, whose administration's war on drugs has been criticized and denounced for alleged extrajudicial killings. With incisiveness, Magsalin remarks: "The tortures and killings by the police have a long history—extrajudicial is kind of traditional."[17] After their identical bags are accidentally exchanged, Chiara is apprehended by policemen for drug possession on the heels of witnessing a shooting by motorcycle-riding gunmen, killing a father and his daughter, a crime explained away by the government's war. What was mistaken for drugs turns out to be the cremains of Magsalin's deceased husband that she intends to bury alongside her mother in Tacloban, her reason for traveling with Chiara to Samar. Like Ludo, who in reality died in New York while writing a script (a task Chiara takes on), Stig dies in the middle of writing a novel that Magsalin then pursues, fictionalizing Stig as the writer Stéphane Réal. The juxtapositions of characters—Magsalin and Chiara; Casiana and Cassandra; Caz and Virginie; Stig and Ludo; Sergeant Gustav Randles of Magsalin's script's representation of the Balangiga Massacre and Sergeant Bernardo Gustavo Randols of the novel's representation of President Duterte's war on drugs—and the juxtaposition of settings and contexts—imperial center and colonial outpost; Vietnam and the Philippines; history and contemporaneity; reality and textuality; fact and fiction—highlight difference and similarity between the foreign and the native as well as rupture and continuity between the past and the present. These are common motifs in postcolonial criticism, elaborated through the well-cited concepts of hybridity, mimicry, and ambivalence.[18] Yet, the narrative strategies of *Insurrecto*, especially its particular use of doubleness, contribute to a nuanced understanding of what makes the Global South a paradigm regarded as "continuing the 'unfinished critique' of postcolonialism."[19]

Postcolonialism, in this view, is the aftermath of the unfulfilled promise of emancipation of Bandung. This has reached an impasse, as evident in the failure of nation-states riddled with oligarchy and authoritarianism, as well as the stale conception of the teleological relation between colonial past and postcolonial present defined by nostalgia for revolution and the desire to overcome structures of oppression. It is also apparent in the muteness in postcolonialism of issues of environmental justice exacerbated by globalization and the role of transnational companies in problems like pollution. The potential for a renewed conception is generated by the understanding of the Global South within the narrative framing of *Insurrecto* as a rethinking of the relation between past, present, and future. In the novel, the retrieval of the horrific episode in the Philippine–American War is certainly an antidote to historical amnesia, a postcolonial anamnesis or a remembering of the past toward overcoming through self-knowledge. This memory work brings to light the desire and derision, or love and hatred, between the colonizers and the colonized that is attended by the disavowal of identity and displacement of self. Leela Gandhi calls this "postcolonial schizophrenia" to which postcolonial theory, in its psychoanalytic orientation, serves as a form of therapeutics.[20]

Opportune, then, is the momentous event of the return to the Philippines of the Balangiga church bells in 2018, the same year of *Insurrecto*'s publication. The tolling of the bells of the Saint Lawrence the Martyr Church on the morning of the Balangiga uprising marked the start of the revolt and were subsequently claimed by the American soldiers as war trophies.[21] The homecoming of the Balangiga bells is a way of reparation toward the strengthening of alliance at a time when the Duterte administration was pivoting toward China, notwithstanding the maritime dispute between the two countries, a reorientation that continues in the face of the continuing health crisis as the Philippine government turns to its southern neighbor for medical aid and vaccine supply.[22] The gesture to repair U.S.–Philippines relations fractured by rising criticism of the Philippine government's war on drugs can also be read into the aid given and relief operations conducted by the U.S. Embassy in the wake of ST Haiyan in 2013.[23] Might this not also be interpreted as reparation for the razing of Samar in 1901? The geopolitics of the present mediates the past and serves as lens through which actions, their complex motivations and consequences, are rendered more visible. It also points to what we might call unfinishability, despite the sense of an ending that comes with this act of return, as international relations are recalibrated in light of the rise and decline of countries in global economy and politics.

Insurrecto powerfully dramatizes the fluid interconnections revealed by the mutual constitution of the past and the present. Apostol remarks of Filipinos and the Philippines: "there's uber-referentiality in the ways we relate to the world ... It's an aspect of colonization, maybe, about being seen awry, from someone else's lens—but that's true of just humans too."[24] This is best given form in her book through the indeterminacy, and thus exchangeability, of the authorship of the dual, and "duel," scripts.[25] At the beginning of the novel and throughout the text, one may easily interpret Cassandra as Chiara's star and Caz as Magsalin's lead, an interpretation arguably prompted by the primary affiliation of the characters based on nationality and ethnicity with *their* central characters. That is the impression until the very last chapter that, should the events be chronologically arranged, is preceded by a cathartic moment shared by Chiara and Magsalin. They both go through an affective experience, one of indignation yet helplessness for the former and mourning and deep vulnerability yet resolve for the latter, after bearing witness to the gunning down of a father and his daughter in the street. This catharsis brings about moral clarification, enabling recognition and an open, even convivial, conversation between the women. In the end, they no longer feel the need to continue on to Balangiga, not out of a sense of accomplishment but a common failure of representation. Magsalin explains her choice of character:

> I wanted to write in a voice strange and distant and foreign—I wanted to get outside of myself. A different lens. And I wanted to write about this unfinished thing—this revolution. A story of war and loss so repressed and untold ... I told, I could not show. The history of that war is beyond my powers to add or detract from the terrible pictures it left behind—those stereo cards in your manila envelope.[26]

She can only tell the story of Balangiga and its Geronima through Cassandra as lens and Cassandra's lens. Mirroring this is Chiara's own feeling of non-fulfillment at telling the story of Ludo through the perspective of the colonized returning the colonial gaze:

> I tried to understand why my father did not follow us when we left Manila, choosing to start a new project instead of saving his marriage. I tried to see him from the lens of the villagers who had witnessed his obsession with his film ... Sometimes I imagine he died from the despair I have, the horror of not knowing him. In the end, I guess, everything is just self-portrait. I could not create a portrait of my father.[27]

This dialogue between the two characters encapsulates the novel's dialogism, a literary device defined by Mikhail Bakhtin as pertaining to linguistic struggle that is an outgrowth of the heterogeneity of languages.[28] In literature, this linguistic struggle can be external or internal. External dialogism is when there are discursive conflicts between characters, and internal dialogism has to do with the inner strife a character experiences signified by their speech. In *Insurrecto*, the struggle between the two scripts transforms into co-creation and a reciprocal processing of personal mourning and national trauma. The analogizing of the personal to the national and vice versa through family history, marital situation, and domicile is captured by the foreign presence in each character's script—Cassandra for Magsalin and Caz for Chiara—an internal differentiation of viewpoint that they deliberately adopt. Such gesture surely entails a bracketing of colonial/imperialist ideology and a voluntary affiliation with the supposed Other. Apostol asserts: "I am hyper-conscious of our multiplicities—how we are quite fragmented, fractured selves but that is not a burden to carry but a means for imagining others more deeply."[29] Imagining the self as well as self-understanding, especially one's grief, is mediated by the Other. It is a process that is inhabited by the Other who is both adversary and ally, or, as represented by Casiana's relationship with the American soldier Frank Betron and Caz's affair with Ludo, lover and enemy.[30]

Magsalin's rewriting of the script is a way of suspending mourning through storytelling. In Chiara's version, Caz leaves Ludo after a heated exchange with her brother in which the latter accuses her of disavowing her past and identity. She defends the movie production, which employs descendants of those who were in the uprising, claiming that it allows victims to come to terms with unnamable and ungrievable suffering. Despite this justification, her leave-taking is a muted assent to the charge of disavowal, an acknowledgment of her complicity with the silencing imposed by the commercially and institutionally validated representation of the colonized. In light of the problems of representation, the importance of photographs of the war that supplement any attempt at narrativizing the Balangiga massacre can be gleaned.

Consistently in the novel is this doubleness or double vision, in itself a kind of unfinishability embodied in character as a fictional element, suggesting that identity is always in formation, a becoming through the Other, and that it is true for both the privileged and subordinated identity. That is to say, what we can also call double consciousness, after W.E.B. Du Bois, is a way of being of both subject-positions: the powerful and the powerless or, in this case, the colonizer and the colonized.[31] What is revealed is the vulnerability of the former, a recognition of the dependency on the Other as cocreator in self-conceptualization and self-realization. Apposite to this analysis of the novel is Russel West-Pavlov's discussion on the Global South: "The 'Global South' does not give us access to 'subalterns' who cannot speak, so much as it opens up spaces in which speech can be invented."[32] Indeed, drawing from the novel, the Global South indicates a reorientation, a speaking *from* the South and a speaking *with* the South rather than the speaking *for* the South by the Global North. It is a dialogic space facilitating mutual recognition, a relationship that is not free of struggle but, instead of a struggle-unto-death, a struggle-unto-life. Only with such mutuality, a consciousness of the Other and by the Other, can the ideals of reciprocity and solidarity in the face of multiple crises be actualized.

To theorize the Global South is to read the Global South. Literary criticism, or interpretation, is how theory can be translated into practice. Conversely, it is how practice generates theory that is oriented toward empiricism: literature is a representation of lived experience, an imaginative writing rooted in reality, history, and futurity. The Global South certainly converges with existing paradigms, such as postcolonialism and the Anthropocene, but what may be considered singular about the Global South is its revisioning and insistence on a dialogic and collaborative relation between self and other as a more ethical mode of addressing the problems—social, political, and environmental—besetting this region in the Anthropocene.

Notes

1 Boaventura de Sousa Santos, *The End of the Cognitive Empire: The Coming of Age of the Epistemologies of the South* (Durham: Duke University Press, 2018), viii.
2 Russell West-Pavlov, "Toward the Global South: Concept of Chimera, Paradigm or Panacea," in *The Global South and Literature*, ed. Russell West-Pavlov (Cambridge: Cambridge University Press, 2018), 2. For details on the Global South and Bandung, see Arjun Appadurai, *Modernity at Large: Cultural Dimensions of Globalization* (Minneapolis and London: Minnesota University Press, 1996), esp. 27–47; Arif Dirlik, "Global South: Predicament and Promise," *The Global South* 1, no. 1 (2007): 12–15; Quỳnh Phạm and Robbie Shilliam, "Reviving Bandung," in *Meanings of Bandung: Postcolonial Orders and Decolonial Visions*, ed. Quỳnh Phạm and Robbie Shilliam (London: Rowman & Littlefield International, 2016); and Duncan M. Yoon, "Bandung Nostalgia and the Global South," in *The Global South and Literature*, ed. Russell West-Pavlov (Cambridge: Cambridge University Press, 2018).
3 See Ella Shohat, "Notes on the 'Post-Colonial,'" *Social Text*, no. 31/32 (1992): 100–101.
4 Dipesh Chakrabarty, *Provincializing Europe: Postcolonial Thought and Historical Difference* (Princeton: Princeton University Press, 2000), 8.
5 Dipesh Chakrabarty, "The Climate of History: Four Theses," *Critical Inquiry* 35, no. 2 (2009): 208.
6 Timothy Clark, *Ecocriticism on the Edge: The Anthropocene as a Threshold Concept* (London: Bloomsbury, 2015), 2.
7 Rob Nixon, *Slow Violence and the Environmentalism of the Poor* (Cambridge: Harvard University Press, 2011), 237.
8 Ibid., 250.

9 Joan Martinez-Alier, *The Environmentalism of the Poor: A Study of Ecological Conflicts and Valuation* (Cheltenham: Edward Elgar, 2002), 10–12. See also Deyna Parvanova, "The industrial revolution was the force behind the New Imperialism," *Essai* 15 (2017).
10 Gina Apostol, *Insurrecto* (New York: Soho Press, 2018), 316.
11 Patricio N. Abinales and Donna J. Amoroso, *State and Society in the Philippines*, 2nd ed. (Quezon City: Ateneo de Manila University Press, 2017), 113.
12 Ibid.
13 Apostol, 25. See also Alvita Akiboh, "The 'Massacre' and the Aftermath: Remembering Balangiga and the War in the Philippines," *US History Scene*, 10 April 2015.
14 Greg Bankoff and George Emmanuel Borrinaga, "Whethering the Storm: The Twin Natures of Typhoons Haiyan and Yolanda," in *Contextualizing Disaster*, ed. Gregory V. Button and Mark Schuller (New York: Berghahn, 2019), 48, 44, 50–53.
15 Apostol, 97.
16 Ibid., 280, 283, 254, 126. See also Danny Petilla, "Lone Woman in Historic Balangiga Uprising Gets Recognition," *Inquirer*, 28 September 2018.
17 Apostol, 150.
18 See, for example, Homi K. Bhabha, *The Location of Culture*, 2nd ed. (London: Routledge, 2004).
19 Yoon, 23.
20 Leela Gandhi, *Postcolonial Theory: A Critical Introduction* (NSW: Allen & Unwin, 1998), 12.
21 See Julie McCarthy, "U.S. Returns Balangiga Church Bells to the Philippines after More Than a Century," *NPR*, 11 December 2018.
22 See Daniel Moss, "The Chinese Antidote to a Covid-Battered Philippines," *Bloomberg*, 21 November 2018.
23 See Jodesz Gavilan, "What Typhoon Yolanda Foreign Aid Looks Like Without US, EU, and UN," *Rappler*, 9 October 2016.
24 Gina Apostol, "Gina Apostol on Her New Book 'Insurrecto,' the Balangiga Massacre, and American Imperialism," interview by Glenn Diaz, *CNN Philippines*, 14 December 2018.
25 Apostol, *Insurrecto*, 99.
26 Ibid., 292.
27 Ibid., 293.
28 Herman Rapaport, *The Literary Theory Toolkit: A Compendium of Concepts and Methods* (West Sussex: Wiley-Blackwell, 2011), 85–89.
29 Apostol, "Gina Apostol on Her New Book."
30 See Gayatri C. Spivak, "Can the Subaltern Speak?" in *Colonial Discourse and Post-Colonial Theory: A Reader*, ed. Patrick Williams and Laura Chrisman (London: Routledge, 2013), 66–111. Spivak identifies two domains or spheres of representation: politics, where representation is the act of speaking for, to be a proxy or a substitute for another; and art as well as philosophy, where it is a depiction of a subject, a portraiture.
31 See W.E.B. Du Bois, *The Souls of Black Folk* (New York: Dover Publications, 1903). For Du Bois, the African-American, rather than self-consciousness, possesses double consciousness, seeing the self only through the lens of others and struggling to assert this hybrid identity, formed by native identity and shaped by foreign influence and imposition, as deserving of respect and societal participation.
32 West-Pavlov, 7–8.

References

Abinales, Patricio N., and Donna J. Amoroso. *State and Society in the Philippines*. 2nd ed. Quezon City: Ateneo de Manila University Press, 2017.
Akiboh, Alvita. "The 'Massacre' and the Aftermath: Remembering Balangiga and the War in the Philippines." *US History Scene*. 10 April 2015.
Apostol, Gina. *Insurrecto*. New York: Soho Press, 2018.
Apostol, Gina. "Gina Apostol on Her New Book 'Insurrecto,' the Balangiga Massacre, and American Imperialism." Interview by Glenn Diaz. *CNN Philippines*. 14 December 2018.
Appadurai, Arjun. *Modernity at Large: Cultural Dimensions of Globalization*. Minneapolis: University of Minnesota Press, 1996.
Bankoff, Greg, and George Emmanuel Borrinaga. "Whethering the Storm: The Twin Natures of Typhoons Haiyan and Yolanda." In *Contextualizing Disaster*. Edited by Gregory V. Button and Mark Schuller. New York: Berghahn, 2019. 44–65.
Bhabha, Homi K. *The Location of Culture*. 2nd ed. London: Routledge, 2004.
Chakrabarty, Dipesh. "The Climate of History: Four Theses." *Critical Inquiry* 35, no. 2 (2009): 197–222.
———. *Provincializing Europe: Postcolonial Thought and Historical Difference*. Princeton: Princeton University Press, 2000.
Clark, Timothy. *Ecocriticism on the Edge: The Anthropocene as a Threshold Concept*. London: Bloomsbury, 2015.
De Sousa Santos, Boaventura. *The End of the Cognitive Empire: The Coming of Age of Epistemologies of the South*. Durham: Duke University Press, 2018.
Dirlik, Arif. "Global South: Predicament and Promise." *The Global South* 1, no. 1 (2007): 12–23.
Du Bois, W.E.B. *The Souls of Black Folk*. New York: Dover, 1903.
Gandhi, Leela. *Postcolonial Theory: A Critical Introduction*. NSW: Allen & Unwin, 1998.
Gavilan, Jodesz. "What Typhoon Yolanda Foreign Aid Looks Like Without US, EU, and UN." *Rappler*. 9 October 2016.
Martinez-Alier, Joan. *The Environmentalism of the Poor: A Study of Ecological Conflicts and Valuation*. Cheltenham: Edward Elgar, 2002.
McCarthy, Julie. "U.S. Returns Balangiga Church Bells to the Philippines after More Than a Century." *NPR*. 11 December 2018.
Moss, Daniel. "The Chinese Antidote to a Covid-Battered Philippines." *Bloomberg*. 12 November 2018.
Nixon, Rob. *Slow Violence and the Environmentalism of the Poor*. Cambridge: Harvard University Press, 2011.
Parvanova, Deyna. "The Industrial Revolution Was the Force Behind the New Imperialism." *Essai* 15 (2017): 96–99.
Petilla, Danny. "Lone Woman in Historic Balangiga Uprising Gets Recognition." *Inquirer*. 28 September 2018.
Phạm, Quỳnh, and Robbie Shilliam. "Reviving Bandung." In *Meanings of Bandung: Postcolonial Orders and Decolonial Visions*. Edited by Quỳnh Phạm and Robbie Shilliam. London: Rowman & Littlefield International, 2016. 3–19.
Rapaport, Herman. *The Literary Theory Toolkit: A Compendium of Concepts and Methods*. West Sussex: Wiley-Blackwell, 2011.
Shohat, Ella. "Notes on the 'Post-Colonial.'" *Social Text*, 31/32 (1992): 99–113.

Spivak, Gayatri C. "Can the Subaltern Speak?" In *Colonial Discourse and Post-Colonial Theory: A Reader*. Edited by Patrick Williams and Laura Chrisman. London: Routledge, 2013. 66–111.

West-Pavlov, Russell. "Toward the Global South: Concept or Chimera, Paradigm or Panacea?" In *The Global South and Literature*. Edited by Russell West-Pavlov. Cambridge: Cambridge University Press, 2018. 1–19.

Yoon, Duncan M. "Bandung Nostalgia and the Global South." In *The Global South and Literature*. Edited by Russell West-Pavlov. Cambridge: Cambridge University Press, 2018. 23–33.

14
QUEERING THE MODEST WITNESS IN THE CHTHULUCENE

Jeff VanderMeer's *Borne* (a New Weird Case Study)

Kristin Girten

> Sweet is the lore which Nature brings;
> Our meddling intellect
> Mis-shapes the beauteous forms of things:—
> We murder to dissect.
>
> *William Wordsworth, "The Tables Turned" (1798)*[1]

Given the deep and wide-reaching ambition that so often tends to characterize modern innovations in science and technology, it is something of an irony that "modesty" was a primary distinguishing feature of the method of empirical witnessing that the forefather of modern science, Francis Bacon, pioneered. By the time Bacon set the stage for such empirical modesty with the publication of his *Novum Organum* in 1620, early European imperialists had already provoked the "Orbis Spike"—a global environmental change that occurred around 1610 as a result of the extermination of approximately fifty million indigenous inhabitants of "the New World" (largely by smallpox). This planetary event was the result of a rapid decline in farming (most significantly, in Latin America), which resulted in a widespread grow-back of trees and, consequently, a depletion of carbon dioxide.[2] However, the kind of modesty Bacon and his followers had in mind—disinterested, detached, and objective—is far from incompatible with such anthropogenic environmental degradation. As many historians of science and ecocritics have shown, Bacon's distinctive variety of modest witnessing appeared to legitimate grand projects of environmental manipulation and exploitation.[3] Baconians may have performed modesty, but their deepest ambitions and most far-reaching projects were anything but humble.

As Steven Shapin and Simon Schaffer explain in their foundational work *Leviathan and the Air-Pump* (1985), "a man whose narratives could be credited as mirrors of reality was a *modest man*; his reports ought to make that modesty visible." He did so by using the form of "the experimental essay," by adopting a "naked way of writing," and by "speak[ing] confidently of matters of fact."[4] These techniques were perceived to allow the scientist to establish and maintain his Baconian "modesty." Over the next century or so, such modesty would come to be known as his *objectivity*, his "view from nowhere," and his basic techniques for achieving it have persisted into the present day.[5] In *Modest_Witness@Second_ Millenium.FemaleMan_Meets_OncoMouse* (1997), multispecies feminist theorist Donna Haraway proposes to "queer" Bacon's modest witness so that we might "enable a more corporeal, inflected, and optically dense, if less elegant, kind of modest witness to matters of fact to emerge in the worlds of technoscience."[6] As Haraway explains, Bacon's modest witness boasts of both neutrality and transcendence.[7] Moreover, empirical modesty is closely tied to and informs the association between technoscience and masculinity—an association whose legacy unfortunately endures in our present day, as the persistent underrepresentation of women in the hard sciences attests. Haraway seeks to queer the modest witness to achieve both a more inclusive science and a more ethical one that not only acknowledges but is fundamentally inflected by humanity's kinship with nonhuman creatures. Whereas Bacon's modest witness transcends nature, Haraway's queer variety remains interwoven with nature. She is, to use a quote from William Wordsworth's poem "A slumber did my spirit seal" (1800), perennially "rolled round in earth's diurnal course / with rocks and stones and trees."[8] As a direct consequence of this radical intermingling—what Haraway calls "entanglement"—she experiences the creatures, both sentient and non-sentient, with whom she inhabits the earth as "kin." For Bacon's modest witness, such creatures are fundamentally Other than himself. In contrast, Haraway's queer modest witness "becomes with" her fellow creatures.[9] She sees herself as bound up with them: "one must be in the action, be finite and dirty, not transcendent and clean."[10] Bacon's method fosters an ontology of detachment; Haraway's, an ontology of kinship. As a result, whereas Bacon's modest witness is perfectly willing to, quoting this essay's epigraph, "murder to dissect"—to sacrifice life for knowledge—Haraway's queer witness is much more circumspect. Bacon encourages an ethic of discovery and advancement; Haraway an ethic of care.[11] Bacon's modest witness pursues progress for its own sake, without much if any concern for the sacrifices it exacts. Haraway's queer witness' pursuit of progress is always accompanied by a deeply felt ecological responsibility.

This chapter analyzes Jeff VanderMeer's postapocalyptic "New Weird" novel *Borne* (2017) through the framework of Haraway's proposal to queer the modest witness and in relation to her call for us to acknowledge our present epoch as "the Chthulucene" (an alternative to the Anthropocene). I argue that *Borne* registers the Chthulugenic nature of our late-capitalist present and, as it does so, offers both a critique of the traditional Baconian modest witness and an inspiring example of how the modest witness may be queered. The eponymous character of the novel is a tentacled shape-shifter who is at times friendly and loving, at other times monstrous. The novel begins as the story's central protagonist and narrator, Rachel, describes having found the strange creature "on a sunny gunmetal day when the giant bear Mord came roving near our home." She goes on to recount, "To me, Borne was just salvage at first. I didn't know what Borne would mean to us. I couldn't know that he would change everything."[12] Change everything, he does. In spite of the swampy dystopic stasis that pervades the novel's landscape, he twists and turns the plot, pulling its central characters, as well as the reader, along in its disorienting wake. As he does so, he invites—indeed, demands—those of us who witness him, and the "nature" by and from which he has been created, to queer our modesty. With Borne's arrival, we are finally compelled at long last to recognize, and reckon with, the fact that the modest anthropogenic retreat into the human self is fundamentally untenable. "Beacon-like" and "strob[ing] emerald green … every half minute or so," he illuminates the radically trans-corporeal, inter-creaturely, forever flowing, and Chthulugenic material reality of Earth's nature.[13] And, as we become privy to this reality, we have no choice but to bear witness to our own reality. We are entangled. We are ourselves Chthulus. Once the privilege of a few, within this New Weird fiction, modesty is no longer an option for any. Entangled within the tentacles of earth's nature, we become queer. We are the species that witnesses, and Borne makes us queer.

It was with his 1620 *Novum Organum* that Francis Bacon pioneered his innovative philosophic method, which was distinguished from the Aristotelian scientific tradition that preceded it by its reliance on experience, experiment, direct observation, and induction. Whereas previous scientific practices regularly tended to be primarily theoretical, speculative, or discursive, Bacon's was fundamentally *empirical* in nature. With his innovation came new challenges. Bacon was particularly concerned with what he called "the idols of the mind." Bacon claims that, "beset" by the idols, "the human understanding is like a false mirror, which, receiving rays irregularly, distorts and discolours the nature of things by mingling its own nature with it." The solution he provides is for the scientist to "free … and cleanse" their "understanding."[14] Bacon suggests that modern science requires that its practitioners purify themselves so they may be set apart and, thus, unencumbered by the very material world they seek to explore and understand. It is this indifferent neutrality, or "modesty," that would eventually evolve into what we now refer to as "objectivity." Still regularly cited as the forefather of "the scientific method," Bacon has had an enduring legacy. Objectivity persists as a requirement of reliable scientific investigation. The scientist, then and now, is expected to be an "independent observer" who resists the temptation to intermingle with, and thus become swayed by, their objects of study.[15]

This expectation of scientific independence has several significant and enduring implications for how science is both perceived and practiced. As Haraway puts it, the scientist "must be invisible": "This self-invisibility is the specifically modern, European, masculine, scientific form of the virtue of modesty. This is the form of modesty that pays off its practitioners in the coin of epistemological and social power."[16] It was not until 1945 that women would be allowed membership in the Royal Society, England's national society of science, which was established in 1660. Founded in 1863, the US National Academy of Sciences was only a couple decades ahead of the Royal Society, electing Florence Rena Sabin as its first female member in 1925. As Haraway explains, "The issue was whether women had the independent status to be modest witnesses, and they did not." Feminine and masculine modesty have been historically perceived as binary opposites. The former is "of the body," enacted by women's preservation of their virginity; the latter is "of the mind," enacted by men's philosophical detachment from matter. Consequently, "within the conventions of modest truth-telling, women might watch a [scientific] demonstration; they could not witness it." From the outset, the modest witness occupied an exclusive and privileged position. Furthermore, as Haraway indicates, "colored, sexed, and laboring persons still have to do a lot of work to become similarly transparent to count as objective, modest witnesses to the world rather than to their 'bias' or 'special interest.'"[17]

Another consequence of scientific modesty and the detachment from matter that it entails is the tendency of science to privilege discovery and progress over ecological health and sustainability. Objective science continues to be associated with the degradation and even "rape" of nature. If he is transcendent above matter, then what is there to oblige the modest witness to care about whatever damage may result from his activities? In a word, nothing. For, untouched by matter, the scientist may have no fear about the material consequences of his activities. He has everything to gain and nothing to lose. No wonder Bacon had such high hopes for his fittingly titled "Instauratio Magna" (1620) or "Great Instauration" (1620). Pursued by the modest witness, scientific progress need know no bounds. The great technoscientific innovations of the Enlightenment era—the steam engine, the spinning jenny, the power loom—were the practical expressions of such unrestrained scientific ambition. It is only over the past few decades that we have begun to reckon with the disastrous consequences of our scientific ambitions. Many scientists, historians, and ecocritics who have proposed an Anthropocene epoch argue that this epoch began in the Enlightenment. According to this line of thinking, Bacon was the father not only of the scientific method but also of the Anthropocene.

Though postapocalyptic "survival," not science, appears as the most prominent theme of VanderMeer's *Borne*, the novel nevertheless poses serious challenges to how we envision and practice science during this period of late capitalism, presenting readers with a scientific allegory.[18] Technoscience, particularly in the form of biotechnology, serves as the backdrop of the novel and appears to be largely responsible for the near uninhabitability of the earth. We are made to believe that an entity known as "the Company" has, in its pursuit of biotechnological innovation, inadvertently produced dangerous monsters. The largest and most threatening of such monsters is Mord, a gigantic flying bear who threatens to kill all who cross his path and whom Rachel depicts as the embodiment of the Company—its "husk," its "ghost." The novel's eponymous character is, we are to presume, also a biotech "monster" of sorts, though whether he is benign or threatening remains uncertain throughout the book.[19] Given that we receive the story through Rachel, who is immediately besot with Borne, most of the time he seems cute and charming rather than sinister.

However, Rachel's perspective is offset by that of her boyfriend Wick, who views Borne as a threat from his first encounter with the creature. With the Company as a looming presence from the novel's outset, readers are immediately invited to be guarded about the scientific and, specifically, scientific innovation. Rachel helps us see another way for science though. When Rachel first brings Borne home, she devotes herself to empirical observation and classification of him: "I upgraded Borne from plant to animal, but still did not reclassify him as 'purposeful.'" Rachel behaves like a biologist, a behavior that is reinforced when she subsequently reminisces of a book her now-dead parents had given her: "a biology book with foldouts showing cross-sections of different environments drawn in detail and in vivid but realistic colors." A page later, she explains how, though she "lost all [her] possessions when [she] came to the city," in her "scavenging" she had come upon "another biology book": "It didn't have foldouts and there were fewer illustrations, but some of the art reminded me of the book I'd loved." She proceeds to give this book to Borne, "along with books on other topics. But the other books were camouflage, really, for what was personal to me."[20] The biology book is the personal book. So, from early on in the novel, VanderMeer invites us to see Rachel as a scientist, albeit an amateur one.

It is curious that Rachel expresses "love" for, and a "personal" connection with, science when the devastation and suffering that plague humanity in the novel's present appear to be a direct consequence of scientific innovation. However, in various ways, the novel asks us to assume that the science that was practiced by the Company must have been fundamentally distinct from that which holds Rachel's affection. From the beginning of the novel, Rachel's hatred of the Company, which she portrays as a "white engorged tick on the city's flank," is palpable.[21] In Rachel's eyes, the Company is a cruel and murderous parasite, a nihilistic thief that has robbed humanity—for at least as far as the imagination can reach—of its sustenance. Though it was once reputed to be the prime source of scientific discovery and progress, time has revealed the Company for what it really is: author of apocalypse. This portrayal evokes the critique of science that Haraway presents. Destruction and death are the direct consequences of the Company's sense of detachment and independence from its research and development. What exactly the Company's goals have been never becomes fully clear, but what does is that it has operated without any significant concern for the consequences of its actions.

Rachel's boyfriend and roommate Wick is a practitioner of technoscience with ties to the Company, and these ties, along with his technological applications, distinguish his science from that which Rachel celebrates. We learn early on in the novel that Wick used to work for the Company, and as the story unfolds, we become increasingly aware that his emotional connection to the organization is far from superficial. Though he, like Rachel, resents the Company for its destructiveness, he nevertheless experiences a sense of loss when he and Rachel return to it and find it in ruins. In fact, earlier in the novel, Rachel detects "nostalgia" in notes Wick took during his time at the Company.[22] Wick has continued to innovate on his own, even after the Company has fallen, leaving a nearly uninhabitable toxic biosphere in its wake. Through much of the novel, Wick evinces scientific tendencies that evoke the traditional modest witness. He has a "taut quality, the armor that almost physically sheathed him when he didn't want to confront something."[23] A desire for self-preservation appears to be his prime motivator.

Whereas Rachel views Borne as "a person" and seeks to protect him, Wick objectifies him and expresses a desire to dissect him:

> "Give it to me. I can find out what it is."
> That made me shudder. "Only by taking Borne apart."
> "Maybe. Yes, of course." ...
> To Wick, Borne was just another variable, something he needed to control to manage his own stress. ... *This was business, this was survival.*[24]

Wick seems to see their world through a telescope. He is oriented to the big picture and is, therefore, well aware of the systems of biopower, and the technoscientific innovations, that continue to rule their lives. Consequently, he is capable of pursuing survival strategically. His empirical modesty—neutrality, detachment—has allowed him to fortify their refuge, The Balcony Cliffs, as effectively as possible. It has equipped him to continue to develop forms of biotech that are valuable on the black market for their mind-altering effects. Wick's success as a modest witness makes him successful at being a protector and a breadwinner.

Later in the novel, though, we discover the sinister history of Wick's technoscientific capabilities and consequently come to critique Wick's scientific practice. As Rachel reveals the history of Mord, the giant flying bear-God whose wrath motivates him to kill all who find themselves in his path (except for his proxies, who help mete out his vengeance), we learn that Wick was involved in Mord's creation. Wick began his biotech career as a participant in the Company's "fish project," which pursued innovation through biotech experiments on and alteration of aquatic animals, many of whom were "dumped," left to suffer and die, in the Company's "holding ponds." Then, as he admits in his letter to Rachel, Wick "helped create Mord. The Company used what we had learned from the fish project to build Mord." Moreover, we learn the depth of cruelty implicit within his creation. As Wick explains,

> the Company wasn't building him from scratch. Not putting a human face on an animal, as happened with the fish. No, they wanted to create an

animal around a human being. Maybe I didn't realize what the Company planned to do to him, but that is no excuse. I should have found a way out, or found a way to get Mord out.[25]

Here, Wick is revealed for who he has really been—a Victor Frankenstein-esque figure who has, on the behest of the Company, sought scientific discovery at the tragic expense of human life. Similarly, Mord is revealed for who he really is—a man-cum-creature who has been made, and then selfishly abandoned, by supposedly "civilized" men. It is no wonder that Mord, like Frankenstein's Creature, turns on his fellow men in the way that he does. Once we learn Mord's story, we sympathize with him and blame the Company (including Wick) for the suffering and death the great bear is obsessed with provoking. The modest witness may appear adept at seeing the big picture and, therefore, at making decisions that serve his own and his close colleagues' and friends' interests. However, we are ultimately called to recognize that he nonetheless misses a lot and is prone to poor judgment because of his detachment. The fallout from his obliviousness and error could hardly be more devastating.

If Wick and the Company signify the conventional modest witness within the allegory of science *Borne* presents, Rachel signifies a thoroughly opposite variety of witness. Whereas Wick and the Company are distinguished by detachment, Rachel is distinguished by a heightened capacity for sympathy and love. Wick is aloof; Rachel is emotional and even sentimental. We might therefore characterize her as a *sensitive* witness. Even though she "refused to call it love," Rachel regularly expresses affection, love, and care for Wick. However, it is in her interactions with Borne that we come to recognize the full depth and range of her sensitivity. When she first comes upon him, the strength of her feeling is immediately palpable: "Borne beat against my chest like a second heart." Whereas Wick wants to dissect Borne, "it was through touch that [Rachel] began to understand [Borne's] complexity," and her touch is gentle, kind, and even loving. In fact, it is not long until she begins to care for him as if she is his mother, even experiencing what she calls "a mother's worry" about him. In the spirit of Haraway, she "becomes kin" with Borne: as Rachel explains, "the more personality Borne showed, the more I felt attached to him." She comes to love Borne and tries "to be a good parent, a good friend," to him.[26] She is "attuned" to him, even able to see the night sky "from his eyes." Her feeling for him is so strong that she continues to care for him even after she has discovered that he has tricked her and Wick by impersonating them to one another, even after she has come to perceive Borne's "monstrous" side.[27] Though at times Rachel seems overly swayed by emotion, we are nevertheless inclined to admire her more than we might criticize her. She achieves what the Company and Wick could—or would—not: she nurtures and educates the biotech that humans have made. In direct contrast to Wick and the Company, Rachel takes on the responsibility of seeing after Borne and helps him become a good reader. It is striking that she, as a sensitive witness, has a greater sense of obligation and responsibility to care for Borne than the modest witness Wick feels for Mord, even though she merely salvages Borne, whereas Wick helps to create Mord.

Rachel is to Borne as Wick is to Mord, and the assonance and consonance in the Mord/Borne pairing serves to emphasize the parallel. (According to the novel's Acknowledgments, "certain aspects" of both monsters were inspired by VanderMeer's "monster cat, Neo, otherwise known as Massive Attack."[28]) Moreover, Rachel and Wick are foils for one another, as are Borne and Mord, to whom Rachel refers during the novel's climax as "our monsters": "the monster I had helped raise fighting the monster Wick had helped create."[29] To return to Haraway, Rachel and Borne together represent kinship and a sense of "becoming-with," whereas Wick and Mord together represent man's modest but willful denial of his material entanglements.[30] As Borne perceptively acknowledges, "Wick, he doesn't say it, but he thinks I'm a freak. A monster."[31] Wick's armor-like modesty causes him to oversimplify and attempt to ostracize Borne. In contrast, Rachel's sensitivity allows her to discover his details, to come to know both his physicality and his personhood. Whereas Wick only sees Borne's monstrosity, Rachel perceives

> the circular tension of the suckers he could create, the waving stubby toughness of the cilia, which looked so delicate but were not, the utter indestructibility where he formed ridges, the glassy imperviousness of those eyes, which had a film over them that hardened as soon as the eye appeared and left only a millisecond before the eye was subsumed in the skin.[32]

As this accumulation of details shows, Rachel is a far better empirical scientist than Wick is. Her sensitivity enhances her empirical aptitude, ensuring the multisensory comprehensiveness of her observations. Much like the "sensors" and "trip wires" she sets for her traps, she is "sensitive to touch and vibration."[33] Though she is ultimately shown not to know all there is to know about Borne, her empirical practice allows her to know far more than Wick does.

Ultimately, too, the plot's unfolding vindicates Rachel's sense of obligation and the sensitivity that informs it. The world is reborn when and only when Borne kills Mord, after having initiated a fight with him. What exactly prompts and enables Borne to kill Mord, "the truest killer of the two," is not fully clear. However, Borne's brief reunion with Rachel appears to be an important motivator, as it inspires him to have this fantasy, which is ultimately partially fulfilled: "And in the end everything will be okay again between us and you can live in the Balcony Cliffs again and I'll move back in with you." VanderMeer implies that Borne's attack on Mord is an expression of his affection for Rachel, which presumably would never have come to be had she not expressed such sympathy with and affection for him. Borne's epic "gift of a better life" to Rachel and Wick is in return for all of the gifts Rachel has given him. Though she is tempted to "make [her] heart hard and not give in" or continue to be sensitive to Borne, there is nevertheless an enduring reciprocity in their relationship that is thoroughly absent in Wick's dynamic with Mord: they both act on an ethic of care, in spite of the fact that both are "weaponized" and, thus, capable of dreadful deeds.[34] Rachel and Borne's mutual love is a "tentacled" and "trans-corporeal" one.[35] They interpenetrate one another. At one point, Rachel even literally hides within Borne's body. In this suspenseful scene, Rachel trans-corporeally enters Borne for the sake of her own survival. Such trans-corporeality is not unidirectional. When Borne impersonates Rachel and Wick, shifting his own shape to mimic theirs, he may be seen to enter them, albeit a simulated form of them, trans-corporeally as well. These important moments of trans-corporeality together emphasize the intertwined nature of their bodies and their fates. Given how self-serving Borne often seems in his childlike innocence, one must presume that Borne saves humanity and the human world at least in part because he has come to see that his own survival is bound up with theirs. That Borne lives and is accommodated to the reborn world (albeit somewhat comically, as a houseplant) only deepens the connection between their entanglement, the mutuality of their survival, and his dramatic act of salvation.

Foils to one another, Rachel and Wick suggest a dichotomy according to which sensitivity is female and objectivity is male. Thus, the novel verges on gender essentialism, albeit one that is gynocentric rather than phallocentric, preferring feminine sensitivity to masculine objectivity. However, the novel ultimately denies such essentialism, advocating queer modesty for both women and men. For one, the power-seeking villainous Magician, whose armor is even stronger than Wick's, shows that not all women are sensitive. Even more importantly, though, the novel concludes with an endorsement of androgyny. By the final pages, Rachel and Wick have transformed, as has their relationship. Once opposites, they ultimately become a unified, androgynous pair. Previously, Wick had been the leader, director of the Balcony Cliffs' development; Rachel the underbuilder and salvager. In the end, though, as the following quote illustrates, they have become equal and united collaborators: "'What now, Rachel?' Wick asked me. 'What do we do now?' 'Whatever we want to do,' I said. So we set to work." "We stand by each other," Rachel explains. It is as if their temperaments, and their modes of witnessing, have merged. They have together become queer modest witnesses: "We sit on the balcony on the good days, Wick and I, and we hold hands and look out at the light on the river at dusk … a river that one day may be truly beautiful."[36] Like Haraway, VanderMeer suggests that hope will come only when we manage to join masculine transcendence and feminine sensitivity together—when we are able to analyze our present, past, and future systematically while at the same time feeling for and becoming-with the "oddkins" like Borne with which we are, by virtue of our shared habitation of the earth, entangled.[37]

In H.P. Lovecraft's origin story, "The Call of Cthulhu" (1928), the tentacled beast is "the thing" that threatens man's sovereignty and, thus, his sanity and survival.[38]

Haraway offers a directly contrary depiction of Cthulhu, whose distinction from Lovecraft's she marks by moving the placement of an "h": "Chthulu." In Lovecraft's portrayal, Cthulhu is an omen of our demise and thus a trigger for the hopelessness and helplessness of human civilization—according to Haraway, a "misogynist racial-nightmare."[39] In contrast, Haraway's Chthulu is humanity's escape hatch. Like many ecotheorists, Haraway recognizes that humanity has found itself—has indeed determinedly if not consciously positioned itself—within the Anthropocene (or, alternatively, the Capitalocene or Plantationocene). However, she refuses to allow the story to end there. She proposes a new era: the Chthulucene. This era is "new" only to our awareness. Like Lovecraft's "Cthulhu," it is as old as time and persists into the present day. It thus coexists with all of the other "-cenes"—the Anthropocene, the Capitalocene, the Plantationocene, as well as the Holocene. It is the story that palimpsestically underlies all other stories and the truth that gives the lie to other stories' fictions. VanderMeer's Borne gives us access to this story. Like Haraway, Borne insists that never has man—or for that matter Earth—been sovereign. Rather, chthulus all, the human and nonhuman creatures of our planet (including not only animals but also "rocks, and stones, and trees") cannot help but intertwine, intermingle, and in-wreath.[40] This is no more and no less than the nature of our planet and the strange shape-shifting tentacled beings that inhabit it.

Notes

1 William Wordsworth, "The Tables Turned," in *Wordsworth: Poetical Works*, ed. Thomas Hutchinson (Oxford: Oxford University Press, 1904), 377.
2 See Simon Lewis and Mark Maslin, "Defining the Anthropocene," *Nature* (2015): 171–180; David Bello, "Mass Deaths in Americas Start New CO_2 Epoch," *Scientific American*, 11 March 2015; and Michael Franco, "'Orbis Spike' in 1610 Marks Humanity's First Major Impact on Planet Earth," *CNET*, 12 March 2015.
3 See, for instance, a special issue of *Telos* devoted to the Anthropocene from 2016 in which the "anthropogenic effects" of Bacon's proposal to "conquer nature" is a common theme. Martin D. Yaffe, "'Anthropogenic Effects' in Genesis 1–11 and Francis Bacon," *Telos* 177 (2016): 16, 19.
4 Steven Shapin and Simon Schaffer, *Leviathan and the Air-Pump: Hobbes, Boyle, and the Experimental Life* (Princeton: Princeton University Press, 1985), 65. The phrase "naked way of writing" is from Robert Boyle, "Proëmical Essay … with some Considerations touching Experimental Essays in General," in *The Works of the Honorouable Robert Boyle*, 2nd ed., ed. Thomas Birch (London: J. & F. Rivington, 1772), 1.318.
5 On the evolution of Baconian modesty into objectivity, see Lorraine Daston and Peter Galison, *Objectivity* (Brooklyn: Zone Books, 2007). The phrase "the view from nowhere" is taken from Thomas Nagel, *The View from Nowhere* (Oxford: Oxford University Press, 1989).
6 Donna J. Haraway, *Modest_Witness@Second_Millenium.FemaleMan_Meets_OncoMouse: Feminism and Technoscience* (New York: Routledge, 1997), 24.

7 As I have elsewhere shown, not all Enlightenment thinkers accepted the effectiveness of such transcendence. For a satirist like Jonathan Swift, it proved to be an apt target of ridicule. See Kristin M. Girten, "Mingling with Matter: Tactile Microscopy and the Philosophic Mind in Brobdingnag and Beyond," *The Eighteenth Century* 54, no. 4 (2013): 497–520.
 8 William Wordsworth, "A Slumber Did My Spirit Seal," in *Poetical Works*, 149.
 9 Donna Haraway, "Anthropocene, Capitalocene, Plantationocene, Chthulucene: Making Kin," *Environmental Humanities* 6 (2015): 160.
10 Haraway, *Modest_Witness@Second_Millennium*, 36.
11 For an earlier "queer witness" and a Romantic precursor to this ethic of care, as founded on an ontology of kinship, see Kristin M. Girten, "Charlotte Smith's Tactile Poetics," *The Eighteenth Century* 54, no. 2 (2013): 215–230.
12 Jeff VanderMeer, *Borne* (New York: MCD/Farrar, Straus and Giroux, 2017), 3.
13 Ibid.
14 Francis Bacon, *Novum Organum*, in *The Works of Francis Bacon*, ed. James Spedding, Robert Leslie Ellis, and Douglas Denon Heath (New York: Hurd and Houghton, 1864), 8.76–77, 99.
15 National Academy of Sciences, National Academy of Engineering, and Institute of Medicine, *Responsible Science: Ensuring the Integrity of the Research Process: Volume I* (Washington, DC: The National Academies Press, 1992), 38.
16 Haraway, *Modest_Witness@Second_Millennium*, 23–24.
17 Ibid., 27, 30, 31, 32.
18 VanderMeer, 167.
19 Ibid., 27, 11.
20 Ibid., 18, 138–139, 140.
21 Ibid., 26.
22 Ibid., 21.
23 Ibid., 135.
24 Ibid., 19.
25 Ibid., 300, 305.
26 Ibid., 56, 64.
27 Ibid., 6, 148, 140, 23, 56, 64, 108, 178–181.
28 Ibid., 325.
29 Ibid., 284.
30 Haraway, "Anthropocene, Capitalocene, Plantationocene, Chthulucene," 160–161.
31 VanderMeer, 173.
32 Ibid., 148.
33 Ibid., 15.
34 Ibid., 262, 279, 312, 314.
35 The term "trans-corporeal" is borrowed from Stacy Alaimo, *Bodily Natures: Science, Environment, and the Material Self* (Bloomington: Indiana University Press, 2010), 2.
36 VanderMeer, 319, 320, 323.
37 Donna J. Haraway, *Staying with the Trouble: Making Kin in the Chthulucene* (Durham: Duke University Press, 2016), 3.
38 See H.P. Lovecraft, "The Call of Cthulhu," in *The Call of Cthulhu and Other Weird Stories*, ed. S.T. Joshi (New York: Penguin, 2016), 139–169.
39 Haraway, "Anthropocene," 160.
40 Wordsworth, "A Slumber Did My Spirit Seal," 149.

References

Alaimo, Stacy. *Bodily Natures: Science, Environment, and the Material Self.* Bloomington: Indiana University Press, 2010.

Bacon, Francis. *The Works of Francis Bacon.* Edited by James Spedding, Robert Leslie Ellis, and Douglas Denon Heath. New York: Hurd and Houghton, 1864.

Bello, David. "Mass Deaths in Americas Start New CO_2 Epoch." *Scientific American.* 11 March 2015.

Boyle, Robert. *The Works of the Honorouable Robert Boyle.* 2nd ed. Edited by Thomas Birch. London: J. & F. Rivington, 1772.

Daston, Lorraine, and Peter Galison. *Objectivity.* Brooklyn: Zone Books, 2007.

Franco, Michael. "'Orbis Spike' in 1610 Marks Humanity's First Major Impact on Planet Earth." *CNET.* 12 March 2015.

Girten, Kristin M. "Charlotte Smith's Tactile Poetics." *The Eighteenth Century* 54, no. 2 (2013): 215–230.

———. "Mingling with Matter: Tactile Microscopy and the Philosophic Mind in Brobdingnag and Beyond." *The Eighteenth Century* 54, no. 4 (2013): 497–520.

Haraway, Donna J. *Modest_Witness@Second_Millenium.FemaleMan_Meets_OncoMouse: Feminism and Technoscience.* New York: Routledge, 1997.

———. "Anthropocene, Capitalocene, Plantationocene, Chthulucene: Making Kin." *Environmental Humanities* 6 (2015): 159–165.

———. *Staying with the Trouble: Making Kin in the Chthulucene.* Durham: Duke University Press, 2016.

Lewis, Simon, and Mark Maslin. "Defining the Anthropocene." *Nature* (2015): 171–180.

Lovecraft, H.P. *The Call of Cthulhu and Other Weird Stories.* Edited by S.T. Joshi. New York: Penguin, 2016.

Nagel, Thomas. *The View from Nowhere.* Oxford: Oxford University Press, 1989.

Responsible Science: Ensuring the Integrity of the Research Process: Volume I. Washington, DC: The National Academies Press, 1992.

Shapin, Steven, and Simon Schaffer. *Leviathan and the Air-Pump: Hobbes, Boyle, and the Experimental Life.* Princeton: Princeton University Press, 1985.

VanderMeer, Jeff. *Borne.* New York: MCD/Farrar, Straus and Giroux, 2017.

Wordsworth, William. *Wordsworth: Poetical Works.* Edited by Thomas Hutchinson. Oxford: Oxford University Press, 1904.

Yaffe, Martin D. "'Anthropogenic Effects' in Genesis 1–11 and Francis Bacon." *Telos* 177 (2016): 16–42.

15
CONTEMPORARY CLI-FI AS ANTHROPOCENE LITERATURE

Kim Stanley Robinson's *New York 2140*

Seth T. Reno

In 2008, journalist Dan Bloom coined the term "cli-fi" (short for climate fiction) to describe a literary and cinematic genre focused on climate change. Most often, cli-fi centers on anthropogenic climate change, or human-caused global warming, though that's not always the case, and climate change can serve as a central theme of the work or as an aspect of the setting or plot. Deriving from sci-fi (science fiction), cli-fi has become one of the fastest-growing literary genres of the twenty-first century, garnering international attention through prominent reports in *The New York Times*, *The Guardian*, and NPR. Researchers in the humanities specializing in fields like ecocriticism, environmental literature, and the environmental humanities have embraced cli-fi, which requires an interdisciplinary approach. As a result, the number of climate-change-themed college courses drawing from cli-fi has grown significantly. It's clear that this is one of the most important literary genres of our time.[1]

However, scholars and readers of science fiction will be quick to point out that SF has always been about climate, to some extent. As contributors in this collection demonstrate, some of the earliest works of SF center on extreme environmental events. Mary Shelley's *The Last Man* (1826), the first Last Man novel in English, is a postapocalyptic tale about a world ravaged by a deadly plague unleashed by global war, industrialization, and colonial exploitation. William Delisle Hay's novella *The Doom of the Great City* (1880) imagines poisonous industrial smog wiping out the population of London. Richard Jeffries' *After London* (1885) similarly imagines an unspecified environmental catastrophe that decimates human civilization and turns London into a deadly, chemical-industrial swamp. And many of H.G. Wells' novels and short stories deal with climate crises, as do many of the most influential works of twentieth-century SF. In other words, climate fiction *is* science fiction, though of a particular kind.

DOI: 10.4324/9781003095347-18

What makes much contemporary cli-fi stand out is its explicit engagement with the science of global warming. Cli-fi novels take climate science and climate change models from the theoretical-scientific realm and place them into tangible narratives, providing realistic examples of how climate change could affect human life in the near future. A recent study on the impact of reading cli-fi reveals that "most readers attested to the value of cli-fi as a tool for enabling the imagination of potential climate futures."[2] What might the planet look like in 50 or 150 years? How will cities and societies adapt to rising sea levels and global temperatures? What new emotions, relationships, and sociopolitical structures might we experience in a world ravaged by global warming? Cli-fi engages these questions and imagines possible futures.

Perhaps no one illustrates these points better than Kim Stanley Robinson, an American author recognized as one of the greatest SF writers of all time. Many of his novels maintain a tri-genre status as science fiction, climate fiction, and "Anthropocene fiction," the latter of which Adam Trexler characterizes as centered on "the historical tension between the existence of catastrophic global warming and the failed obligation to act."[3] According to Trexler, Anthropocene novels focus on the complex connections between economics, politics, and ecology that drive our globalized world. Anthropocene fiction, then, is a particular kind of cli-fi with a distinctive geological and sociopolitical viewpoint. Rebecca Evans goes even further, arguing for a sub-genre of "Anthropocene science fiction," stories that dismantle the idea of a single, often Western, story about how anthropogenic climate change developed and what it's doing to the planet.[4] Robinson's work fits nicely into Evans' category, as his Anthropocene fiction both writes the Anthropocene and emerges from it: industrial capitalism, imperial colonialism, and fossil fuel culture have produced the Anthropocene, along with this new literary genre. The distinction between cli-fi and Anthropocene fiction is therefore fluid, though one distinguishing factor in the most recent works of Anthropocene fiction is the author's explicit engagement with or acknowledgment of the Anthropocene as a new geological epoch.

Robinson's 2017 novel *New York 2140* exemplifies this new kind of Anthropocene novel. This genre-bending novel presents a near future when much of Manhattan is under water after catastrophic glacial melting causes sea levels to rise fifty feet. Robinson uses the term "Anthropocene" several times throughout the novel, and the Anthropocene concept acts as a thread, a grounding concept through which Robinson imagines a potential future based on the planet's current trajectory. He structures the novel around eight economic concepts (which title the book's eight parts), emphasizing the relationship between capitalism and climate change. In many important ways, capitalism creates the Anthropocene; the two are bound together. The accumulating metaphors of a nation and world drowning in debt literally produce a world drowning in rising sea levels and socioeconomic inequality. *New York 2140* demonstrates how living in the Anthropocene means that we can never really escape the past, as it remains materially embedded in the waters, atmosphere, and economic infrastructure of the present—and the future.

Kim Stanley Robinson: Hero of the Environment

In Robinson's vast body of work, which spans over thirty years and includes over twenty novels and numerous short stories, several major themes consistently drive his writings: environmentalism and sustainability; the relationship between climate change, science, and capitalism; and the political and economic modes of resistance to addressing climate change. These are all hallmarks of cli-fi and Anthropocene fiction, and readers and critics alike praise Robinson as one of the most realistic and scientifically informed writers of these genres.[5] And he really knows his stuff: Robinson was dubbed a "Hero of the Environment" by *Time* magazine in 2008, an award that recognized the world's most influential environmentalists, and, in addition to his writings, speeches, and teaching, Robinson works for the Sierra Nevada Research Institute, which funds interdisciplinary research to promote sustainability and other ways to address climate change.

Robinson is well known for a number of climate-based trilogies, including his Science in the Capitol trilogy (2004–2007), which focuses on a group of scientists, politicians, and Buddhist monks in Washington, D.C., during a climate change disaster in the early twenty-first century. The first novel, *Forty Signs of Rain*, contains one of Robinson's most well-known lines, which could just as easily appear in *New York 2140*: "Easier to destroy the world than to change capitalism even one little bit."[6] This is a riff on a famous quote from theorist Fredric Jameson, who was Robinson's PhD advisor at UC San Diego: "it is easier to imagine the end of the world than to imagine the end of capitalism."[7] Both Robinson and Jameson critique the illusion that capitalism is a natural order of the world; rather, they suggest, it is destroying the world. As many chapters in this collection illustrate, capitalism and its consequences—globalized industrialization, imperial colonialism, concentration of wealth, uneven distribution of resources, climate change—are key features of the Anthropocene epoch. The end of capitalism *is* the end of the world—unless we shift to a different political and economic order. Robinson imagines possible futures of and alternatives to capitalism in many of his novels, including *New York 2140*.

In a 2014 interview, Robinson reveals some of his thinking about the political and economic aspects of the Anthropocene, and the means by which we might live in the Anthropocene in a more sustainable manner. In order to "make it through this current, calamitous period," he says, we first need to establish "how many of us constitutes a carrying capacity given our consumption, and then figure out the technologies and lifestyles that would allow for that carrying capacity while also allowing ecosystems to thrive."[8] Carrying capacity here refers to how many humans can live on Earth in a sustainable manner. Humans' current consumption of natural resources is far outpacing Earth's ecosystems, mainly by the actions and policies of the wealthiest nations. One solution, Robinson suggests, is lifestyle change: less consumption, more renewable resources, and so on. But the second, and more important bit, is much more challenging: acting globally with "a set of laws" everyone would follow. He explains:

> We need a global economic system that is designed specifically for sustainability. We already have a global economic system in the form of institutions like the World Bank and the International Monetary Fund. Together, their agreements make up a comprehensive system. But right now, this system cheats future generations by systematically underpricing the true costs of our exploitation of the biosphere. It sets the prices of the Earth's natural resources by establishing what is basically the aggregation of supplies and demands. But this process is biased toward pricing things lower and lower, because of pressure from buyers and the need for sellers to stay in business. As a result, sellers sell their products for less than they cost to make, which should lead to bankruptcy for the seller, but it doesn't because parts of the costs have been shifted onto future generations to pay. When practiced systematically it becomes a kind of multi-generational Ponzi scheme, and leads to the mass extinction event of the early Anthropocene, which we have already started.[9]

This is difficult to accomplish. Changing the global economic system suddenly doesn't really work, but we don't have a lot of time to make major changes. Robinson suggests altering the current system "so that the global rules of the World Bank, etc., require ecological sustainability as their main criterion." The problem with enacting such rules is capitalism itself:

> Capitalism as we know it is represented as natural, entrenched, and immutable. None of that is true. It's a political order and political orders change. What we want is to remember that our system is constructed for a purpose, and so in need of constant fixing and new tries.[10]

These are the exact issues and future possibilities he takes up in *New York 2140*.

The most immediate contexts for *New York 2140* are the Great Acceleration (1950–present) and the Great Recession (2007–2009), and the way these two Great phenomena interact. The Great Acceleration refers to the unprecedented growth in human activity since the mid-twentieth century, and the term is used almost exclusively in discussions of the Anthropocene epoch. The booms in human population, water use, chemical manufacture, fossil fuels, and transportation have resulted in accelerated effects of global warming, including species extinction, acidification of the oceans, sea level rise, and widening social inequalities.[11] The Great Recession is a product of this Acceleration; it resulted from the kind of global economic Ponzi scheme Robinson claims is partly responsible for the environmental disasters that typify the Anthropocene. Robinson emphasizes this point in epigraphs to many of the chapters, which quote major financial figures during the lead up to and aftermath of the Great Recession. Here's what happened:

After nearly a decade of unsustainable financial growth in the largely unregulated US financial industry throughout the 1990s and early 2000s, the market crashed when the US housing bubble "popped": a large number of people who had taken out risky subprime mortgages to buy homes could no longer afford to pay their loans, and those loans had been extended out tenfold by various investment banks through a variety of mortgage-backed securities and investments. In essence, financial companies were selling loans and making bets on the market *backed* by the promise of future mortgage payments. The result was a two-year recession in the United States followed by a global economic disaster in 2009—followed by government-backed bailouts of some of the largest banks. Despite failing spectacularly, the capitalist system regenerated itself, as no other alternative seemed possible. The Great Recession also occurred at a time in US history when political engagement with climate change was at an all-time low.[12] Similar to the prospect of ending capitalism, climate change presents itself in politics as an impossible challenge, something immutable and "natural" rather than a product of human behavior and activity. In *New York 2140*, Robinson imagines this cycle of capitalism and climate change continuing more or less along the same trajectory for another 100 years.

Anthropocene, Capitalocene, and *New York 2140*

What might New York City look like in 100 years if humans continue with business as usual? Robinson imagines an eerily plausible future in *New York 2140*. A series of two "Pulses," as he calls them—sudden rises in the global sea level resultant from melting glaciers—inundates much of Manhattan. Robinson projects a fifty-foot sea level rise over forty years, going with the extreme end of current climate change models; average scientific estimates put sea level rise around ten to twenty feet by 2100. Still catastrophic, but not nearly as much as fifty feet (though that's still possible). Along with these Pulses, world financial markets tank, and, each time, governments step in to bail out the big banks and keep capitalism chugging along. In essence, Robinson imagines two more Great Recessions of much greater severity. But "New York is still New York," as characters repeatedly claim throughout the novel.[13] The mega-rich buy up property in the dry, upper side of Manhattan. Groups redesign and repurpose buildings as cooperatives in midtown. New and more radical neighborhoods develop in intertidal areas. The gulf between the rich and poor is more pronounced, and capitalists and traders begin betting on the future of this New New York. There's a lot of new technologies—hover boats to travel around waterways that used to be roads, materials that insulate buildings to protect them from flooding and water damage, cities built on gigantic platforms that float in the sky—but the same human behaviors keep capitalism churning out the Anthropocene.

Capitalism is the driving force of the Anthropocene in *New York 2140*. Yet, despite specific references to the Anthropocene throughout the book, the novel could just as easily be read as a work of the Capitalocene—that is, an alternative name for Earth's new geological epoch, emphasizing the central role of capitalism, and the handful of wealthy nations most responsible for global warming, rather than humans acting as a collective whole.[14]

The opening chapter of the novel establishes this critique of capitalism. The chapter is a dialogue between Mutt and Jeff, two freelance programmers for financial markets who have become disillusioned with the capitalist system. In a comical, though deeply informed, exchange in emulation of the absurdist-postmodern plays *Waiting for Godot* (1952) and *Rosencrantz and Guildenstern Are Dead* (1966), the pair decide to do exactly what Robinson claims is necessary: change the rules of the global economic system to make ecological sustainability the main criterion. In their rather surreal and suspended state of existence, this plan is feasible: like their counterparts in the plays just mentioned, they're more like embodiments of philosophical ideas than real people, dialogue without bodies, an ongoing intellectual conversation outside of the novel's fiction. As Jeff states,

> The prices are always too low, and so the world is fucked. We're in a mass extinction event, sea level rise, climate change, food panics, everything you're not reading in the news … Things are sold for less than it costs to make them.[15]

Although the characters exist in 2140, their assessment of the Anthropocene is a not-so-subtle description of the early twenty-first century. So, being the genius programmers they are, they recode the financial system on the spot. But they are immediately "caught," and their code "corrected," after just a few seconds. In later chapters, we learn that their fix involved eliminating tax havens, instituting a progressive tax going up to 90% on people who make over 100 million dollars, and funneling money to the US Securities and Exchange System to fund new financial laws and regulations that take into account ecological sustainability and environmental impacts.[16] Fearing for their lives—they are eventually kidnapped—they escape into the sunken city to hide from the angry capitalists on their heels.

Mutt and Jeff's opening conversation and disappearance not only set in motion the plot of the novel, which focuses on the convergence of a diverse cast of characters living in the MetLife building, but also establish its focus on the often-unseen and misunderstood role capitalism plays in shaping Earth's physical environments. Many people think of capitalism in the abstract: it's a sprawling economic and political system based on private property, private control of a nation's industries and resources, financial competition, and the goal of accumulating as much wealth as possible. But all of those characteristics translate into humans' relationship to the physical environment: economics is more important than ecology; the human world is more important than the nonhuman world; making money is more important than making sustainable communities and environments. And since the advent of industrial capitalism in the eighteenth century, this system has been linked directly to anthropogenic climate change through the extraction, sale, and consumption of fossil fuels: first coal, then oil, then gas (and now, in the early twenty-first century, all three). Burning up all of those fossil fuels led to great innovations, wealth, and better lives for many people (though not all), but it's all on borrowed time: fossil fuels are finite, and they stick around in the atmosphere, building up, modifying ecosystems in drastic ways. The increase of carbon dioxide in Earth's atmosphere causes global warming, as well as the imagined Pulses in Robinson's novel. Capitalism generates rising sea levels, acidification of the oceans, air pollution, and the new natures of the Anthropocene. But as Robinson makes clear in his novel, capitalism can also benefit from the problems that it creates—there's no persuasive financial reason, from the perspective of capitalism, to end business as usual. Or so it seems. Mutt and Jeff show that the financial gains of the present borrow from the future in a doomed-to-fail Ponzi scheme that comes crumbling down every so often and will continue to regenerate itself until a new system takes its place.

In contrast to Mutt and Jeff, Franklin Garr is in love with capitalism. Garr is a successful stock trader and inventor of the Intertidal Property Pricing Index (IPPI), which allows traders to bet on sea level rise in relation to housing prices and thus real estate investments. As Garr explains, his IPPI values property in the intertidal zone of New York, which is currently in a bubble; traders are betting and creating derivatives based on how many buildings are collapsing and how many are being renovated and thus suitable for investment. He imagines questions a skeptic might pose: "Spoofing? No. Ponzi scheme? Not at all! Just *finance*. Legal as hell."[17] Garr is the only character narrator in the novel, giving readers special insight into his perspective on the relationship between financial systems and climate change. The night Mutt and Jeff disappear, Garr notices a dip on the Chicago Mercantile Exchange, a result of the duo's fix: all of the gains turned into losses, just for a few seconds, as banks suddenly had to factor in the future. But Garr is undeterred, in the first half of the novel, anyway: "Am I saying that the floods, the worst catastrophe in human history, equivalent or greater to the twentieth century's wars in their devastation, were actually good for capitalism? Yes, I am."[18] Capitalism drives and profits from climate change.

Interjecting throughout the plot of the story is "the citizen," an irreverent character who directly addresses readers, providing sweeping historical and cultural commentary. It's unclear exactly who the citizen is: they could be a resident of New New York; a "future historian," as Spencer Adams argues;[19] and/or a mouthpiece for Robinson himself. Most of what readers learn about the Pulses comes from the citizen, but they also provide a deep history of New York from the last Ice Age (that is, about 11,000 years ago), when water from melting glaciers flooded valleys, creating the bays, rivers, and islands that came to be known as New York. The sea level rose by 300 feet over a few thousand years. The newly formed area was an ideal place to set up shop for indigenous peoples, and, later, European colonialists, who quickly transformed the forest of trees into "a forest of skyscrapers."[20] And then, the citizen explains, there came another sea level rise event: the two Pulses of the late twenty-first century, when New York was inundated again, producing New New York, with its hellish outer boroughs (now polluted, poisonous swaps) and half-drowned island of Manhattan. What Robinson does here is place human history over geological history, showing how the two are no longer separable in the Anthropocene.[21] There's a sense of historical déjà vu here: the floods at the start of the Holocene epoch that created the contours of New York are repeated, seemingly within the blink of a geological eye, in the Anthropocene epoch, reshaping New York. But anthropogenic sea level rise only took a few decades. Human activity is now on par (and arguably surpasses) with powerful natural processes that shape continents and atmospheres over millions of years.

In later chapters, the citizen links the Pulses directly to capitalism. After the First Pulse, when the sea level rose ten feet in ten years during the 2060s, things were bad, but it was too late for any meaningful change. Despite massive decarbonization efforts and attempts to cool the global climate artificially through aerosol sprays (a technique scientists have proposed in the early twenty-first century), global warming "was baked in by then and could not be stopped by anything the postpulse people could do."[22] The citizen sarcastically states that these efforts were needed fifty years earlier, but no one did anything, because

> no one saw it coming, but no, wrong: they did. Paleoclimatologists looked at the modern situation and saw CO2 levels screaming up from 280 to 450 parts per million in less than three hundred years, faster than had ever happened in the Earth's entire previous five billion years, (can we say "Anthropocene," class?).[23]

Of course, Robinson is providing commentary on the state of climate science and public perception of global warming at the time he wrote the novel, in the second decade of the twenty-first century. It's a direct call to readers: we need to do something now! In the Second Pulse, oceans warmed in an unstoppable feedback loop with carbon levels in the atmosphere. Antarctica melted, and the sea level rose forty feet in a decade. It was an "anthropogenic mass extinction event, the term often used. End of an era. Geologically speaking it might rather be the end of an age, period, epoch, or eon, but that can't be decided until it has run its full course."[24] In other words, this is the Anthropocene, or Capitalocene, or whatever you want to call it.

But capitalism returns to business as usual. The citizen recounts how, for a few years, people of the world united to create new sustainable forms of infrastructure and power: nations adopted half-earth land usage modifications, and everything went carbon-neutral. These changes were expensive; economists asked, "Could we afford to survive?"[25] Apparently not: governments ultimately bailed out the big banks (again), most people faced food shortages and financial disaster, and all the bankers kept getting superrich. Capital moves around a bit, mainly from New York to Denver, to keep growing itself, its own entity ruling the world. The superrich hire private armies to protect them from "regular people." As investors leave New York, these regular people move back in and set up alternative, collective forms of society, which are quite successful—utopian, even—and all of sudden, New York is desirable again. And so, the investors come back (that's where the novel is in 2140). Basically, capitalism won out, and the rich doubled down on the same policies that created the Anthropocene.[26]

Robinson pits competing views and trajectories of the Anthropocene against one another. *New York 2140* is both apocalyptic and utopian: it depicts a world ravaged by catastrophic global warming *and* revitalized by the kinds of ecological thinking and carbon-neutral technologies required to sustain human life on Earth. Mutt and Jeff give voice to necessary institutional changes to global financial markets. Other characters living in the MetLife building and intertidal areas depict alternative lifestyles. And even Garr, the pro-capitalist character in the novel, modifies his worldview by the novel's end, investing more of his time and money into sustainable infrastructure. Garr is the only character who really changes throughout the novel: in one of the final scenes, he confronts his mentor, who, readers learn, was behind a sabotage project on the MetLife building in a bid to buy out the residents. In a searing image of capital flight, his mentor half-heartedly apologizes, then boards a hovering city full of partying billionaires, flying off into the sky. While the "good guys" won, the superrich are not hurt. They'll be back.

Yet, *New York 2140* is ultimately an optimistic, utopian work of cli-fi. As Brent Ryan Bellamy points out, Robinson includes ecological disaster in his novel, but it's not the focus: in the novel's myriad depictions of self-sustaining residential cooperatives, carbon-neutral and carbon-negative technologies, and utopian practices, "Robinson's hypothesis is that, in the wake of catastrophic climate change and sea-level rise, human beings will have found a way to live together and share the work in a highly localized, self-sustaining way."[27] Robinson himself has said that he's "much more interested in the utopian response" to climate crises, writing that "our technological abilities and the energy flows on the planet are such that a 'good anthropocene' is still physically possible." One way to create this "good anthropocene" is by "inventing post-capitalism."[28]

In the penultimate chapter of *New York 2140*, the citizen outlines such a post-capital world. In 2143, progressives win a series of government elections, and global financial markets factor in sustainability: banks are nationalized; there's a progressive tax on capital assets and a 91% tax on capital flight; new labor and environmental laws are enacted to protect people and the planet; and the country gets universal health care, guaranteed employment, and a year of mandatory national service. This is something of a wish list for Robinson, what he (and many others) argues is necessary to combat climate change and to live sustainably in the Anthropocene. Because there's no stopping the Anthropocene: we're already in it, so we must learn to live in this new epoch. And that means rejecting business as usual. The citizen wryly asks, "That making people secure and prosperous would be a good thing for the economy was a really pleasant surprise to [the ultrarich]. Who knew?"[29] But it's not an entirely happy ending. The citizen/Robinson makes clear that this all could change at any moment: "the immense black-hole gravity of greed and fear" is always there, always ready to "push back" against progressive change, capitalism always waiting patiently to squeeze back in "between the glass walls of law" and justice.[30]

Conclusion

New York 2140 asks readers to imagine a potential future of New York, and, by extension, potential futures of other cities—your city—and of the world. Where is the Anthropocene headed? What will your hometown look like in 100 years? How can we move away from capitalism? We don't know. But if major industrial nations like the United States keep on the same path with the same policies as the early-twenty-first century, things could very well turn out like they do in Robinson's novel. This is really the essence of Anthropocene fiction and contemporary cli-fi: these works force upon readers the transitory nature of our lives and our own historical moment, while simultaneously emphasizing the long-lasting implications of the momentous time in which we now live. What humans do throughout the 2020s will affect Earth's ecosystems for thousands of years. Geologic and human history have collapsed in on themselves, and this is an eerie, strange, uncanny phenomenon. How do we make sense of this collapse? How do we understand humans' newfound geophysical power? How do we feel in the Anthropocene? How do we move forward? Science gives us data, facts, and projections, while literature gives us narratives to understand the emotional and human implications of that data—and cli-fi (as Anthropocene literature) is where the two meet.

Notes

1 See Angela Evancie, "So Hot Right Now: Has Climate Change Created a New Literary Genre?" NPR, 20 April 2013; Kyle Plantz, "Move over Sci-Fi: 'Climate Fiction' Finds Its Way into Classrooms," *Reuters*, 10 April 2015; J.K. Ullrich, "Climate Fiction: Can Books Save the Planet?" *The Atlantic*, 14 August 2015; Claire L. Evans, "Climate change Is So Dire We Need a New Kind of Science Fiction to Make Sense of It," *The Guardian*, 20 August 2015; Rio Fernandes, "The Subfield That Is Changing the Landscape of Literary Studies," *The Chronicle of Higher Education*, 21 March 2016; and John Abraham, "CliFi—A New Way to Talk About Climate Change," *The Guardian*, 18 October 2017.

2 Matthew Schneider-Mayerson, "The Influence of Climate Fiction: An Empirical Survey of Readers," *Environmental Humanities* 10, no. 2 (2018): 482.
3 Adam Trexler, *Anthropocene Fictions: The Novel in a Time of Climate Change* (Charlottesville: University of Virginia Press, 2015), 9.
4 Rebecca Evans, "Nomenclature, Narrative, and Novum: 'The Anthropocene' and/as Science Fiction," *Science Fiction Studies* 45, no. 3 (2018): 484–499.
5 See, for example, the chapter on Robinson in Fredric Jameson, *Archaeologies of the Future: The Desire Called Utopia and Other Science Fictions* (London: Verso, 2005), 393–416.
6 Kim Stanley Robinson, *Forty Signs of Rain* (New York: HarperCollins, 2004), 140.
7 Fredric Jameson, "Future City," *New Left Review* 21 (2003): no page.
8 David Grinspoon, "An Astrobiologist Asks a Sci-fi Novelist How to Survive the Anthropocene," *Nautilus* 15 (31 July 2014): no page.
9 Ibid.
10 Ibid.
11 See Will Steffen, et al., "The Trajectory of the Anthropocene: The Great Acceleration," *The Anthropocene Review* 2, no. 1 (2015): 81–98; J.R. McNeill, *The Great Acceleration: An Environmental History of the Anthropocene Since 1945* (Cambridge: Harvard University Press, 2014); and www.igbp.net/globalchange/greatacceleration.4.1b8ae20512db692 f2a680001630.html
12 Trexler notes an explosion of cli-fi and Anthropocene fiction written during the second term of US President George W. Bush (2005–2009), which marked a low point in American leadership on environmental issues. See Trexler, 9.
13 Kim Stanley Robinson, *New York 2140* (Orbit, 2017), 33.
14 See Jason W. Moore, ed., *Anthropocene or Capitalocene? Nature, History, and the Crisis of Capitalism* (Oakland: PM Press, 2016).
15 Robinson, *New York 2140*, 4.
16 Ibid., 150–152.
17 Ibid., 123.
18 Ibid., 118.
19 Spencer Adams, "Staging the Speculative: On Kim Stanley Robinson's *New York 2140*," *Qui Parle* 27, no. 2 (2018): 533.
20 Robinson, *New York 2140*, 33.
21 This Anthropocenic "deep history of humans" was on Robinson's mind in the 2010s: in his novel *Shaman* (2013), a work of "prehistoric fiction," he follows a group of humans living during the last Ice Age. See Michael Gaffney, "The Ice Age and Us: Imagining Geohistory in Kim Stanley Robinson's *Shaman*," *Science Fiction Studies* 45, no. 3 (2018): 469.
22 Robinson, *New York 2140*, 139.
23 Ibid., 140.
24 Ibid., 144.
25 Ibid., 381.
26 For an essay on the relationship on these issues in the novel, see Roberto J. Ortiz, "Financialization, Climate Change, and the Future of the Capitalist World-Ecology: On Kim Stanley Robinson's *New York 2140*," *Soundings* 103, no. 2 (2020): 264–285.
27 Brent Ryan Bellamy, "Science Fiction and the Climate Crisis," *Science Fiction Studies* 45, no. 3 (2018): 418.
28 Kim Stanley Robinson, "Story Spaces of Climate Change," *Science Fiction Studies* 45, no. 3 (2018): 427.

29 Robinson, *New York 2140*, 603.
30 Ibid., 604.

References

Abraham, John. "CliFi—A New Way to Talk About Climate Change." *The Guardian*. 18 October 2017.

Adams, Spencer. "Staging the Speculative: On Kim Stanley Robinson's *New York 2140*." *Qui Parle* 27, no. 2 (2018): 521–538.

Bellamy, Brent Ryan. "Science Fiction and the Climate Crisis." *Science Fiction Studies* 45, no. 3 (2018): 417–419.

Evancie, Angela. "So Hot Right Now: Has Climate Change Created a New Literary Genre?" NPR. 20 April 2013.

Evans, Claire L. "Climate change Is So Dire We Need a New Kind of Science Fiction to Make Sense of It." *The Guardian*. 20 August 2015.

Evans, Rebecca. "Nomenclature, Narrative, and Novum: 'The Anthropocene' and/as Science Fiction." *Science Fiction Studies* 45, no. 3 (2018): 484–499.

Fernandes, Rio. "The Subfield That Is Changing the Landscape of Literary Studies." *The Chronicle of Higher Education*. 21 March 2016.

Gaffney, Michael. "The Ice Age and Us: Imagining Geohistory in Kim Stanley Robinson's *Shaman*." *Science Fiction Studies* 45, no. 3 (2018): 469–483.

Grinspoon, David. "An Astrobiologist Asks a Sci-fi Novelist How to Survive the Anthropocene," *Nautilus* 15 (31 July 2014): no page.

Jameson, Fredric. *Archaeologies of the Future: The Desire Called Utopia and Other Science Fictions*. London: Verso, 2005.

———. "Future City," *New Left Review* 21 (2003): no page.

McNeill, J.R. *The Great Acceleration: An Environmental History of the Anthropocene Since 1945*. Cambridge: Harvard University Press, 2014.

Moore, Jason W., ed. *Anthropocene or Capitalocene? Nature, History, and the Crisis of Capitalism*. Oakland: PM Press, 2016.

Ortiz, Roberto J. "Financialization, Climate Change, and the Future of the Capitalist World-Ecology: On Kim Stanley Robinson's *New York 2140*." *Soundings* 103, no. 2 (2020): 264–285.

Plantz, Kyle. "Move over Sci-Fi: 'Climate Fiction' Finds Its Way into Classrooms." *Reuters*. 10 April 2015.

Robinson, Kim Stanley. *Forty Signs of Rain*. New York: HarperCollins, 2004.

———. *New York 2140*. New York: Orbit, 2017.

———. "Story Spaces of Climate Change." *Science Fiction Studies* 45, no. 3 (2018): 426–427.

Schneider-Mayerson, Matthew. "The Influence of Climate Fiction: An Empirical Survey of Readers." *Environmental Humanities* 10, no. 2 (2018): 473–500.

Steffen, Will, et al. "The Trajectory of the Anthropocene: The Great Acceleration." *The Anthropocene Review* 2, no. 1 (2015): 81–98.

Trexler, Adam. *Anthropocene Fictions: The Novel in a Time of Climate Change*. Charlottesville: University of Virginia Press, 2015.

Ullrich, J.K. "Climate Fiction: Can Books Save the Planet?" *The Atlantic*. 14 August 2015.

INDEX

Anasi, Obumneme F. 136, 144n26
Anthropocene: bomb spike 3–5, 39, 44–45; Capitalocene 5, 6, 17, 27, 65, 71, 77, 78, 108n2, 168, 175–178; Chthulucene 65, 71, 159–160, 168; dating of 3–6, 14–17, 39–40; Eurocene 5, 7, 64–68, 70–71; Great Acceleration 5, 17, 26–27, 65, 68–70, 89, 142n4, 174–175; Orbis spike 3–4, 39–40, 65–66, 159; Plantationocene 5, 7, 65, 71, 76–84, 168; white supremacy scene 76, 134; *see also* climate change, global warming
antiblackness 65–66, 71, 79
Apostol, Gina 149–155
Austen, Jane 39, 42–44

Bacon, Francis 159–162
Burke, Edmund 6, 32–33

capitalism 3, 5, 6, 17, 26–34, 39, 52–53, 55, 57, 60, 65, 67–68, 71, 77, 82, 84, 85n23, 89, 100, 103, 126, 145, 147–148, 162, 172–180
Chakrabarty, Dipesh 119, 127
Clark, J.P. 134–142
climate change 14, 19, 22, 27, 44, 50, 64–65, 67, 69, 76, 79–81, 112, 114–116, 125–131, 150, 171–180; *see also* Anthropocene, global warming
climate fiction 171–180; *see also* science fiction, Shelley, Mary, VanderMeer, Jeff, Wells, H.G.

Colebrook, Claire 141, 144–145n37
Columbian Exchange 3, 17, 65–67, 70, 89
COVID-19 92, 100, 103, 147
Crutzen, Paul 1, 3, 14, 42, 100, 118–119, 125

Darwin, Charles 31, 119–120
Davies, Jeremy 1, 93n7, 118–119
Davis, Heather 50, 53, 134

economics 3, 5, 26–35, 122, 172, 177
energy humanities 3, 6, 38–46
environmental justice 2, 7, 50–60, 79, 152
environmental racism 3, 7, 39, 45, 50–60, 84, 89, 141, 147
extinction 2, 5, 15, 17, 23, 26, 29, 174, 176, 178
extraction: fossil fuel 17, 136, 138, 177; resource 41, 51–52, 55, 59, 89, 145; uranium 52, 54, 56–57

Garrard, Greg 126–127, 131
gender 7, 58, 76–80, 83–84, 125–130, 135, 138, 141, 167
global warming 5, 15, 22, 39, 126, 171–172, 174, 176–179; *see also* Anthropocene, climate change
Global South 89, 134, 140, 147–149, 152, 154–55; *see also* postcolonial

Index

Haraway, Donna 80, 107n2, 160–163, 165–168
Hogan, Linda 57–60
Hume, David 28–29

Indigenous studies 7, 16–17, 50–60, 64–72, 77, 134–135; *see also* Native American studies
Industrial Revolution 3–4, 17, 39, 41–44, 65, 67–68, 100, 112–113, 125–126, 129–130, 149

Linnaeus, Carl 29

Malthus, Thomas 31
Marx, Karl 26–27, 33–34, 102, 108n8
Morton, Timothy 17, 22, 93n6

Native American studies 7, 40, 50–60, 64–72; *see also* Indigenous studies

Ortiz, Simon 54–57, 60
Otu, Oyeh 136, 144n26

plague 99–101, 107
postcolonial 40, 135, 139, 148–150, 152, 155; *see also* Global South

queer theory 3, 7, 20, 81–84, 90, 160–161, 167

retrovirus 99, 106–107
Robinson, Kim Stanley 171–180
Ruskin, John 126, 129–30

scarcity 6, 27, 29–32, 34, 41
science fiction 171–172; *see also* climate fiction, Shelley, Mary, VanderMeer, Jeff, Wells, H.G.
settler colonialism 7, 39, 50–59, 65, 67, 69–72
sexuality 20, 52, 57, 76–78, 80, 82–83, 90, 125–126, 134–135, 138, 140–141, 148; *see also* gender, transgender
Shakespeare, William 39–41
Shelley, Mary 3, 99–107, 119, 171
slavery 3, 7, 39, 41–44, 46, 65–71, 78–80, 134–135, 140, 142
Soyinka, Wole 39, 44–45
Spillers, Hortense 73n19, 78–79

Tangerine 76, 80–84
Thomson, James 29
Thoreau, Henry David 111–116
Todd, Zoe 50, 53, 134
transgender 7, 76–84

VanderMeer, Jeff 159–168

Wells, H.G. 119–123
White, Gilbert 29–30
Wollstonecraft, Mary 104–106, 108n17, 109n20
Woolf, Virginia 125–131
Wordsworth, William 101–102, 159, 160

Yusoff, Kathryn 50, 52–53, 68, 77, 81, 134–135, 140–142